A Multilevel Approach
to the Study
of Motor Control
and Learning

A Multilevel Approach to the Study of Motor Control and Learning

Debra J. Rose
Oregon State University

Allyn and Bacon

Boston London Toronto Sydney Tokyo Singapore

Executive Editor: Suzy Spivey
Editorial Assistant: Lisa Davidson
Marketing Manager: Quinn Perkson
Editorial Production Service: Thompson Steele Production Services
Manufacturing Buyer: Suzanne Lareau
Cover Administrator: Linda Knowles

Copyright © 1997 Allyn & Bacon
A Viacom Company
Needham Heights, MA 02194

Library of Congress Cataloguing-in-publication Data

Rose, Debra J.
A multilevel approach to the study of motor control and learning / Debra J. Rose.
p.   cm.
Includes bibliographical references and index.
ISBN 0-02-403621-8
1. Motor learning.   2. Afferent pathways.   I. Title.
QP301.R65 1997   96-24476
152.3--dc20   CIP

Printed in the United States of America

10 9 8 7 6 5 4   01 00 99

Photo Credits: Photo credits are found on page 315, which should be considered an extension of the copyright page.

*To my mother, Valerie, who taught me
that all things are possible*

CONTENTS

CHAPTER 4
Sensory Contributions to Action   84

■ *HIGHLIGHT*
The "Length-Detecting" Muscle Spindle / 92

CHAPTER 5
Vision and Action   117

SECTION TWO
Motor Learning

CHAPTER 6
The Nature of Motor Learning   141

■ *HIGHLIGHT*
*Applying Motor
Learning Princi-
ples to Clinical
Settings / 280*

PREFACE

The writing of this textbook was prompted by my fascination with the intricacies of human motor behavior and a mounting frustration, as teacher and student of motor control *and* learning, at not being able to find a textbook that encompassed a discussion of both areas of study. Having now spent three years writing such a textbook, I better understand why so few previous authors attempted the endeavor. One reason for avoiding such an undertaking is no doubt the rapid expansion of our knowledge about human motor control and learning. New and exciting theories have emerged that not only offer a different perspective on both areas but also challenge us to look in a very different way at how we control and learn movements.

Of course, as is often the case with new ideas, controversy emerges as a result of new perspectives being juxtaposed with existing viewpoints. Some of that controversy will be presented in this textbook. In those chapters where it surfaces, an attempt is made to describe the essence of each alternative viewpoint. Readers are encouraged to form their own opinions on the merits of each viewpoint after carefully considering the various types of evidence that research has provided. It is my hope, as a teacher, that presenting the information in this way will lead to meaningful exchanges about the subject matter in the classroom. The quotes that precede each chapter should also serve as a catalyst for discussion of chapter content.

THE TARGET AUDIENCE

This book has been written for upper-division undergraduate and entry-level graduate students who have already acquired a strong background in the areas of anatomical and mechanical kinesiology. It is also assumed that the reader has a basic understanding of central nervous system operations (neural transmission, terminology, and anatomy). Students are now preparing for a broader spectrum of careers that include, in addition to physical education, such areas as physical therapy, athletic training, and corporate and industrial fitness management. Sections devoted to a discussion of the compromised motor behavior associated with a number of neurological disorders are also included in most chapters of the book to further accommodate the interests of a broader audience.

APPROACH OF THE TEXTBOOK

The book is divided into two sections: Motor Control and Motor Learning. The first section introduces the reader to the theories and concepts of motor control that have shaped the research process during the last 50 years. In a departure from the approach taken by many other textbooks devoted to a discussion of motor control issues, this first section, in particular, describes the underlying mechanisms of motor control at both a psychological and a neurological level of analysis. In this way, the two theoretical areas that have contributed most to our current understanding of human motor control and learning are acknowledged. Adopting a multilevel approach to the subject matter also serves to provide the student with a better appreciation and understanding of the many layers of complexity that characterize changing human motor control.

The second section of the book focuses on the concepts that underlie the acquisition and retention of movement skills. In this section the book assumes a more practical emphasis, discussing the issues related to how skills should be introduced and practiced for optimal retention and transfer. The section closes with a chapter devoted to shaping the learning process by providing augmented feedback.

FEATURES

A number of pedagogical elements have been incorporated into each chapter of the text to enhance the reader's understanding of the material. Each chapter begins with chapter objectives and a quote that exemplifies the content to be covered. Throughout each chapter, dialog boxes are highlighted in the margin to emphasize the major points and serve as quick chapter reviews for students. "Highlight" boxes are included throughout the text as a means of describing pivotal research findings, further explaining important theoretical constructs, or illustrating how research can be applied to practice. Examples from movement, skill, and clinical settings to illustrate and apply the major concepts are integrated throughout the text. This is in response to the more diverse student population in a field once devoted exclusively to the preparation of physical educators. Each chapter concludes with a summary, a listing of important terminology, suggested further readings, "test your understanding" review questions and an "about the quote" section. I hope that this textbook will help you, the reader, find the area of human motor control *and* learning as fascinating as I do.

ACKNOWLEDGMENTS

I want to acknowledge the assistance and support provided by a number of people throughout this project. A debt of gratitude is owed to Dr. Robert Christina, the mentor who shaped my early vision of the field and the research process; to Ann Castell, the original editor associated with this project; to my colleagues at Oregon State University; to past and present undergraduate and graduate students who provided me with excellent feedback on the early versions of this book; and to Dr. Jody Jensen, University of Oregon, who reviewed the early chapters and offered an insightful critique of the chosen content from the "outside." Finally, my sincere and heartfelt thanks to a very special person whose unwavering support and encouragement sustained me during the many periods of frustration that inevitably accompany a project of this magnitude.

REVIEWERS

Judy Chandler, University of Kansas; Mark Guadognoli, University of Nevada; Joseph R. Higgins, Columbia University; Charlotte A. Humphries, University of North Dakota; Leon E. Johnson, University of Missouri; Brenda Lichtman, Sam Houston State University; Michael Manley, Anderson University; Alphadine Martin, Sam Houston State University; Glenn M. Roswall, Jacksonville State University; Patricia Shewokis, Bowling Green State University; Gary Wicks, University of St. Olaf; Emily H. Wughalter, San Jose State University; and John Zody, Fort Hays State University.

A Multilevel Approach
to the Study
of Motor Control
and Learning

THE NATURE OF MOTOR CONTROL

CHAPTER OBJECTIVES

- Understand the importance of adopting a multilevel approach to the study of motor control and learning.

- Become familiar with the prominent theories of motor control that have guided research and practice over the past century.

- Understand the strengths and weaknesses of each theory of motor control in describing the important characteristics of human action.

- Understand and be able to describe the various processes by which the available degrees of freedom within the human system can be coordinated and controlled to produce skilled action.

> *"What we observe in human skilled behaviour is the rich intermingling of various levels of control as a function of the task demands, the state of learning of the subject and the constraints imposed on the task and subject by the environment."*
>
> —Pew (1974)

The book you are about to begin reading is quite unlike most of the textbooks currently available to students interested in learning more about human motor behavior. How is it different? It is different in two important ways. First, it attempts to explore the principles governing both the control *and* the learning of movements in a single textbook, and second, it adopts a multilevel approach to the study of motor control and learning. Not only does it seek to explore the learning and control of human actions at a behavioral, or psychological, level of analysis, but where possible, it also conducts a similar exploration at the neuromotor level of analysis.

By adopting a multilevel approach, we acknowledge the two most important bodies of knowledge that have shaped the field of study known as motor control and learning: neurophysiology and psychology. And we also reveal the many levels of complexity that characterize the learning and control of movement. Historically, writers of motor control and/or motor learning textbooks have tended to describe human motor behavior by drawing from only one of the two bodies of knowledge (Brooks, 1986; Magill, 1993; Schmidt, 1988). After reading such textbooks as a student, and later as a teacher of motor control and learning, I was always left feeling that only a few pieces of the total motor control and learning puzzle had been provided. I found myself wondering how the psychological processes referred to as "encoding," "response selection," and "response execution" at a behavioral level of analysis were actually accomplished by the neurological and musculoskeletal systems and how we could learn to perform movements we had never experienced before. My overwhelming need to know more as a student of the area inspired the multilevel approach that characterizes this textbook. I hope this multilevel approach also provides you, the reader, with more pieces to the puzzle known as motor control and learning.

DEFINING MOTOR CONTROL

> Motor control: The study of postures and movements and the mechanisms that underlie them.

What exactly *is* the nature of motor control and how broadly should the term be applied when describing movement? For example, should the term be reserved for describing the quality of movement expressed by accomplished athletes such as the gymnast pictured on the cover of this textbook? Or can it also be used to describe the movements of an infant attempting to stand for the first time, a child swinging and missing a pitched baseball, and a frail adult attempting to negotiate a corridor with the assistance of a walking frame? Perhaps the best way to begin to address this question is by defining the term *motor control*. Simply stated, **motor control** is the study of postures and movements and the mechanisms that underlie them. This definition suggests that all movements and postures, irrespective of quality, are expressions of motor control.

In order to understand the nature of motor control, it is necessary to discover *what* is actually being controlled and *how* the various processes governing that control are organized. Although it is clear that muscles and joints are the final targets of motor control, the process by which

> Theories of motor control must address the "what" and "how" of human control.

these agents of movement are recruited remains a subject of considerable interest and controversy among researchers. Throughout the years, systematic research efforts have led to the development of a number of theories and related models of motor control, each of which has contributed significantly to our understanding of human motor control. Let's begin by

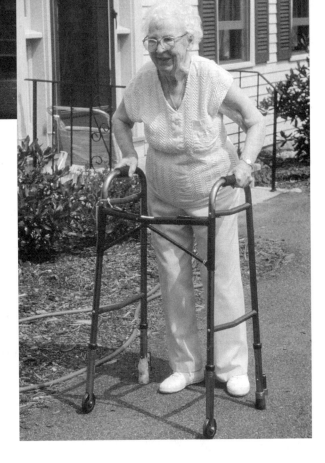

All movements and postures, regardless of
quality, are expressions of motor control.

reviewing a small cross section of theories that have attempted to address both the "what" and the "how" of human motor control.

THEORIES OF MOTOR CONTROL

Three general categories of theories have dominated the literature related to motor control during the past century. These include reflex theories, hierarchical theories, and (more recently) dynamic systems theory. The predictions associated with each of these theories have been tested using a variety of measurement techniques and levels of analysis. Whereas some researchers have worked primarily at a behavioral, or psychological, level of analysis, others have employed animal models in an attempt to identify the actual neurological mechanisms underlying action. Let us begin by discussing the defining characteristics of each theory and their respective contributions to our present understanding of human motor control.

Reflex Theories

One of the earliest neurologically based **reflex theories** developed to explain how movements are controlled was based on the work of Sherrington (1857–1952), a prominent neurophysiologist who considered the reflex to be the fundamental unit of motor control. A basic assumption of this theory was that physical events occurring in the environment served as the **stimulus** for action, triggering a chain of individual reflex circuits that were responsible for producing a movement **response.** According to Sherrington (1906), "the outcome of the normal reflex action of the organism is an orderly coadjustment and sequence of reactions" (p. 8). Consistent with this theory is the idea that the individual is a passive recipient of externally produced sensory input. Sensory receptors in the skin, muscles, and joints are stimulated, triggering other sensory systems that, in turn, excite motor systems responsible for producing motor output in the muscles and joints that were originally stimulated.

> Sherrington considered the reflex to be the fundamental unit of motor control.

To test his ideas, Sherrington conducted a series of experiments that involved severing the spinal cord of animals immediately below the brain. This procedure greatly simplified the circuitry of the nervous system and made it possible to study the mechanisms of the spinal cord in isolation from the higher cortical centers. In this way, Sherrington could focus his attention on what he believed to be the elementary unit of behavior: the reflex.

During the 1920s and 1930s, various forms of reflex chaining models of motor control were also being studied at a psychological level of analysis by a group of psychologists who came to be known as the behaviorists (Skinner, 1938; Thorndike, 1927). This group of researchers viewed the acquisition of movement patterns and motor skills as the linking of individual movements into a chain of behavior. A chain of action was thought to be triggered by some external stimulus that resulted in an observable movement response. This response would then generate a second stimulus for subsequent action. Behaviorists were primarily interested in studying observable movement outcomes, as opposed to the underlying processes responsible for producing the outcomes. Thus the theories developed during this period offered little insight into how the motor system was being organized to produce movement.

Although the reflex model of motor control provided a straightforward explanation of how movements are controlled, it was much too simple to account for a person's ability to perform a wide variety of goal-directed actions. The inadequacies of this theory are particularly evident when we begin to consider the vast array of voluntary movements that require us to anticipate changes in the environment, rather than wait for them to occur. As we are well aware from our sports activities and daily living experiences, many of our actions must be proactive—as opposed to reactive—in order for us to avoid undesirable consequences.

A player tending goal during a game of soccer or ice hockey, for example, has no time to wait for the ball or puck to be contacted before deciding on his or her own plan of action. Instead, by carefully watching the movements of a number of key offensive players for important clues, the goalie must attempt to *predict* which player will attempt the shot on goal. In this way the goalie can begin to plan his or her movements before the ball or puck is actually struck. Similarly, drivers who have previously experienced winter road conditions drive at significantly lower speeds, decelerating as they approach curves in the road where ice is known to accumulate. In situations such as these, the performer must draw on existing knowledge about the situation and anticipate changes in the environment in order to be successful.

A second weakness of reflex theories of motor control is their inability to account for movements performed in the absence of sensory feedback. This **open-loop control** of movement has been demonstrated not only in studies using animals subjected to **deafferentation**, the surgical cutting of sensory

> Behaviorists were more interested in studying observable outcomes than underlying processes.

> Sensory feedback is not essential for the execution of all movements.

Many movement situations require that performers anticipate the actions of others rather than waiting for them to occur.

pathways between peripheral receptors and spinal cord/brain (Grillner, 1975; Taub & Berman, 1968) but also in human sensory block studies (Kelso, 1977; Smith, 1969) and in clinical observations of patients who have sustained damage to sensory pathways (Lashley, 1917). The collective findings of these studies have demonstrated that sensory feedback is not essential for the execution of all movements, an argument that directly contradicts Sherrington's own research findings and the basic assumptions underlying reflex theories of motor control.

Although reflex theories are no longer used to explain how voluntary movements are controlled, it is interesting to note that a number of treatment approaches that are still widely used in physical therapy are founded on reflex models of motor control (see Gordon, 1987). An example of one such reflex-based approach is the neurodevelopmental treatment (NDT) system developed by Bobath (1965; 1978). The primary goal of this treatment method is to elicit reflexes considered normal while suppressing or inhibiting abnormal reflexes. NDT continues to be a popular method used to treat children with cerebral palsy and adults with acquired hemiplegia.

Hierarchical Theories

In stark contrast to earlier, reflex theories, **hierarchical theories** of motor control assume that *all* aspects of movement planning and execution are the sole responsibility of one or more cortical centers representing the highest command level within the hierarchy of the CNS. This cortical "executor" contains all the information necessary for action and directs lower centers within the nervous system to carry out the prescribed movement. Moreover, it is capable of coordinating and regulating movement with or without referring to externally generated sensory feedback.

> Higher cortical centers command lower centers to carry out prescribed movements.

One of the first models developed to test the predictions of these hierarchical theories of motor control was devised by Hughlings Jackson in the 1850s. Jackson argued that movements were represented in the higher levels of the brain and then were used to guide subsequent performances. Accordingly, he believed, the flow of information is unidirectional. That is, higher centers convey information for action to lower subordinate centers, and no other communication occurs. This rigid "top-down" view of motor control has since been modified to allow for communication between levels within the hierarchy, the lowest spinal centers conveying information to higher cortical centers in the form of feedback related to how the movement is being carried out. Although some theorists refer to this modified view as a **heterarchical model** of motor control (Greene, 1972), the idea that motor control begins at the highest centers of the brain is common to both models.

According to hierarchical theories, representations of movement are stored in memory in the form of plans or programs for movement. These **motor programs** are believed to consist of prestructured sets of motor commands that are constructed at the highest cortical level and then conveyed to the lowest centers in the hierarchy responsible for executing the movement. This view of motor control has guided the interpretations of motor control theorists since the first operational definition was provided by Keele in 1968. He defined the motor program as "a set of muscle commands that are structured before a movement sequence begins, and that allow the entire sequence to be carried out uninfluenced by peripheral feedback" (p. 387).

> Motor programs are prestructured sets of motor commands developed in the cerebral cortex.

The strongest empirical support for both hierarchical theories and motor program control of voluntary movements has been provided by application of the same types of deafferentation techniques that led to the demise of reflex accounts of motor control. The use of psychological measures such as

Closed- versus Open-Loop Control of Movement

One important theoretical debate that received a great deal of attention in the motor behavior literature for a number of years revolved around the question of whether the control of movement should be characterized as closed-loop or open-loop in structure. The central issue in the debate concerned the perceived role of sensory feedback in the control of movement. Whereas closed-loop models of motor control emphasized the essential role of sensory feedback in the planning, execution, and modification of action, open-loop descriptions focused on the *a priori* generation of action plans by a central executor somewhere

Actions, like those of this skilled pianist, that must be performed quickly require an open-loop mode of control.

in the cerebral cortex. Once generated, the action plan was executed without regard to sensory feedback.

Of course, we now know that neither of these theoretical accounts can adequately describe how movements are controlled in every possible movement situation. It is more likely that we utilize the mode of control that is best suited to the type of environment in which we are moving and to the goal of the action we have chosen to solve a given motor problem. For example, when performing movements that require precision, we are most likely to choose a closed-loop mode of control. In this mode of control, we rely strongly on the use of sensory feedback not only to guide the action but also to make numerous small corrections to the movement as it unfolds. Threading a needle, performing a beam sequence, and reaching to pick a fragile object up from a table are movements to which a closed-loop mode of control is best suited. Conversely, actions that must be performed quickly require an open-loop type of control. In these situations, it is more likely that

a plan of action will be formulated in advance of the action and then executed without regard to the available sensory feedback. This type of control is evident in movement skills such as typing and piano playing and in a variety of sport skills such as pitching, throwing, and pistol shooting.

One additional factor that influences the *degree* to which movements are performed in a closed-loop versus an open-loop fashion is the skill level of the performer. Novice performers must rely heavily on sensory feedback to guide their performance, but more skilled performers are capable of performing most, if not all, aspects of a chosen movement without resorting to sensory feedback. Contrast the slow and frequently interrupted playing of novice piano players, who must carefully follow the notes displayed on the sheet music in front of them, with the rapid finger movements of experienced pianists. Very often, highly skilled pianists are capable of playing complex musical pieces without sheet music.

reaction time (RT), described in more detail in the next chapter, also provided support for the idea that many voluntary movements, particularly those that must be executed quickly, can be planned in advance (Henry & Rogers, 1960; Rosenbaum, Inhoff, & Gordon, 1984; Sternberg, Monsell, Knoll, & Wright, 1978). This unique feature of hierarchical theory better explains how it is possible for goalkeepers and drivers to plan their actions before changes actually occur in the environment.

Although Keele's original definition of a motor program was to serve as an important catalyst for several research endeavors in the early 1970s, the definition has since been modified to account better for an individual's ability to perform a wider range of actions, particularly movements considered novel. (A broadening of the definition was also considered necessary because storing a motor program for every conceivable movement would place too great a demand on memory.) A more important role for sensory feedback has also been incorporated into more recent versions. In contrast to the often superfluous role prescribed for feedback in Keele's earlier definition of a motor program, it is now acknowledged that sensory feedback is used to ensure a movement's accuracy when enough time is available. The importance of sensory feedback in the control and learning of movements will be discussed in more detail in later chapters of this book.

The Generalized Motor Program (GMP) Concept. By the late 1970s, a broader definition of the motor program had emerged, largely thanks to the research efforts of Schmidt and colleagues (Schmidt, 1976; 1982; 1988; Shapiro, 1978; Shapiro, Zernicke, Gregor, & Diestal, 1981). Although the **generalized motor program (GMP)** described by Schmidt (1991) still consists of a stored pattern of movement, its actual structure is more abstract than the one first described by Keele. It can also be applied to a wider range of movements and can be altered or modified during execution in response to changing environmental conditions. Central to this more general concept is the existence of **parameters,** some variant, some invariant, that are applied to the GMP in order to specify how a particular movement pattern is to be expressed. These parameters specify such things as the overall duration of a movement, the overall force needed to accomplish the movement, the temporal phasing of the movement pattern, and the spatial and temporal order in which the components of the movement are to be executed.

> A generalized motor program is more abstract in structure and can be applied to a broader range of movements.

A generalized motor program that can be used to perform a large number of similar movements simply by adding the appropriate set of movement parameters to the abstract plan of action considerably reduces the number of programs one must store in memory. The idea of a generalized motor program also accounts for our ability to achieve the same movement outcome using different muscle groups. For example, it explains how it is possible to write by using very small print on a check or much larger print on a blackboard (Merton, 1972). To write in larger print, one need only "scale up" the same general movements, using the larger muscle groups of the arm. This ability to produce the same movement outcome with a variety of different muscle groups is called **motor equivalence.** Parameter specification also makes it possible for an individual to perform novel movements adequately on the first attempt, an ability not accounted for in the more limited motor program concept expressed by Keele.

Dynamic Systems Theory

In more recent years, a quite different approach to the study of motor control has emerged. The antecedents of this new **dynamic systems theory** (or action systems theory, as it is also called) can be traced back to the early work of Bernstein (1967), a Russian physiologist who contributed much to our understanding of how movements are controlled at a neurological level, and of the psychologist J.J. Gibson (1966; 1979), who studied action at a perceptual level of analysis. Although neither researcher is alive today, many of their ideas have been incorporated into this contemporary theory of motor control by theorists such as Kelso, Kugler, Reed, Turvey, and others (Kelso & Tuller, 1984; Kugler & Turvey, 1987; Reed, 1982; Turvey, 1990).

Dynamic systems theory differs from hierarchical theories of motor control in two very important ways. First, it reestablishes a role for the environment as an important source of information for action. It does this by focusing on the relationship between the performer and the environment in which the action is to take place. In fact, the strongest advocates of this new theory (Reed, 1982; Turvey & Carello, 1981; 1988) would argue that *all* the information for action is available in the environment and can be directly perceived by the performer. Thus the planning of actions does not require elaborate cognitive processing, because information provided by the environment is immediately meaningful.

> Dynamic systems theory reestablishes a role for the environment as an important source of information for action.

The second way in which this new theory of motor control differs from earlier theories is related to how the action is actually produced. Recall that in hierarchical theories of motor control, a cortical executor, or control center at the level of the cortex, was the primary source of motor control. Dynamic systems theorists do not believe that any such rigidly defined cortical mechanism is solely responsible for controlling action. Instead, they argue that motor behavior results from the interaction of multiple subsystems (neurological, biological, musculoskeletal). No subsystem has priority over another or is the only one capable of controlling or prescribing how the action will unfold. The term that dynamic systems theorists apply to this phenomenon is **self-organization.**

> Motor behavior is self-organized. It results from the interaction of subsystems, and no one subsystem is capable of prescribing the entire action.

Despite its recent emergence as a viable theory of motor control, the action systems (or dynamic systems) approach has already contributed much to our understanding of how movements are controlled. First, it has emphasized the relationship between the performer and the environment in the planning and control of action. According to this theory, actions are shaped by the intentions of the performer *and* the constraints imposed by the environment. Second, the greater responsibility afforded to the spinal and skeletomuscular levels better accounts for our ability to produce a number of highly sophisticated patterns of coordination (such as locomotion) without the need for cortical guidance. Third, the greater role played by the lower control centers provides a mechanism for the automatic postural adjustments that accompany a number of voluntary movements. Reflexive modification of actions on the basis of sensory feedback is also made possible by this lower-level control mechanism.

> Actions are shaped by the intentions of the performer and the constraints imposed by the environment.

Although at first glance the dynamic systems theory of motor control appears to stand in stark contrast to earlier theories, the ideas expressed in this theory are similar to many that are currently being developed by neuroscientists and psychologists alike. These new theories are often called distributed parallel processing theories or neural network theories. In a manner reminiscent of the self-organizing principles that characterize the dynamic systems framework, these alternative theories also distribute the responsibilities for producing action among a number of autonomous neural centers (Grossberg & Kuperstein, 1986; Rumelhart, McClelland, & PDP Research Group, 1986). Moreover, unlike the neural centers described in hierarchical theories, these centers are not restricted to the cortex but are distributed throughout subcortical, spinal, and even musculoskeletal levels of the nervous system (Pew, 1984). Empirical testing of these alternative theories of motor control is still in its early stages, but they offer hope for bridging the gap between psychological and neurological explanations of how movements are organized.

CHARACTERISTICS OF HUMAN ACTION

> Any theory of motor control must be able to account for multiple characteristics of human action.

Having briefly outlined the major assumptions underlying the three most prominent theories of motor control, let us now begin to explore how the defining principles associated with reflex, hierarchical, and dynamic systems theories can be used to describe certain characteristics associated with human action. To help us in this task, Sheridan (1984) has identified four important characteristics of human motor behavior that he believes any theory of motor control must address. These are flexibility of action, uniqueness of action, consistency of action, and modifiability of action.

Flexibility

Flexibility of action is thought to be achieved by recruiting different muscles and joints to achieve the same action. This characteristic enables us to write legibly even when we control the pen with limbs other than our

The same action, that of pushing open a door, can be achieved by recruiting different muscles and joints.

| Flexibility of action is achieved by recruiting different muscles and joints to perform the same action. |

fingers (Raibert, 1977), and it helps us push open doors and turn on light switches using other body parts when our arms are laden with parcels. In this way, the many degrees of freedom available in the human motor system can be used to our advantage in a number of movement situations. In an earlier section of this chapter, we used the term *motor equivalence* to describe this ability. A more thorough description of this concept is provided in the highlight *The "Degrees of Freedom" Problem* featured later in this chapter.

Uniqueness

The uniqueness of action—the fact that no two movements are ever performed in exactly the same way—is a second characteristic of human action that any theory of motor control must account for. One has only to watch an accomplished tennis player hitting balls projected by a ball machine to see that every forehand stroke is performed differently.

No two movements are ever performed in exactly the same way.

Slight variations are evident in how the body is positioned prior to ball contact and in how the striking limb is moved through space during each successive stroke. This suggests that the movement pattern underlying the forehand stroke is not rigidly constructed.

> No two movements are ever performed in exactly the same way.

Consistency and Modifiability

The third characteristic described by Sheridan involves the consistency with which actions can be reproduced. That is, the temporal and spatial characteristics of the movement remain relatively stable from one performance to the next. The final characteristic for which any theory of motor control must account is a skilled performer's ability to modify an action, even as it is being executed. How many times have you observed skilled performers change the path of their movements as a result of a change in the situation that was not apparent before the movement began? (One example is a defender jumping to obstruct a forward's view of the basketball rim.) This is a particularly important ingredient

> The temporal and spatial characteristics of a movement remain relatively stable between performances.

for successful performance in varied or unstable environments, whether they are associated with a sport or with conditions that arise in daily life (such as walking along a busy sidewalk).

How well does each of the three types of theories account for these characteristics of skilled action? It is clear that a reflex theory of motor control is unable to provide an adequate explanation for at least three of the characteristics identified by Sheridan. Certainly it describes no mechanisms that would permit actions to be modified in any way, particularly during their execution. Recall that a stimulus or set of sensory inputs triggers a response, which then serves as the stimulus for the subsequent response. Nor does this theory's rigid framework explain our ability to produce unique and/or novel actions on subsequent attempts. Only the characteristic of consistency can be explained in terms of a reflex theory of motor control. The direct link between the stimulus and response provides a mechanism for achieving spatial and temporal consistency between movement attempts.

> Only the characteristic of consistency of action can be explained by using a reflex theory of motor control.

Hierarchical theories, on the other hand, are better able to address each of the characteristics identified by Sheridan. According to these theories, flexibility of action is achieved simply by adding different movement parameters to the same generalized motor program. This might involve applying more force to an object you wish to throw overhand in order to achieve a greater throwing distance. This same mechanism can also account for our ability to produce unique actions—at least those that belong to the same class of actions as those already represented in memory. For example, even though some readers may never have seen or participated in the game of cricket, many could successfully hit a cricket ball that was bowled to them with the batting implement used in the game. How? Simply by drawing on the generalized motor program that represents previously experienced striking actions associated with other games or activities in which the individual has participated (such as baseball or golf). Although it is unlikely that the first few attempts will resemble a well-learned batting stroke, previous striking experiences will ensure production of a movement pattern that grossly approximates a batting action similar to one used in cricket.

> Skilled performers are capable of modifying their action, even as it is being executed.

Hierarchical theories are also able to account for our ability to modify actions in progress, at least up to a point determined by the amount of time available to the performer. If one has enough time to use sensory feedback, then it is possible to alter the motor program being used to guide the action. In the case of ballistic actions, however, the action proceeds too quickly to permit any modification during its execution. By way of consolation, however, the sensory feedback that was available during the movement can be used to modify the next movement attempt.

The fact that certain movement parameters applied to any general plan of action are invariant whereas others are variant ensures our ability to achieve consistency in our actions. By manipulating the parameters of force and time, we are able to preserve the spatial and temporal patterning of a movement even though different muscle groups are used. This ability was nicely demonstrated by Hollerbach (1978), who asked a group of subjects to write the word *hell* in both small and large print. Measurement of the two different acceleration patterns created by the moving pen revealed a surprisingly consistent temporal pattern in the application of force despite the fact that the level of overall force applied varied between the two print sizes. It appears that the same underlying plan of action was being used even though the goal of the task was to write using larger print.

Finally, how does the more recently developed dynamic systems theory address each of the characteristics identified by Sheridan? The self-organizing properties embodied within the dynamic systems model provide for flexibility and modifiability of action in that no one structure within the nervous system is responsible for producing the action.

As a result, none of the details of the action exists before the start of the action; all simply emerge as the performance unfolds. Immediate adjustments for any sudden disturbance or obstacles encountered are therefore possible within groups of muscles that are only temporarily constrained to perform the action. This same temporary organization of muscle groups also allows for uniqueness of action. Lacking the permanence of "hard-wired" reflexes, these functional muscle groups can be reorganized in an almost infinite number of ways to produce variations in action that may be considered unique. The very fact that no representations of specific movement patterns are stored also facilitates unique action.

The final characteristic identified by Sheridan, consistency of action, is accounted for within a dynamic systems model by the **topological invariance** that exists among the various coordinated muscle groups. To illustrate this idea, let us consider the act of walking. Although the speed of the locomotor pattern can be increased by altering the cadence, or number of steps completed per minute, and by increasing the amount of force delivered to the muscles involved in the action, the relative pattern of coordination among the limbs remains highly invariant. The fact that muscles never work alone, according to this theory, but are constrained to operate within a functional group to achieve a common task goal also ensures consistency of action.

Despite their vastly different operating principles, both the hierarchical and the dynamic systems theories of motor control can account for each of the characteristics of human action identified by Sheridan. How then does one determine which of the two models better explains human motor control? As yet, no answer to this question exists, and researchers aligned with each of the two theoretical frameworks continue to argue the merits of both. This ongoing debate has been coined "the" motor-action controversy. It has been the focus of much interest in recent literature published in the area of motor control (Meijer & Roth, 1988; Colley & Beech, 1988).

> Both the hierarchical and the dynamic systems theories of motor control are able to account for multiple characteristics of human action.

Although both theories provide very plausible explanations for action in a number of movement contexts, neither theory has been able to explain how actions are produced in all circumstances. Perhaps it is not a question of which theory is better, but rather, of how the strengths of both theories can be integrated into a more comprehensive view of human motor control. Indeed, a growing number of writers have already begun to encourage such a direction for future research (Colley, 1989; van Wieringen, 1988).

COORDINATION VERSUS CONTROL OF ACTION

So far we have focused on the control of action, but it is also important to consider a second, equally vital component of action: coordination. Although it is not uncommon to see the terms *control* and *coordination* used interchangeably in the motor control literature, advocates of natural–physical perspectives on motor control (i.e., action systems, or dynamic systems, theorists) argue that each term represents a different aspect of motor behavior and therefore warrants its own definition (Kugler, Kelso, & Turvey, 1982; Newell, 1985). These writers contend that the coordination and the control of a skill can be independently manipulated. That is, the goal of an action can be achieved by altering one or both of these components. Moreover, it is possible to observe and measure each of these components independently. As you read the next chapter, you will discover that certain kinetic and kinematic measures are used to study the control of an action and that other measures are specifically intended to study its coordination.

> Coordination: The process by which an individual constrains, or condenses, the available degrees of freedom into the smallest number necessary to achieve the goal.

How does coordination differ from control? According to Sparrow (1991), **coordination** is the process by which an individual constrains, or condenses, the available degrees of freedom into the smallest number necessary to achieve the goal. These degrees of freedom may be represented by the many different joints in the body, by individual muscles, or even by the many hundreds of thousands of motor units that activate groups of muscle fibers. How many degrees of freedom each of these possible units of motor control exhibits is determined by the number of different ways in which the unit of control is capable of moving.

> Control: The process of manipulating the constrained behavioral unit.

The constrained degrees of freedom form a behavioral unit that can then be manipulated in a variety of ways (Kugler, Kelso, & Turvey, 1980). The process of manipulating this behavioral unit is described as **control**. At a behavioral level, coordination can be described in terms of the relationship between segments within the same limb (intralimb coordination) or between multiple limbs (interlimb coordination). Conversely, control is described in terms of the absolute magnitude of the movement observed within or across limbs (i.e., the level of force, velocity, or displacement observed).

In order to reach a level of performance similar to that exhibited by skilled athletes, musicians, and dancers, we must begin to experiment with many different ways of constraining, or condensing, the many available degrees of freedom. At the same time, we also begin assigning different values of particular movement parameters (such as force and velocity) until an optimal set of values has been assigned. Once this point in the process of skill acquisition has been reached, the best solution to the motor problem has been found and the performer has developed **skill.**

A skilled performer is one who has found the best solution to the motor problem.

Exactly how do we attempt to reduce the number of muscles, joints, and/or motor units needed to perform a given movement task? Three mechanisms that help us achieve better coordination have been identified. The first of these three mechanisms involves the central nervous system, the second relies on exploitation of certain properties of the musculoskeletal system, and the third involves the use of sensory inputs arising from performance of the movement itself. A discussion of the first two mechanisms is presented in the next section of this chapter. The role that sensory inputs play in both the control and the coordination of movement will be discussed in detail in Chapter 4.

Muscle Response Synergies

One method of coordinating, or reducing the number of available degrees of freedom, is for the CNS to constrain a group of muscles, often spanning multiple joints, to act as a single behavioral unit. This type of organization has the net effect of reducing the number of varying dimensions, or movements, possible within the motor system. Some of

Although some muscle response synergies are believed to be functional at birth, most are developed throughout life as specific ontogenetic skills, such as rollerblading, are learned.

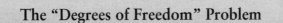

The "Degrees of Freedom" Problem

degree of freedom (1867):   any of a limited number of ways in which a body may move or in which a dynamic system may change.

(Webster's dictionary, 1986)

One of the many issues that contemporary theorists in the area of motor control and learning have been trying to resolve is *what* is actually being controlled within the human system when we perform a movement and *how* the various units of action are organized to pro-

duce coordinated action. In an excellent series of chapters, Turvey and colleagues (Turvey, Fitch, & Tuller; Tuller, Turvey, & Fitch; Fitch, Tuller, & Turvey, 1982) outline a perspective on motor control that has its origins in the writings of Bernstein (1967). A central concern

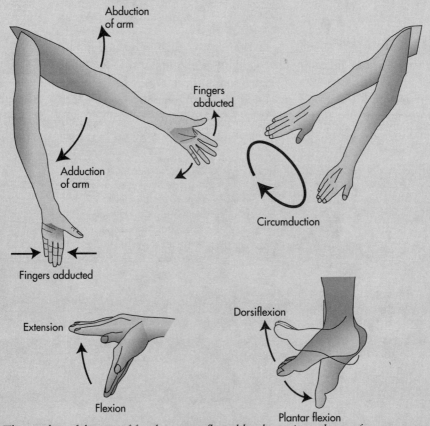

The number of degrees of freedom are reflected by the various planes of movement available at each joint in the body.

From *Human Anatomy* by Marieb and Mallatt. © 1992 by Benjamin/Cummings Publishing Company. Reprinted by permission.

for Bernstein was to understand how the human performer coordinated and controlled a complex system of bony segments, linked by joints and layers of musculature, that is capable of moving in a variety of different planes. The term **degrees of freedom** has often been used to describe the number of ways in which any given unit of control is capable of moving. These units of control may be described in terms of joints, muscles, or even motor units.

If what we control during movement are the joints, Turvey and colleagues estimate that a total of seven degrees of freedom must be controlled just to move the arm. Three degrees of freedom are available at the shoulder, one at both the elbow and the radio-ulnar joint, and two at the wrist joint. If we go a step further and consider the muscle the unit that is controlled during movement, the number of degrees of freedom available rises dramatically. In order to move that same arm successfully, we must now regulate a minimum of twenty-six degrees of freedom: at least ten muscles at the shoulder joint, six more at the elbow joint, four at the site of the radio-ulnar joint, and six controlling the different movements of the wrist

joint. As you might expect, the estimated number rises exponentially when the motor unit is considered the unit of control.

The overwhelming problem of controlling the many hundreds and thousands of degrees of freedom available within the human motor system has prompted a number of researchers to reject the idea of an executor, or central motor program, whose role is to specify *all* the details of a movement by delivering motor commands to each individual muscle involved in the action. Bernstein and the dynamic systems theorists, in particular, contend that such a method of control is unrealistic in light of the anatomical and mechanical sources of variability that characterize the human system. Moreover, to send out a fixed plan of action to the various muscles would severely limit our ability to modify a movement in response to changing environmental constraints. Although our understanding of the human system continues to develop, the problem of how the various systems collectively control the available degrees of freedom within the human operator remains an enigma.

these **coordinative structures** or **muscle response synergies,** as they are often called, are believed to be functional at birth (examples include reaching, grasping, and locomotion). The majority of these synergies, however, are developed throughout life as specific ontogenetic, or cultural, skills are learned. Examples of learned cultural skills include rollerblading, ice skating, tennis, and volleyball.

Unlike those synergies inherent in the dynamic human system, the second group of muscle response synergies are less rigidly organized and are often only temporarily constrained for the purpose of simplifying a particular motor act. For

> One mechanism of coordination is to organize groups of muscles into muscle response synergies.

example, the muscle response synergies we recruit to lift an object to the mouth are not the same as those muscle synergies organized to assist us in lifting a chair from the floor. The size of the movement being performed, in and of itself, often determines the number and types of muscle response synergies recruited.

Mechanical Properties of Limbs

A second mechanism available to make the coordination of action easier exploits the properties of the musculoskeletal system by allowing movements of the limb without the need for concurrent muscle activation. This is certainly evident during the swing phase of locomotion, when passive forces generated by the mechanical properties of the muscles and their physical connections with ligaments at the various joints are sufficient to move the limb through space. Movements that are initiated at one joint invariably affect the movements of other limbs because the limb segments are linked. Swinging the hip forward, for example, naturally influences the movements of the knee and ankle joints below.

The "spring-like" qualities of the muscle can also be exploited by the CNS to assist us in accurately positioning our limbs in space. To

> A second mechanism of coordination is to exploit the inherent properties of the musculoskeletal system.

Movements that are initiated at one joint invariably affect the movements of other limbs because of the physical linking of the limb segments and the mechanical properties of muscles.

accomplish such goals, the stiffness of the involved musculature is manipulated, often before the movement is begun. This ability to prepare the muscles prior to movement is called **pretuning** or **feedforward**. As we will see in later chapters, this feedforward ability serves us well in a variety of movement situations.

A coordinated movement requires the effective manipulation of multiple muscle groups and of the joints controlling each limb involved in the action. This is best achieved through a combination of resources: the assembly of various muscle response synergies into functional units of action, exploitation of the mechanical properties of limbs and muscles, and a continuous stream of sensory information triggered by performance of the movement itself.

SUMMARY

Despite the importance of movement as a vehicle for interacting with our immediate environment, our understanding of the mechanisms that govern such interactions remains incomplete. Although experimental research has culminated in the development of a number of theories of motor control over the past century, many questions about how movements are controlled remain. Perhaps no one theory will ever be sufficient to describe just how we are able to accomplish every type of movement possible in every environmental context.

IMPORTANT TERMINOLOGY

After completing this chapter, readers should be familiar with the following terms and concepts.

control	motor programs
coordination	muscle response synergies
coordinative structures	open-loop control
deafferentation	parameters
degrees of freedom	pretuning
dynamic systems theory	reflex theories
feedforward	response
generalized motor program	self-organization
heterarchical model	skill
hierarchical theories	stimulus
motor control	topological invariance
motor equivalence	

SUGGESTED FURTHER READING

Abernethy, B., & Sparrow, W.A. 1992. The rise and fall of dominant paradigms in motor behaviour research. In *Approaches to the study of motor control and learning,* ed. J.J. Summers, pp. 3–45. North-Holland: Elsevier Science Publishers B.V.

Meijer, O.G., & Roth, K., eds. 1988. *Complex Movement Behaviour: "The" motor-action controversy.* North-Holland: Elsevier Science Publishers B.V.

Morris, M.E., Summers, J.J., Matyas, T.A., & Iansek, R. 1994. Current status of the motor program. *Physical Therapy,* 74, 8, 738–752.

TEST YOUR UNDERSTANDING

1. Briefly describe the major assumptions associated with each of the following theories of motor control: (a) Reflex, (b) Hierarchical, (c) Heterarchical.

2. Briefly describe the type of empirical evidence that was advanced in support of hierarchical theories of motor control.

3. How do heterarchical theories differ from hierarchical theories of motor control?

4. Describe three ways in which the dynamic systems theory of motor control has contributed to our understanding of how movements are controlled.

5. Describe the four characteristics of human action that any theory of motor control must account for. Provide one practical example to illustrate each of these four characteristics.

6. Briefly describe how the reflex, hierarchical, and dynamic systems theories account for each of the four characteristics of human action described in Question 5.

7. Compare and contrast the terms *control, coordination,* and *skill.*

8. Identify the three mechanisms that are used to constrain the number of degrees of freedom available in the human system.

About the Quote

Pew is describing the importance of the interplay that occurs between the environment and the learner in any movement situation. In contrast to earlier views expressed by advocates of the hierarchical theory of motor control, Pew advocates a more distributed processing view wherein a number of independent centers of activity at cortical, subcortical, spinal, and even muscular levels all contribute to the production of coordinated action. As he writes in a later article (Pew, 1984), "each independent processing entity can act in response to a query from another system" (p. 19).

Whether the processing center that responds to the query is at the cortical, spinal, or some other level is also influenced by two other factors: the nature of the task to be completed and the skill level of the performer undertaking the task. In the case of a performer in the early stages of skill acquisition, processing centers at the level of the cortex are strong contributors to the planning and direction of the action. As skill level increases, however, responsibility for action is given over to other levels within the CNS: the spinal and muscular levels in particular. How this distribution of control is possible should become more clear as you read Chapter 3. Finally, the complexity of a task influences the nature of the processing required. The more complex the task to be completed, the higher the level of motor control required.

CHAPTER 2
SCIENTIFIC MEASUREMENT AND MOTOR CONTROL

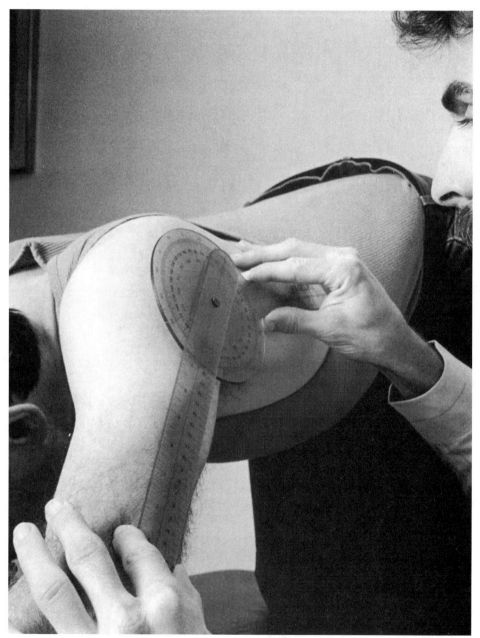

CHAPTER
OBJECTIVES

- Be able to identify and differentiate between measurement techniques used to describe the outcome of a movement and those used to describe the process by which the outcome was achieved.

- Become familiar with the various chronometric measures used to study the timing and duration of the cognitive operations involved in the planning and execution of actions.

- Become familiar with the various error scores used to determine whether a particular movement outcome was achieved and the nature of the error observed.

- Understand and be able to differentiate between behavioral measures used to quantify the observable form of a movement and those used to quantify the various internal and external forces that influence that observable form.

- Understand and be able to differentiate between measurement techniques used to describe the changing patterns of limb coordination and those used to describe how a particular movement is controlled.

- Be able to identify the different types of neurological measures used to describe and investigate the inner workings of the nervous system.

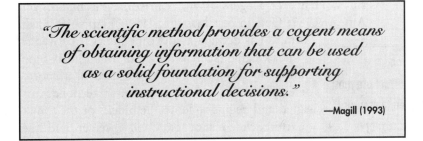

"The scientific method provides a cogent means of obtaining information that can be used as a solid foundation for supporting instructional decisions."

—Magill (1993)

Each of the theories of motor control described in Chapter 1 is the outcome of many years of systematic research using many different and increasingly sophisticated measurement techniques. This chapter describes different types of scientific measurement techniques that are used to test the validity of various models of motor control. These measurements range from noninvasive psychological measures to considerably more invasive experimental procedures designed to monitor and/or alter CNS function directly during movement.

PSYCHOLOGICAL MEASURES

The types of measures that have been used at a psychological level of analysis to test the validity of the three models of motor control can be divided into two basic categories: outcome and process measures. The measures applied to test the early reflex models of motor control were used primarily to describe the end result, or response outcome, observed as a function of manipulating one or more experimental variables. However, the assumptions underlying the more recent hierarchical and dynamic systems models have been tested using research paradigms and measurement techniques designed also to describe *how* the movement was controlled to achieve a particular outcome. We will begin this section with a discussion of two commonly used response outcome measures: chronometry and performance errors.

Response Outcome Measures

The **chronometry,** or timing and duration, of the cognitive operations involved in the planning of voluntary movements (as described in hierarchical models of motor control) has been extensively explored by a number of researchers using different types of **reaction time (RT)** measures (Henry & Rogers, 1960; Christina, Fischman, Vercruyssen, & Anson, 1982; Goggin & Christina, 1979; Klapp, 1975). In its simplest form, RT is defined as the time interval between the presentation of a signal (such as a light or an auditory tone) and the initiation of movement. It can be used in a sports situation to determine how quickly a sprinter responds to the starter's signal and begins to leave the blocks or the time required by a quarterback to spot an open receiver and then begin the throwing action. Although both of these performance situations involve RT, they provide us with different types of information about the decision-making processes involved.

> Chronometry and performance errors are most commonly used to measure response outcomes at a psychological level of analysis.

Simple, Choice, and Discrimination Reaction Times.   The first example describes a **simple reaction time (SRT)** situation, because the movements of the sprinter are in response to the presentation of a single stimulus, the firing of the starter's gun. Conversely, the football example describes a **choice reaction time (CRT)** situation, because many possibilities for action are available to the quarterback. Depending on how the movement situation unfolds following the snap, the quarterback may choose to throw to any one of a number of possible receivers or may even decide to run with the ball. A third type of RT situation, which also involves the presentation of multiple signals, is called **discrimination reaction time (DRT)**. Instead of requiring a particular movement response to a specific signal, as is the case in CRT, performers in a DRT setting are required to respond to only one of several signals presented. (The coach has instructed the quarterback to throw to a particular receiver even though

Simple reaction time and choice reaction time measures are used in the laboratory to study the speed of the decision-making processes observed in a number of different types of movement situations.

several others are available.) All of these RT situations can be easily replicated using simple movement tasks in a controlled laboratory setting. Such laboratory-based RT studies have provided researchers working at a psychological level of analysis with an important means of testing certain predictions associated with hierarchical models without resorting to more invasive measurement techniques.

Fractionated Reaction Time.   In recent years, a more precise RT method has been used by a small number of researchers to study more closely the cognitive processes involved in the planning of action (Anson, 1982; Christina & Rose, 1985; Clarkson & Kroll, 1978). This more precise measurement, referred to as **fractionated reaction time (FRT)**, requires the use of surface **electromyography (EMG)** to partition RT into two parts: **premotor time (PRMOT)** and **motor time (MOT)**. Premotor time is the time that elapses between the presentation of a reaction signal and the first change in EMG activity in the muscle that is identified as the prime mover in the action being observed (see Figure 2.1). The prime mover might be the biceps brachialis muscle in simple flexion movements at the elbow or the middle deltoid when the movement to be performed is in a lateral direction.

> The fractionation of RT into premotor and motor components has made it possible to separate cognitive from mechanical processes.

Premotor time reflects the time required to receive and interpret the sensory signal presented, develop an action plan, and convey it to the appropriate musculature. Motor time begins with the first change in

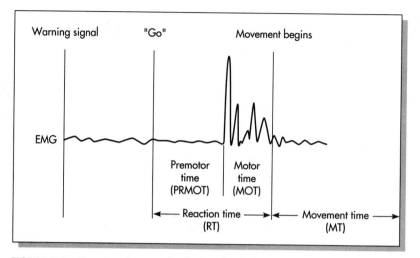

FIGURE 2.1 Reaction time can be further divided into a premotor and motor time component.

electrical activity recorded in the prime-moving muscle and continues until the movement begins. Unlike premotor time, this second component is not directly observable and must be calculated by subtracting premotor time from the overall reaction time. This technique makes it possible to separate the more purely cognitive processes from the mechanical processes, providing researchers with more precise information about the action planning process.

The value of FRT has been demonstrated in a number of studies involving large-scale movements (Anson, 1982, 1989; Christina & Rose, 1985). It has enabled researchers to identify a number of movement characteristics (such as movement complexity, accuracy demands, and the anatomical characteristics of the responding limb) that appear to influence the speed of the decision-making process significantly. (For a detailed review of this literature, see Christina, 1992.) Moreover, the partitioning of RT into a central and a motor component has made it easier to discern whether delays in the initiation of movement are due to the slowing of certain cognitive processes or are purely mechanical characteristics associated with the limb(s) performing the movement (e.g., size of limb and muscle fiber type).

Variables Influencing Reaction Time. All of the RT measures have been used in more formal experimental settings in an effort to learn how certain variables affect the time needed to plan and execute movements. Proponents of hierarchical models of motor control have found RT measures particularly useful in their quest to identify the types of variables most likely to influence each of the hypothetical mental processes (stimulus identification, response selection, and response programming) involved in preparing a given action.

As a result of their experimental manipulations, researchers have identified a number of variables that significantly influence the time required to complete the mental processes believed to precede the actual movement. These include such factors as the number of response choices available to the performer, the complexity of the response to be performed, the accuracy demands associated with the movement, and the amount of practice provided on a specific task. As we will see in later chapters, the practitioner must consider the influence of each of these variables when developing and implementing strategies designed to facilitate the learning or relearning of movements.

In addition to its many applications in sports, RT methodology has also been used to investigate the impact of various types of neurological diseases and traumas on the time required to plan and initiate rapid movements. For example, both SRT and CRT measures have been used to assess the ability of patients with Parkinson's disease to prepare to execute a variety of different actions (Stelmach, Garcia-Colera, & Martin, 1989; Stelmach, Worringham, & Strand, 1987). The movement preparation abilities of individuals with cerebral palsy have also been explored using the more precise FRT technique (Parks, Rose, & Dunn, 1989).

Movement Time.   A second chronometric measure used in conjunction with RT is **movement time (MT)**. This measure represents the time interval between the start of a movement and its completion. MT has proved to be a particularly useful means of demonstrating a well-known phenomenon in motor control known as the **speed–accuracy trade-off**. This phenomenon is most likely to occur in movement situations where the

> Speed–accuracy trade-offs can be demonstrated using RT and MT measures of motor performance.

performer is required to move quickly *and* accurately. In a slalom kayak event, for example, the paddler strives to complete the course in the shortest period of time while also correctly negotiating several gates placed along the course. In order to be successful in this event, the paddler must delicately balance speed with accuracy, because each time the paddler hits or misses a gate, unwanted seconds are added to the overall score. Recording MT in this type of situation therefore provides some insight into the strategy a performer uses to optimize success.

The measurement of MT and RT can also provide important clues to whether a particular movement is being planned in advance of the movement or during its execution. Researchers have demonstrated that

Many movement situations require that performers move both quickly and accurately in order to be successful.

in certain movement situations, subjects plan only a portion of the movement in advance and then continue to plan later segments as the movement progresses (Rosenbaum, Inhoff, & Gordon, 1984; Stelmach, Worringham, & Strand, 1987) . This is particularly evident in situations where movement sequences comprise multiple segments or exceed 500 milliseconds in duration.

Performance Errors.   The recording of performance errors is a practice commonly used by teachers to assess performers' ability to perform a particular skill or how well they are progressing in learning a new sport skill. Similarly, a quick review of team batting averages or fielding errors provides the coach with valuable information on which to base future practice sessions. Researchers also use different types of error scores to determine whether the goal of a movement was actually achieved. For example, did the performer succeed in hitting the target or execute the movement sequence in its correct order? In addition to telling us whether a particular movement outcome was achieved, certain error scores can also help us better understand why a particular movement

HIGHLIGHT

Using Chronometry to Measure the Effects of Movement Disorders

Measures of reaction time and movement time have been extensively used to understand better the effects of various movement disorders on a person's ability to plan and execute movements effectively. One movement disorder that has been investigated using various RT and MT measures is Parkinson's disease. This disease disrupts the functioning of the basal ganglia, neurological structures known to contribute to the planning of action. Two very common symptoms of the disease are difficulty in the initiation of movement (akinesia) and slow execution of movement (bradykinesia). These and other symptoms lead to significant changes in gait and posture.

RT and MT research studies have yielded a number of interesting conclusions. For example, individuals with Parkinson's disease demonstrate choice reaction times that are not disproportionately longer than those displayed by individuals without the disease, which suggests that the disease does not adversely influence movement planning in certain movement situations (Stelmach, Worringham, & Strand, 1987). As the level of L-dopa declines in the basal ganglia, however, choice reaction times have been shown to increase dramatically among Parkinson's patients.

Researchers have also found that as the overall complexity of a movement task to be planned is increased, individuals with Parkinson's disease do not plan the action in its entirety prior to the signal to move. Instead, they plan only the first portion before beginning the movement. Once the movement is begun, they continue to plan the remainder of the movement. This tendency was not reflected in the CRT findings but showed up in the significantly longer movement times observed for the first segment of the movement. Including multiple measures, particularly when they are known to measure different aspects of motor control, therefore seems advisable for researchers interested in learning more about the effects of movement disorders on various aspects of motor control.

In addition to the specific information they can provide about the effect of a particular neurological disease on the planning and control of movements, RT and MT measurements can also be used to gain greater insight into the specific contributions of various brain structures to the skilled control of movement. Of course, a number of structures and/or areas within the CNS are integral to effective motor control. Thus the motor deficits observed in Parkinson's patients may also be due to other subsystems in the CNS having been adversely affected by the loss of the important neurotransmitter dopamine.

outcome occurred. For example, certain error scores can tell us whether performers undershot or overshot a target and how consistently they performed over multiple attempts.

The error scores we will discuss are absolute error (AE), variable error (VE), constant error (CE), absolute constant error (|CE|), and total error (E). Given that each error score provides slightly different information about the nature of the error, it is customary for researchers to calculate several error scores in experiments.

The error score that is quickest to calculate and the one most commonly used to evaluate performance is **absolute error (AE)**. This error score simply measures the amount of error associated with a particular performance. In the case of target pistol shooting, the total score obtained after 60 shots might be calculated. AE does not, however, provide us with any information about the direction of the error. For example, it would be helpful to know where each shot penetrated the target relative to the 10 ring and how often the shot landed in a particular area of the shooting zone.

> Absolute error measures the overall amount of error in a performance.

To obtain this type of information, two other error scores must be calculated. The first of these is **variable error (VE)**, a score that represents the degree of consistency, or the *variability*, associated with a given performance. This error score is obtained by calculating the standard deviation of the shooter's total score for 60 shots. The lower the standard deviation, the more consistent the performance.

> Variable error represents the degree of consistency or variability associated with a performance.

The second error score that provides useful information about the nature of the error is **constant error (CE)**. CE provides a measure of response bias, because it considers not only the amount of error but also the *direction* of the error. For example, if we were to divide the shooting target in half and assign a negative (−) value to the left side and a positive (+) value to the right side, we could determine whether the shooter tended to shoot more to one side of the 10 ring than to the other. From a practical perspective, the coach could use this information to help a performer alter his or her shooting technique. For a shooter whose shots continually land to the left of the 10 ring, the correction may be as simple as adjusting the sights on the shooter's pistol to eliminate this tendency. Simply recording AE would not have provided the coach with this meaningful piece of information.

> Constant error is used to measure the level of bias in a performance because it considers both the amount and direction of error.

As useful as this second type of performance error is when we are evaluating the performance of individuals, it offers a less accurate indication of performance bias when applied to a group of performers. This is because the score of one performer negates the score of a second performer when both record the same magnitude of error in opposite directions. If one shooter scored a 7 for a shot that landed on the left side of the 10 ring, and a second shooter fired a shot that landed on the right side in the 7 ring, then the two scores, when summed, would be equal to zero. To overcome this problem, Henry (1974) and Schutz (1977) suggested that the absolute values of both performers' CE scores be averaged. The overall bias of the group is then determined by comparing the number of positive and negative values associated with each individual's score. This alternative performance error score is called **absolute constant error (|CE|)**. It is reported more often in research studies than constant error because of its greater validity. One alternative to calculating both CE and VE is to use a composite score that combines these two measures (Henry, 1974). **Total error (E)** measures the total variability surrounding a particular performance. Using this error score is often considered the best means of capturing both response bias and variability in a single measure.

Response Process Measures

A shift in interest from simple motor skill situations involving movements of a single joint to situations characterized by complex interactions between mover and environment has prompted the use of measurement techniques designed to capture the moment-to-moment control of movement. These process-oriented measures not only have facilitated more precise descriptions of movement but also have provided a more comprehensive means of testing the validity of hierarchical and dynamic systems models. Four of the most popular measurement techniques currently used to describe and quantify the coordination and/or control of movement are kinematic, or form-related, measures; electromyography, kinetic, or force production indices; and angle–angle diagrams and phase plane portraits. Let's look at each of these measurement techniques and review their contributions to our understanding of how movements are produced.

Kinematic Descriptors.   Advances in filming equipment, coupled with the increasing availability of commercial software packages that incorporate mathematical and statistical programs (Peak Performance Systems, Qualisys, Watsmart), have given researchers an opportunity to quantify more objectively the **kinematics**—that is, the motion qualities without regard to force—that characterize the performance of a variety of motor skills. This type of technique provides the researcher with a vast array of information about limb displacement, acceleration, velocity, and other important movement-related parameters (see Figure 2.2). Kinematic analyses have helped us identify important components of particular movement patterns and explain differences in

> Kinematic analyses can be used to identify important components of a movement pattern and also to demonstrate how an action's goal can shape the observed behavior.

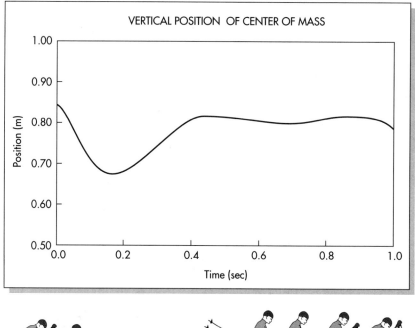

FIGURE 2.2 Kinematic analyses have been used to identify important components of a particular movement pattern that often differentiate skilled from unskilled performers.

movement outcomes. They also constitute an important set of measures for studying the control of action.

More recently, kinematic descriptions have been used to demonstrate how the overall goal associated with an action can shape the observable movement pattern. In one such study (Martenuik, Leavitt, MacKenzie, & Athenes, 1990), subjects were required to reach and grasp a disk located on a table in front of them and then perform one of two possible actions: throw the disk into a large cardboard box or place it into a well with a small opening. Careful review of the kinematic data describing the limb's movement during the two phases of the movement indicated that differences existed not only during the second phase of the movement, when subjects were required to handle the disk differently, but also during the first phase of the movement, which required exactly the same movement pattern for both tasks. The kinematic data showed that subjects who were required to perform the more precise of the two movements tended to decelerate the arm for a longer time before reaching the disk.

On the basis of these findings, the authors concluded that the spatial demands associated with the second component of the movement influenced how *both* components were planned and then ultimately controlled. None of the outcome-oriented measures we have described could have provided this insight into the nature of the planning and control processes used to perform these two very different types of movements. These findings have also proved troublesome for dynamic systems models that do not include a role for cognitive mediation in the production of movement.

Electromyography (EMG).   We noted earlier that electromyography (EMG) has enabled researchers to fractionate RT into a central and a peripheral component. It has also provided valuable information about a muscle's activity during movement. Recording electrodes are usually placed on the surface of the skin above the muscles of interest for the purpose of measuring the level of electrical activity that occurs in agonist and antagonist muscle groups during a particular movement. Once the raw EMG signal obtained from each muscle has been amplified and filtered, important spatial and temporal characteristics of the movement can be identified from the resulting output. An EMG wave form can answer questions related to the amount of force exerted by a given muscle, its amplitude and duration of contraction, and, in the case of multiple recordings, the temporal coordination between the various muscle groups.

Multiple EMG recordings have been used to describe how the various muscle groups in the leg and trunk are activated when we attempt to maintain and/or restore postural stability in a variety of environmental conditions. As Figure 2.3A and B illustrates, when the surface below us is relatively flat and broad, balance is restored after a **perturbation** by using an ankle synergy. This synergy is characterized by a muscle activation pattern that begins in the ankle joint muscles opposing the sway perturbation and then progresses to the proximal muscles in the thigh and lower trunk on the same dorsal or ventral aspect of the body. However, when the support surface below us (a narrow beam, for example) is shorter than the feet are long, a different postural synergy comes into play to help us maintain an upright posture. In this situation, muscles in the thigh and lower trunk muscles are activated on the opposite aspect of the body to those activated on the broader support surface. This activation pattern usually begins

> Multiple EMG recordings have been used to describe how the various muscle groups in the leg and trunk are activated when we attempt to restore balance.

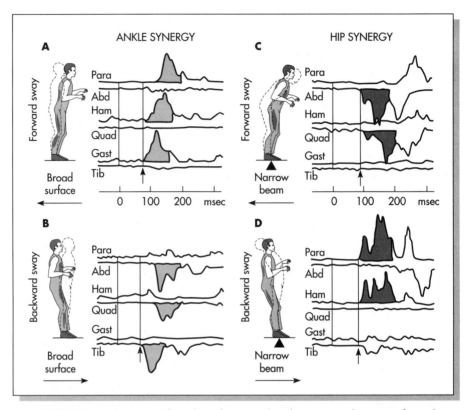

FIGURE 2.3   EMG recordings have been used to demonstrate the types of muscle response patterns to forward (top) and backward (bottom) sway perturbations. An ankle strategy is used on a normal, broad surface (A and B), whereas a hip strategy is used on a narrow surface (C and D).

within 100 milliseconds after the support surface is moved in a forward or backward direction. Figure 2.3C and D clearly indicate that a hip synergy is now being used to restore the body to an upright stance.

Kinetic Descriptors.   The analysis of any movement is really not complete until all the various internal and external forces acting on the body are considered. These can be measured with various types of equipment, including force platforms and smaller force transducers placed between the moving limb and the apparatus being moved. For example, force transducers can be used to describe the transfer of force between a rower's hands and the oar being pulled or the force of impact on a tennis player's racket hand as the ball is contacted in the serve. Once the amount of force applied by various limbs throughout the course of the movement has been analyzed and graphically

> Kinetic measures help us to understand why it is possible to achieve similar movement outcomes using different levels of force.

represented, researchers can determine how it is possible to achieve a similar movement outcome using different levels of force.

Angle–Angle Diagrams: Measuring Coordination.   The coordination within segments of a limb can be nicely described by plotting an **angle–angle diagram.** These diagrams can be used to illustrate the change in both the spatial and the temporal relationships of limb segments during the course of a movement sequence. Although angle–angle diagrams are most commonly used to represent cyclical activities such as walking and running, discrete actions of short duration can also be described via this measurement technique (Newell, 1985). Let us consider two studies in which angle–angle diagrams were used to examine intra-limb coordination patterns.

> The nature of the intra-limb coordination between segments of a limb can be described by plotting angle–angle diagrams.

Enoka and colleagues (Enoka, Miller, & Burgess, 1982) plotted the movement of a skilled runner's left knee joint against that of the left thigh during the course of a single stride (Figure 2.4A) and then compared the resulting angle–angle diagram to those constructed for three below-knee amputee runners (Figure 2.4B, C, and D). When we compare the topology of the curve for the skilled runner with those developed for the below-knee amputees, clear differences in the pattern of intra-limb coordination emerge, particularly during the stance phase of the stride (i.e., IFS to ITO). In contrast to the characteristic knee joint flexion–extension sequence observed during the stance phase in the skilled running gait, the knee–thigh diagram for each of the three amputees reveals a very different pattern. This pattern indicates that the knee is not being flexed during stance but is rather held at a constant angle. The amputees were using the left limb as a rigid lever about which to rotate while the prosthetic foot was in contact with the ground. Enoka (1988) suggests that these types of diagrams could be very useful to the clinician who is trying to help an amputee develop a gait pattern that more closely approximates a normal pattern.

Applying the same procedure to a discrete skill, McIntyre and Pfautsch (1982) constructed angle–angle diagrams to both describe and compare the intra-limb coordination of baseball batters who were considered effective opposite-field hitters with the pattern exhibited by ineffective opposite-field hitters. The relative motion of the hitter's bat and left forearm was plotted against the left elbow angle during a baseball batting swing to the same side or to the opposite side of the field. As Figure 2.5 indicates, the angle–angle diagrams of the effective and the ineffective batters are quite different. Whereas the profiles for same-field and opposite-field batting swings are quite similar for the effective

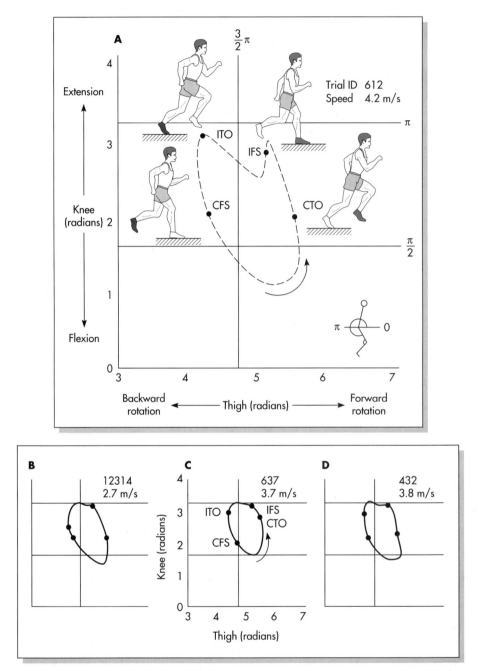

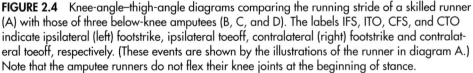

FIGURE 2.4 Knee-angle–thigh-angle diagrams comparing the running stride of a skilled runner (A) with those of three below-knee amputees (B, C, and D). The labels IFS, ITO, CFS, and CTO indicate ipsilateral (left) footstrike, ipsilateral toeoff, contralateral (right) footstrike and contralateral toeoff, respectively. (These events are shown by the illustrations of the runner in diagram A.) Note that the amputee runners do not flex their knee joints at the beginning of stance.

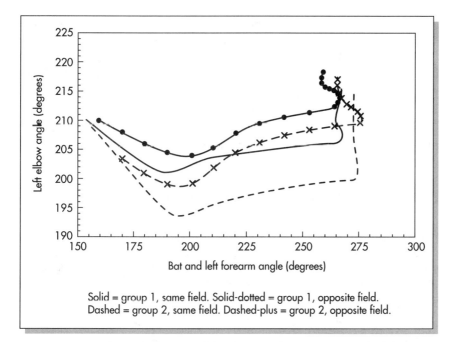

Solid = group 1, same field. Solid-dotted = group 1, opposite field.
Dashed = group 2, same field. Dashed-plus = group 2, opposite field.

FIGURE 2.5 Angle–angle diagram of the elbow angle and the bat and left forearm angle during a baseball batting swing to either the same field or the opposite field by effective (group 1) and by ineffective (group 2) opposite-field hitters.

hitters (group 1 in the diagram above), this is not true for the ineffective opposite-field hitters (group 2). Significant differences are also evident when the magnitudes of the joint angles for same-field batting are compared across the two groups. It would seem that these diagrams could also serve as a very useful tool for coaches in diagnosing and correcting persistent errors in technique.

Phase Plane Portraits: Measuring Control. The use of topological portraits, or **phase plane portraits,** to describe how movements are being controlled is an important measurement technique used by researchers to explore the qualitative dynamics associated with coordinated behavior within the framework of dynamic systems theory. Phase plane diagrams similar to those shown in Figure 2.6A–D are geometric representations of movement that are obtained by continuously plotting the relationship between two kinematic variables of interest. In contrast to the angle–angle diagrams just described, the dynamic position of a particular joint is plotted against a movement parameter (angular velocity) rather than the position of a second limb

> Phase plane portraits are used to illustrate how a particular movement is controlled during a movement.

segment. In this way, the manner in which a particular limb is coordinated *and* the way it is controlled can be measured concurrently.

Winstein and Garfinkel (1985) suggest that displaying the relationship between joint angular velocity and the position of a particular joint as a phase plane portrait provides a pictorial summary of the relationship between the changing velocity of a limb and its effect on joint position. Depicting the relationship between the two kinematic variables in this way also eliminates the need to review multiple graphs of single variables plotted against time (e.g., limb velocity vs. time and limb position vs. time), as the more traditional approach requires. Winstein and Garfinkel used this method to compare the trajectories of movement

FIGURE 2.6 (A) Normal phase plane trajectory of knee angle plotted against its angular velocity for one gait cycle. (B–D) Phase plane trajectories plotted for each of three hemiparetic patients. These phase plane portraits illustrate the different levels of control exerted by the knee joint during walking.

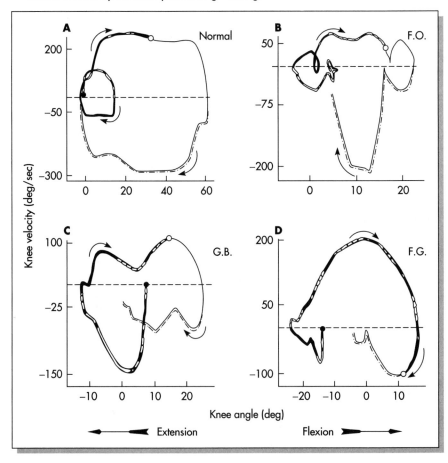

observed in unimpaired locomotor behavior with the disordered locomotor patterns exhibited by neurologically impaired individuals. They
were particularly interested in learning more about the underlying control mechanisms and how they influence the resulting action.

As Figure 2.6 indicates, clear differences are evident between the
phase plane trajectories exhibited by an unimpaired individual (A) and
those exhibited by three hemiparetic patients (B, C, and D). The authors
identify at least four qualitative features that differentiate disordered
from unimpaired locomotor patterns: (1) the absence of a square phase
plane trajectory, indicating the loss of appropriate timing and focused
control, (2) the absence of certain phase-dependent features, (3) smaller
overall movement trajectories and velocities, and (4) the presence of
cusps or "catches" in the movement trajectory that may indicate inappropriate activity of flexor and extensor muscle groups. Winstein and
Garfinkel suggest that further development and implementation of this
type of qualitative measurement technique may eventually allow
researchers to identify "qualitative signatures" that characterize certain
motor control pathologies.

Dynamic phase plane portraits are being used with increasing frequency to evaluate emerging models of motor control (Cooke, 1979), to
assess the effectiveness of certain therapeutic treatments (Knutsson,
1983; Winstein & Garfinkel, 1985), and to compare the qualitative differences in motor control that result from various pathologies (Beuter &
Garfinkel, 1985; Knutsson & Richards, 1979). Researchers interested in
better understanding how the control of movement changes with age are
also finding phase plane portraits a meaningful descriptive tool (Clark,
Whitall, & Phillips, 1988; Thelen, 1986).

NEUROLOGICAL MEASURES

The fact that we know as much as we do about the inner workings of
the nervous system is largely due to advances in recording techniques
and instrumentation that have taken place since the turn of the century.
These techniques have proved useful to researchers studying hierarchical models of motor control at a neurological level of analysis. A
variety of scientific measurement techniques have been used in this century, but we will focus on five measurement techniques currently
employed by scientists interested in discovering how the CNS contributes to the control and learning of action. These techniques are surface and intracellular electrical recordings, lesions, ablations, and brain
scanning techniques.

Surface Recordings—Evoked Potentials

One very useful and noninvasive technique designed to record event-related electrical activity within the brain involves averaging raw electrical signals recorded at the surface of the scalp. These averaged signals, or **evoked potentials (EPs),** have been shown to coincide with the presentation of certain sensory signals designed to elicit movement. A better understanding of the timetable involved in the planning and execution of voluntary movements has resulted from the use of this recording technique. The timing sequence that these scalp recordings suggest is involved in preparing to execute movement has been confirmed by intracellular recordings obtained from the same cortical regions in monkeys required to perform similar movements (Strick, 1983; Thach, 1978).

> Evoked potentials enhance our understanding of the timetable involved in the planning and execution of voluntary movements.

Intracellular Recordings

The development and refinement of intracellular recording techniques has provided neuroscientists with the means to explore directly the internal operations of brain cells during the execution of movement. To accomplish this goal, a micropipette with a very sharp tip is inserted directly into the brain and used to record intracellular potentials as a movement proceeds. Although the use of this invasive technique is limited to animal studies, it has provided us with a better understanding of the role of certain neurological structures in the planning and execution of movements. For example, intracellular recordings of cell activity in the basal ganglia have shown it plays a much more diverse role in the planning and control of movement (Connor & Abbs, 1991; DeLong & Georgopoulos, 1981) than was previously thought. Similarly, recordings obtained from certain cells of the cerebellum have elucidated its functions in the control and learning of movements (Brooks, 1984; Gilbert & Thach, 1977).

Lesions and Ablations

Another type of experimental method used to identify the possible role(s) played by various structures within the CNS during movement involves either the ablation (cutting out) of certain well-known structures in the CNS or the introduction of lesions to the same structures. The invasive nature of these two techniques restricts their use to animal applications. In these studies, the ability of animals to control and/or learn new movements is carefully studied after the removal or lesioning of the structure of interest. Although the results of such animal studies have enriched our knowledge base about the functions of individual structures and the residual capabilities of other connecting structures within the CNS, one must be cautious in applying these findings to human nervous system function.

An alternative to the use of animal models to describe CNS function has been the development of pathological models of motor control based on clinically diagnosed populations. Despite the distributed processing that characterizes the human nervous system, wherein responsibility for action planning and execution is shared by a number of cortical and sub-cortical structures, several neurological disorders affect specific brain structures and motor behavior in clearly identifiable ways. For example, studies conducted with individuals suffering from Parkinson's disease (Della Sala, Lorenzo, Giordano, & Spinnler, 1986; Stelmach, Worringham, & Strand, 1986), known to selectively affect basal ganglia function, have yielded considerable insight into the role of the basal ganglia in the planning and coordination of movement. Clinical observations of patients with damage confined to the cerebellum (Hallett, Shahani, & Young, 1975; Nashner & Grimm, 1978), another important structure involved in the planning and coordination of movement, have also yielded valuable information about normal CNS function. In the next chapter, we will discuss in greater detail the roles of the basal ganglia and cerebellum in motor control.

> Pathological models of motor control based on clinical populations provide a viable alternative to the use of animal models to describe CNS function.

Brain Scanning Techniques

During the course of the last decade, further advances in technology have made it possible to visualize the CNS on a grand scale. One particular technique known as **nuclear magnetic resonance imaging** (**NMRI**) provides high-resolution computerized scans of the brain's anatomy that can be used to detect abnormalities in areas of the CNS that would not be visible using x-ray imaging such as **computer tomography** (**CT**) scans. NMRI has been extremely helpful in identifying lesions associated with multiple sclerosis and abnormalities in the spinal cord area (Kent & Larson, 1988).

A more recently developed brain scanning technique that has enabled scientists to study dynamic brain function is **positron emission topography** (**PET**). These scans are made possible by injecting certain tracer substances into the brain. Unlike the static NMRI techniques, PET scans monitor changes

> The development of positron emission topography has enabled researchers to study dynamic brain function.

Positron emission topography (PET) has enabled researchers to study dynamic brain function.

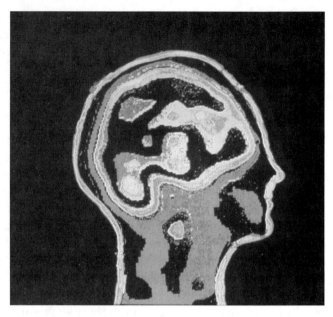

in regional blood flow during the performance of various motor and language tasks. Increased blood flow in certain regions is thought to indicate their level of involvement in the processing activity under way. The images produced show the distribution of metabolic processes (such as glucose utilization) that are associated with electrical activity.

This technique has enabled researchers not only to assess the level of functional damage in the CNS that often leaves brain structures intact but also to study the localization of higher functions (such as language abilities). Still more recently, PET and NMRI have been successfully used together to study the effectiveness of neural transplant surgery conducted in a small number of patients suffering from Parkinson's disease (Sawle & Myers, 1993). As effective as this brain scanning technique appears to be in the study of dynamic brain function, its complexity, invasiveness, and high cost have limited its application in the area of motor control.

SUMMARY

Researchers have employed a variety of measurement techniques in their attempts to understand how the human system produces an infinite number of motor actions. At a psychological level of analysis, researchers have used a combination of measurement techniques in an effort to describe what elements of the human system are being controlled and how the processes underlying performance are organized. These techniques have focused largely on the use of various kinematic, kinetic, and electromyographical descriptors of movement and innovative techniques for qualitatively representing the dynamic elements of action (e.g., angle–angle diagrams and phase plane portraits).

Chronometric measures (e.g., measures of reaction time and movement time) have been used to explore the timing and duration of cognitive operations that researchers hypothesize are involved in the planning and execution of action plans believed to be prepared in advance of the actual movement. Various types of performance error measures have been used to learn more about the nature of the movement outcome. Recent technological advances have also permitted the use of neurological measurement techniques to study how a particular action is organized to achieve a given goal. These more objective process measures have contributed many pieces to the puzzle of human motor control.

There are still many more questions than answers in the area of motor control. The continued development of new measurement techniques should enable us to test ever more effectively the predictions of present and future models of motor control.

IMPORTANT TERMINOLOGY

After completing this chapter, readers should be familiar with the following terms and concepts.

absolute constant error (|CE|)
absolute error (AE)
angle–angle diagrams
choice reaction time (CRT)
chronometry
computer tomography (CT)
constant error (CE)
discrimination reaction time (DRT)
electromyography (EMG)
evoked potentials (EPs)
fractionated reaction time (FRT)
kinematics
kinetics
motor time (MOT)
movement time (MT)
nuclear magnetic resonance imaging (NMRI)
perturbation
phase plane portraits
positron emission topography (PET)
premotor time (PRMOT)
reaction time (RT)
simple reaction time (SRT)
speed–accuracy trade-off
total error (E)
variable error (VE)

SUGGESTED FURTHER READING

Snyder, C.W. Jr., & Abernethy, B. In press. *Understanding human action through experimentation.* Champaign, IL: Human Kinetics.

Sparrow, W.A. 1992. Measuring changes in coordination and control. In *Approaches to the study of motor control and learning,* ed. J.J. Summers, pp. 147–162. North-Holland: Elsevier Science Publishers B.V.

TEST YOUR UNDERSTANDING

1. Describe the various types of measurement that have been categorized as (a) response outcome measures and (b) response process measures.

2. How does the type of information obtained by using fractionated reaction time differ from that obtained by using other types of reaction time measures?

3. Describe three task-related variables that influence how quickly a movement is initiated.

4. Identify the performance error measures that convey each of the following kinds of information about a performance.
    (a) The total amount of error observed.
    (b) Whether the performer undershot or overshot a target.
    (c) The amount of variability observed in a performance.

5. Briefly explain what the term *speed–accuracy trade-off* means. In what type of movement situations is it likely to occur?

6. Compare the type of information obtained by using kinematic descriptors with that obtained by using kinetic measures.

7. Briefly describe how angle–angle diagrams and phase plane portraits contribute to our understanding of motor control. Provide examples of sports and/or clinical situations in which these two different types of measurement techniques have been used.

8. Describe the measurement techniques that are employed at a neurological level of analysis and provide us with a dynamic view of CNS function during movement.

About the Quote

The scientific method to which Magill refers involves the systematic and objective observation of potential relationships among variables. Each time we read a research article describing the outcome of one or more experiments, we witness the use of the scientific method to describe, explain, and predict on the basis of the information obtained from the experimental process. In order to study the variable or variables of interest, however, the researcher must control for, or eliminate, all other variables that might interfere with or further complicate the relationship of interest. This requires careful planning on the part of the experimenter(s), who must consider how best to organize the experiment to answer the question(s) posed and the most appropriate form of measurement to use. You now have some understanding of the different types of measurement used to examine motor control.

The need for careful control over the number of parameters allowed to vary freely in an experiment often leads to frustration for the practitioner who reads such articles. This is because the experimental tasks may be very unlike those performed in a "real world" setting or because the setting itself may seem too contrived to yield any useful information. Fortunately, as experimentation progresses and the robustness of the relationship is established, more variables can be introduced. The relationship can be investigated in a more realistic setting, and the tasks being performed can more closely resemble those performed in everyday living and sports settings. It is only by putting an instructional or clinical technique to the scientific test that a practitioner can be assured of its value to the learner and/or patient.

CHAPTER 3
DEVELOPING AND EXECUTING A PLAN OF ACTION

CHAPTER OBJECTIVES

- Understand and be able to describe the cognitive and neuromotor processes involved in the planning and execution of goal-directed actions.

- Understand and be able to describe the various mechanisms available in the spinal system for the ongoing control and modification of movement.

- Understand and be able to describe the primary mechanisms by which the appropriate amount of force for a given motor action can be generated.

- Understand how the musculoskeletal system influences the production of force.

- Understand and be able to describe how movements can be controlled and/or modified at a subconscious level.

> *"Motor action is the product of a whole company of players, not of individual performers."*
>
> —Brooks (1986)

Interaction with our environment is achieved through a variety of goal-directed postures and movements. Consider an infant attempting to take those first, uncertain steps or a prima ballerina performing a virtuoso sequence of dance steps. The observable motor behavior of both requires the cooperation of the nervous and musculoskeletal systems. Whereas the nervous system is largely responsible for orchestrating the plan of action, the musculoskeletal system is ultimately responsible for its execution and ongoing control.

Despite the fact that we still do not know exactly *how* information flows between the two systems or *what* movement variables are controlled by the CNS, it has become increasingly clear that motor control is not localized within the brain but rather is distributed throughout the CNS. Various brain and spinal centers work together to produce coordinated movement, and cooperation among the neural centers is made possible by a rich network of feedback loops. These reciprocal connections facilitate communication, comparison, and correction at all levels of the CNS.

> Motor control is not localized within the brain but is distributed throughout the CNS.

This chapter is intended to provide the reader with a general understanding of how we plan and execute goal-directed actions. We will conduct our discussion at both the cognitive and the neuromotor level of analysis in order to achieve a more comprehensive understanding of the action planning process. We will begin with a brief description of the types of cognitive processes involved in the planning and execution of action plans. Then we will consider the areas of the nervous system that appear to be involved in carrying out these cognitive processes. Although our discussion of the processes involved in the planning and execution of action will be sequential, always remember that many cognitive processes are occurring simultaneously and that other areas within the CNS are also active at various times during the planning and execution of action. Much is known about the operations of the CNS, but much more remains to be discovered.

PLANNING THE ACTION

Making the Decision to Act

At a cognitive level, the action-planning process begins with a decision or intention to act. This decision may be the result of an internally generated goal or may occur in response to changes in the surrounding environment. During this aspect of the action-planning process, illustrated in Figure 3.1, the performer receives and analyzes a myriad of inputs from the various senses within the body but also acknowledges a large amount of information from the external environment. These inputs may then be matched with an existing goal for action or used to develop the goal the performer thinks will best fit the constraints imposed by the surrounding environment. For example, during the course of a game, a tennis player may decide to return the ball as close to the baseline as possible so that she or he can run in close to the net and prepare to follow up with a short, angled volley return to win the point (the goal).

> The action planning process begins with a decision or intention to act.

Before acting on the goal, however, it is important for the player to monitor carefully all the associated sensory input, such as the opponent's position on the court, the movement of the ball off the opponent's racket, and the player's own responding movements and court location. In this way, the player can best determine, on the basis of the incoming sensory input, whether the intended goal is realistic. It is quite likely that the player who does not attend to certain relevant cues in the environment will develop a less-than-optimal plan of action. This would cer-

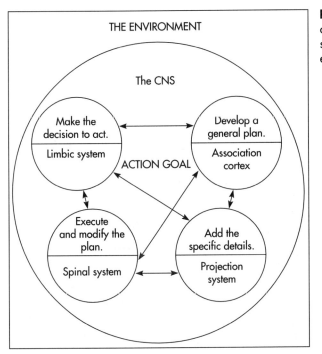

FIGURE 3.1 A multilevel view of the cognitive operations and functional task systems involved in the planning and execution of goal-directed actions.

tainly be the case if the opponent's return forced the player to run deep into the corner of the court and make a weak return stroke that barely passed over the net. Given this change in the environmental conditions, it would be necessary to rethink the goal of the action.

Developing a General Plan

Once the decision to act has been made, the planning process continues with the development of a very general plan of action. How appropriate is the plan of action that is subsequently developed will be determined by a variety of factors. Important among these are the performer's previous experience with the movements to be executed and how well the movement situation was initially evaluated. If the performer has experienced the same or a similar movement situation before, then it is likely that his or her evaluation of the environment and choice of action will be more accurate. Experienced players of golf, for example, are more likely to choose the most appropriate approach shot to the green because they have experienced a similar situation on many previous occasions. In contrast, the novice player has little idea what stroke or golf club is most appropriate for the situation.

> The quality of the action plan is influenced by the performer's previous experience and by how well the movement situation was initially evaluated.

Adding Details to the Plan

Specific details must be added to the general plan in order to accomplish the movement goal.

Once the general plan of action has been developed, the individual begins to add the specific details of the action. These details involve selecting the various movement parameters (e.g., force, velocity, displacement) necessary to accomplish the original goal of the movement. The decision to propel a ball at a particular target, for example, is not sufficient to prompt or ensure a successful outcome. Before this is possible, the performer must also decide which body part will be used to propel the object, what level of force is needed, and the direction and amount of limb displacement.

In addition to considering the goal of the movement itself, the performer must also consider the existing environmental constraints. These might include the distance from the target, its overall size, and whether it is fixed or moving in space. Unless all these variables are accounted for during the planning process, it is unlikely that the emerging action will adequately reflect the intended goal. Having said this, however, we must also recognize that many actions fail to achieve the intended goal because of factors outside the control of the individual. For example, the environment may be changing too quickly as the action is being planned to allow sufficient time for the performer to make the necessary modifications.

Executing the Plan of Action

The specific plan of action is finally performed by various parts of the musculoskeletal system, and a movement outcome is produced. The process does not stop here, however, because it is important to know whether the movement outcome adequately reflected the original goal. This all-important evaluation is made possible by feedback derived from sources that are either internal or external to the performer. Examples of internal sources include the various subsystems involved in the planning and execution of the action and the various muscles and joints performing the action. The surrounding movement environment also provides an extremely important source of feedback to the performer and, very often, determines the shape of the movement outcome. The ability to recognize the available sensory feedback and prioritize its use often distinguishes the skilled from the novice performer, because it is on the basis of this movement-based feedback that the performer is able to elaborate and/or modify aspects of the action plan at all stages of its development and implementation. As we will also see in the section of this textbook on motor learning, movement-based feedback is essential for helping us develop knowledge about our movement-based experiences that is then used to make the learning of new motor skills or the refinement of existing skills easier.

THE NEUROMOTOR LEVEL OF ANALYSIS

As informative as it is to describe the cognitive processes involved in the formulation and implementation of action plans, descriptions based only at a cognitive level do not tell the whole story. Not only do they fail to identify the actual mechanisms responsible for transforming our many thoughts into action, but they also leave us with the impression that information follows a specific and unidirectional route through the four cognitive processes shown in Figure 3.1. One has only to observe skilled actions to realize that there are many ways in which a movement goal can be achieved. Instead of producing a specific movement pattern on each attempt, the skilled performer chooses the action plan that produces the best match between his or her own performance goals and the constraints of the environment in which the movement is to be performed. Moreover, it is rare that only one action plan is being developed at any given moment. In reality, the performer is often planning future actions while still implementing earlier ones. Any or all of the systems illustrated in Figure 3.1 could be active at any moment in time.

> The skilled performer develops the action plan that produces the best match between the performance goal and the environmental constraints.

In order to better understand how goal-directed behavior is accomplished, it is necessary to describe the action-planning process at the neuromotor processes level. Describing action at this level helps us begin to identify the actual neurological mechanisms that are involved in the planning and execution of any particular action. As is evident in Figure 3.2, the human brain can be divided into several anatomical regions that serve different but complementary functions. Some regions are primarily responsible for vision, hearing, speech, and higher intellectual thought, whereas others are intricately involved in the orchestration of movements. It is to these movement-related areas of the brain that we now direct our attention.

Let us begin by identifying the various neural centers that have been shown to be involved in some aspect of the planning and/or execution of action. To guide us in this discussion, a review of Figure 3.1 is in order. Four areas within the CNS appear to be actively involved in the cognitive processes underlying the planning and execution of action.

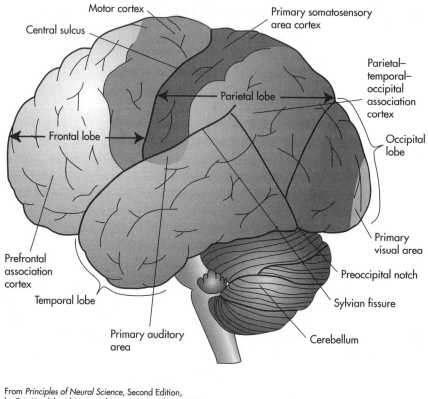

From *Principles of Neural Science*, Second Edition,
by Eric Kandel and James Schwartz. Copyright © 1985
by Appleton and Lange. Reprinted by permission.

FIGURE 3.2 The human brain from an anatomist's viewpoint.

These include the limbic system, the association cortex, the projection system, and the spinal system. These areas are identified not in terms of their anatomical location within the CNS but, rather, according to the way they function during the planning of actions. Brooks (1986) has collectively described these areas as functional neural "task systems" (p. 19).

The Limbic System

The intention to act is associated with a set of interconnected neural

The limbic system helps fulfill our desire to act.

structures that surround the upper brainstem area within the cerebrum. The **limbic system** helps us fulfill our desire to act in response to the demands of the environmental context. This desire to act provides us with the goal for action and thereby triggers subsequent events in the planning process. Important components within this system include the fornix, amygdala, cingulate gyrus, mamillary bodies, and regions of the hypothalamus. An additional component of this system that appears to be an important memory structure is the hippocampus. The role of this structure in the development of memory representations will be discussed further in Chapter 8.

The Association Cortex

Because the association areas distributed throughout the cortex receive partially processed sensory inputs from other areas within the CNS, it is likely that these areas play an important role in the planning of actions. A second look at Figure 3.2 confirms the distributed nature of the **association cortex;** association areas are located in the frontal, temporal, and parietal lobes of the brain. Among the primary functions attributed to these areas are the recognition, selection, and integration of relevant sensory inputs reaching the higher levels of the cortex. A sophisticated network of nerve pathways that connects the limbic system with the association cortex also provides the means by which the decision to act or not act can be communicated to the entire association cortex. It is within this widely distributed area of the cortex that a general plan for action is thought to be first formulated. Of course, the development of this plan is also influenced by the incoming sensory inputs that receive their final processing in the association cortex. In this way, the association cortex has information relevant to the needs of the performer and to the state of the environment in which the action will be executed.

> The general plan of action is developed within the widely distributed association areas of the cortex.

The Projection System

Yet another set of cognitive processes related to the planning and execution of action resides in a set of midbrain and cortical structures that make up the **projection system.** A large body of neurological research has indicated that one of the primary functions of this system is to determine how the action is to be carried out. The projection system is responsible for adding the movement dynamics necessary to shape the general action plan into one that best fits the performer's goal and the environmental constraints of the moment. The projection system consists of both the sensory and motor areas of the cortex in addition to various other subcortical nuclei. Two subcortical structures and one cortical structure—the basal ganglia, the cerebellum, and

> Structures within the projection system determine how the action is to be executed by adding the details needed to shape the general plan.

the motor cortex—are integral to the successful functioning of this task system. In light of the fact that these three components are thought to be instrumental in the development of more specific action plans, a discussion of their respective roles in the formulation of action plans is warranted.

Basal Ganglia. The specific role of the basal ganglia (BG) in motor control has been examined using a variety of research methods. Most of these have involved (1) intracellular recordings obtained from certain BG nuclei in awake animals performing voluntary movements or (2) induced lesion studies also performed using animals. In addition, the quantitative analysis of movement deficits resulting from BG damage has provided much insight into the specific operations performed by the nuclei that compose this structure. Analyses of this type have been conducted primarily in clinical settings with patients suffering from either Parkinson's or Huntington's disease. On the basis of this research, it is believed that the BG play a key role in the scaling of specific parameters of movement (e.g., velocity, direction, and amplitude), while also assisting with preparations for action. One has only to observe the difficulty with which Parkinson's patients attempt to initiate movements or maintain their amplitude to appreciate the importance of the role the basal ganglia play in both the planning and the execution of action.

> The basal ganglia appear to play an important role in the scaling of specific movement parameters.

Cerebellum. The cerebellum (or "little brain," as it is often called because it, like the larger cerebrum, is composed of two hemispheres) has also been shown to play a vital role in the control of action. By virtue of its elaborate connections with the spinal system, brainstem, and cerebral cortex, the cerebellum is able to compare information arriving from peripheral receptors with that being sent out from the cortex and other areas within the projection system. Comparison of these multiple inputs enables the cerebellum not only to coordinate and regulate the quality of the action produced but also to serve as a major center for the detection and correction of movement errors. Indeed, many theorists consider the cerebellum the site of the **efferent copy** or "blueprint for action." This copy of intended movement is compared to sensory inputs arriving from the periphery that provide moment-to-moment updates relative to joint movement and muscle tension and length, in particular. In this way, any mismatch between what was intended and what is actually occurring can be quickly detected and addressed.

As was the case with the basal ganglia, many of the functions attributed to the cerebellum have become known through systematic analysis of the movement behaviors of individuals with various forms of cerebellar dysfunction. These studies have confirmed that the cerebellum is involved in the coordination and regulation of movements. They have also demonstrated the important role played by the cerebellum in the maintenance of postural stability and smooth locomotor patterns. The recording of neuronal activity in certain cells of the cerebellum has also provided support for cerebellar involvement in the acquisition of new movement patterns.

> The cerebellum serves as a mechanism for error detection and correction.

Motor Cortex.   As early as 1870, Fritsch and Hitzig discovered that the direct application of electrical current to a particular area of the cortex resulted in movement. Unfortunately, this discovery led a number of researchers to conclude erroneously that the area known as the motor cortex controlled the execution of all voluntary movements. Current research suggests that the motor cortex plays an integral part in the planning and execution of movements, but its role is considerably more specialized than was previously thought. That is, the motor cortex appears to be selectively involved in the production of skilled movements, particularly those that demand finely discriminated hand and finger movements. This ability can be observed in a skilled seamstress threading a needle or in a musician performing a musical piece on a classical guitar. A second but related function of the motor cortex seems to be regulation of the development of muscular force during movement. This is an important feature of slow movements that demand precision and of those that entail controlled acceleration and/or deceleration. These abilities are certainly integral to successful performance in a variety of sports and many activities associated with daily life.

> The motor cortex appears to be selectively involved in the production of fine motor actions and the regulation of muscle force during movement.

Although the specific functions of the basal ganglia, cerebellum, and motor cortex have been highlighted in this section, it is important to remember that the motor behavior we observe cannot be attributed solely to any one of these three components—or even to the larger projection system to which they belong. Rather, as we said earlier, the emerging motor behavior is the result of an interaction among the many subsystems within the nervous system, and no one subsystem is able to produce the movement or even to dictate how it is to be performed. This last statement has important implications for the physical therapist who helps patients relearn functional movement patterns that can no longer be accessed or organized in the ways they were before.

> The emerging motor behavior is the result of an interaction among the many subsystems within the CNS. No one subsystem has priority over another.

Motor Pathways

Information specific to the movement to be performed reaches the spinal system via two important sets of motor pathways: the **pyramidal tract** and the **extrapyramidal system** of pathways. Once the information is conveyed to this system, it becomes the responsibility of specialized neurons (alpha, or skeletomotor, neurons) to carry the information out to the various muscle response synergies (a group of muscles constrained to act together) that will ultimately perform the action. The alpha motoneuron therefore serves as the final pathway linking the CNS with the skeletal muscular system.

The Pyramidal Pathway. As Figure 3.3 indicates, the axons associated with the pyramidal (lateral and ventral corticospinal tract) system of pathways are some of the longest axons in the human CNS. From their origin in the motor and sensory areas of the cerebral cortex, the axons that make up this system of pathways descend uninterrupted to the spinal cord, where they synapse indirectly, and, sometimes directly, with motoneurons distributed throughout its various levels. This anatomical feature, coupled with the large diameters of the axons of this motor system, ensures that movement-related information reaches its final destination in the spinal system with considerable speed. It is not surprising, then, that the primary function of the pyramidal system is to assist in the control of rapid and precise movements of the extremities. This motor system is also capable of influencing reflexive actions by selectively inhibiting or exciting spinal cord motoneurons responsible for innervating muscle.

> The pyramidal system assists in the control of movements that are both rapid and precise in nature.

Extrapyramidal Pathways. In contrast to the faster-conducting pyramidal pathway, the second major system of motor pathways transmits information at considerably slower speeds. This is largely because the axons composing the extrapyramidal system are frequently interrupted, particularly in the subcortical areas of the brain. Although these many synaptic connections rule out a role for this system in the production of rapid movements, this feature provides an important modifying function in motor control. Unlike the pyramidal system, the extrapyramidal system is a well-distributed and complex network of pathways originating in both the cerebral cortex and the subcortex.

These pathways interconnect areas within the cerebral cortex, basal ganglia, and thalamus and several areas within the brainstem. Less attention has been directed to uncovering the specific functions of the

FIGURE 3.3 Pathways of the pyramidal system (the lateral and ventral corticospinal tracts) carry motor impulses to skeletal muscles.

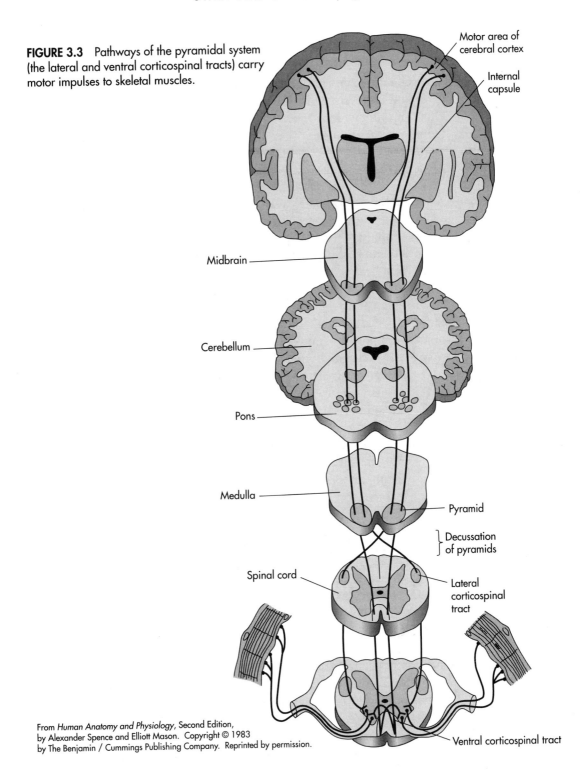

From *Human Anatomy and Physiology*, Second Edition, by Alexander Spence and Elliott Mason. Copyright © 1983 by The Benjamin / Cummings Publishing Company. Reprinted by permission.

extrapyramidal pathways, largely because of their overwhelming complexity. It is likely, however, that this system of interconnecting pathways enables us to modify actions—before they are executed in some cases and certainly while they are being executed in many more cases. One can only imagine how inflexible our actions would be without the modifying capabilities of the extrapyramidal system.

The Spinal System

Many of the final details related to the actual execution and ongoing control of movements are left to the **spinal system,** which directly regulates the timing of the various muscle activation patterns in those parts of the **skeletal muscular system** that will actually perform the desired movement. Minor adjustments to the movement pattern can also be made at this level through regulation of the firing levels of motoneurons responsible for activating the various muscle response synergies involved in the performance of the action. How the spinal system functions in the moment-to-moment control of action is the subject of the next section.

The spinal system directly regulates the timing of the various activation patterns of the muscle response synergies involved in the action.

Although this description of the neuromotor processes might also suggest that information flowing through the various areas in the nervous system follows a specific and unidirectional route, this is simply not the case, particularly when one considers that the various task systems are all interconnected via an elaborate network of internal feedback loops (see Figure 3.1). These interconnections allow the CNS to make comparisons at various points in the planning process and to determine whether the movement currently being executed will effectively achieve the goal originally conceived. It is not always possible to make adjustments in the plan before the movement begins, but continuous feedback from areas both within and external to the CNS can certainly be used to modify, or even curtail, movements already in progress.

MOMENT-TO-MOMENT CONTROL

Once the plan of action has been developed by the various subsystems within the CNS, all that remains to be done is recruitment of the appropriate muscle response synergies to execute the action plan. As the reader will recall from our discussion in Chapter 1, these groups of muscles, constrained to act as a single functional unit, enable us to reduce the number of degrees of freedom we must individually control. This has the net effect of simplifying the decision-making process for the CNS. How then does the CNS decide which muscle response synergies are actually recruited for a given action? McCrea (1992) suggests that the final decision as to which muscle groups will be activated is largely governed by two factors: the type of action produced at the joint(s) spanned by the muscle response synergy and the total number of synergies needed to generate enough force to produce a desired action. This force may be generated for the purpose of propelling an object such as a javelin, or may be exerted against the ground and air as we perform the final approach run and take-off in the high jump.

It has become increasingly clear in the last two decades that the ongoing control and coordination of movement is not the sole responsibility of higher cortical structures, as hierarchical models of motor control had assumed. Instead, coordinated movement is made possible by the interactions between multiple subsystems located at all levels of the CNS. This change in perspective has been fueled by a resurging interest among researchers in the operations performed by lower levels within the CNS (such as the spinal cord) and the musculoskeletal system with which these lower levels are ultimately interfaced.

The collective results of these many studies have prompted researchers to both modify and extend the widely held view that the spinal system serves as a passive conduit for neural messages traveling between higher cortical levels and the skeletomuscular system. This older view has now been replaced with a considerably more dynamic view of spinal cord function. In this view, the spinal system is accorded greater responsibility for the ongoing control and coordination of a broad range of voluntary movements, and other subsystems within the CNS play a complementary rather than a dominant role. Let us begin at a neurological level by describing the different types of motoneurons found throughout the spinal cord and their respective roles in movement production and modification.

Types of Motoneurons

Alpha or Skeletomotor Neurons.   Once the information for action has been conveyed to the spinal system, a number of neurons distributed throughout the various segments of the spinal cord are activated. One of these types of neurons assumes the responsibility of carrying the neural impulses to the appropriate muscle response synergies. This is the function of the **alpha motoneuron** or **skeletomotor neuron**, which

> The alpha motoneuron serves as the final pathway linking the CNS with the skeletal muscular system.

forms the final common pathway leading from the CNS to the peripheral musculature. These alpha motoneurons are organized into groups, or pools, within the spinal cord and are collectively responsible for the innervation of specific skeletal muscles.

Gamma or Fusimotor Neurons. The second type of motoneuron present within the spinal system is the **gamma motoneuron** or **fusimotor neuron.** This second type of motoneuron is activated by the same neural impulses that activate the alpha motoneurons in a process called **alpha–gamma coactivation.** Unlike the alpha motoneurons, however, which send their impulses to the extrafusal fibers of skeletal muscle, the gamma motoneuron carries its message to a specialized receptor called the **muscle spindle,** which is located deep within the muscle. Although the role of this extensively studied receptor in the ongoing control and modification of voluntary movement is still not completely understood, it is considered an extremely important mechanism for detecting and correcting movement-related errors. We will describe exactly how the muscle spindle can serve this function in a later section of this chapter.

> Gamma motoneurons carry their message to the muscle spindles, specialized receptors located deep within the muscle.

Interneurons. The third type of neuron located in the spinal system is the **interneuron.** The exact role played by interneurons in the ongoing control and modification of movement has yet to be elucidated, but it is clear that sophisticated networks of interneurons exist both within and between segments of the spinal cord. Advances in cell-recording technologies have provided further evidence that these networks are responsible for integrating the internally generated information arriving from other subsystems within the CNS. They are also responsible for integrating the various sensory inputs that enter the CNS at various levels of the spinal cord.

How are interneurons able to serve such a complex function? It is primarily because of their ability either to excite or to inhibit the pools of motoneurons with which they synapse. In this way, certain muscles can be inhibited while others are excited to produce coordinated movement. This process of simultaneous excitation and inhibition, or **reciprocal inhibition** as it is most often called, not only permits us to make the automatic adjustments in posture necessary when we touch a hot item or step in a hole while running but also assists us in voluntarily coordinating our limbs when performing the many activities associated

> Coordinated action is achieved through the simultaneous activation and inhibition of motor neuron pools serving different muscle groups.

with daily life. What is perhaps even more interesting is the fact that these neural circuits comprising inhibitory and excitatory interneurons appear capable of orchestrating movements without being directed to do so by other subsystems within the CNS. These hypothetical neural circuits are often referred to as **central pattern generators** (see the accompanying Highlight).

Muscle Activation and Force Production

As mentioned earlier, the final link between the spinal and musculoskeletal subsystems is created by the alpha motoneuron synapsing with extrafusal muscle fibers at a site known as the **neuromuscular junction** or motor end plate. At this juncture, the electrical energy conveyed by the alpha motoneuron is converted to chemical energy in the form of a neurotransmitter substance (e.g., acetylcholine) that penetrates the membrane of the muscle. If the potential generated at the neuromuscular junction is sufficient in magnitude, it will be converted to a muscle action potential. The generation of this muscle action potential then triggers a second chain of muscular events that culminate in the interaction of two very important contractile proteins (actin and myosin) within the muscle itself. This two-step process, which is called **excitation–contraction coupling,** is responsible for transforming action potentials into muscular force.

The connection between a single alpha motoneuron and the extrafusal muscle fibers innervated by it forms the most fundamental unit of motor control, a **motor unit.** The exact size of these motor units is determined by the total number of muscle fibers innervated by one alpha motoneuron. Some alpha motoneurons (e.g., muscles of the leg and trunk) innervate as many as 2000 muscle fibers; others (e.g., muscles of the eye and fingers) innervate as few as 10 to 15 muscle fibers. These large differences in innervation ratios influence the level of motor control available in certain muscles. Innervation ratios that are very low facilitate movements requiring fine motor control, whereas larger innervation ratios make it possible to generate the large amounts of force characteristic of more gross movements.

> The fundamental unit of motor control is the motor unit.

Motor Unit Recruitment.   How is it that individual motor units can be activated to assist us in generating just the right amount of force necessary to produce different levels of motor control? Two mechanisms are available to the CNS to accomplish this goal. The first is related to how

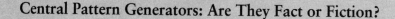

HIGHLIGHT

Central Pattern Generators: Are They Fact or Fiction?

The conclusion that certain stereotypical movement patterns, such as locomotion, could continue to be generated without any control being exerted by the cerebral cortex has been formed on the strength of the results of a number of research studies involving "spinal" animals (animals in which the spinal cord has been disconnected from higher cortical levels and peripheral sources of information). When these posturally supported spinal animals are placed on moving treadmills and electrically stimulated, they are able to produce a locomotor pattern very similar to that of an intact animal (Grillner, 1981; Forssberg, 1985; Forssberg, Grillner, & Rossignol, 1977). How is this continued locomotion possible in the absence of higher cortical involvement?

Researchers aligned with hierarchical theories of motor control hypothesize that flexible networks, or circuits of neurons located within the spinal cord, are responsible for producing certain rhythmical movements such as locomotion and breathing. Although these circuits are triggered in the spinal animals by electrical stimulation, it is believed that in the case of intact humans and animals, these circuits are first "turned on" by neural impulses reaching the spinal cord from one or more "command" neurons located in higher regions of the CNS (the brainstem and cortex). Once triggered, these neural circuits, which are known as central pattern generators (CPGs), are capable of independently maintaining a locomotor pattern through alternating bursts of activity in flexor and extensor muscle groups of the legs.

In addition to being able to generate the locomotor pattern continuously, CPGs are also thought to be capable of adjusting the locomotor pattern in response to peripheral feedback from cutaneous, muscle, and joint receptors in the moving limbs. This capability has been observed when the speed of the tread-

the respective motor units are *recruited* during muscle contraction, and the second involves the *rate* at which individual motoneurons are activated. The discovery of the first of these two mechanisms can be attributed to a set of observations made by Denny-Brown (1938), who reported that motor units appeared to be recruited in a very orderly sequence. Some time later, Henneman (1957; 1979) discovered that the recruitment pattern first observed by Denny-Brown appeared to be determined by the size of the motor unit. This hypothetical explanation, referred to as the **size principle**, is thought to apply irrespective of whether force is being increased or decreased within a given set of muscles. According to the size principle, smaller motor units are activated first because they require only low levels of electrical stimulation to fire. As the amount of electrical stimulation increases, however, progressively

mill below a spinal animal is increased. Within moments of the change in surface speed, the animal's locomotor pattern is adjusted to accommodate the altered surface conditions.

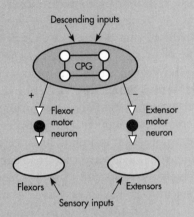

Once triggered by descending inputs, neural networks known as central pattern generators (CPGs) are believed to maintain a given movement pattern through alternating bursts of activity in flexor and extensor muscle groups.

Although the concept of CPGs is repeatedly used to demonstrate the hierarchical control of locomotion even in humans, the exact nature of their structure and pattern-generating characteristics is still not well understood. Moreover, dynamic systems theorists argue that reproduction of a coordinated pattern of action in an isolated cat spinal cord under carefully controlled experimental conditions cannot begin to be equated with the operations necessary to carry out functionally appropriate actions in intact animals. As Thelen and Smith (1994) argue in a recently published book describing the development of cognition and action according to a dynamic systems perspective, the notion of a CPG lacks the plasticity, responsiveness, and sophistication needed to capture the essence of locomotion in a "real-life" setting. According to Thelen and Smith, concepts like the CPG "simply do not account for what we really observe in developing organisms." (p. 10)

larger motor units are activated until all the available motor units innervating a given muscle are firing.

The type of movement we wish to perform largely determines the number of motor units recruited in a given motoneuron pool. In the case of activities requiring only small amounts of force, not all motor units available to us need to be recruited. As our force requirements increase during the performance of ballistic activities or of maximum-power activities such as sprinting or jumping for maximum height, all available units are progressively activated. Not only does the orderly recruitment of motor units provide us with a mechanism for grading force production according to the type of movement being performed, but it also reduces the complexity of the decision-making process

According to the size principle, smaller motor units are activated before larger motor units.

occurring within the CNS. Given this orderly recruitment of motor units, the subsystems involved in developing the action plan need only specify which muscle response synergies are to be recruited in advance of the movement. The actual selection of motor units has already been determined on the basis of the size principle.

Rate Coding.   In addition to the differences in motoneuron size that are believed to influence how soon they are recruited during force production, a second important property associated with motor units is also believed to influence the level of force generated in a given muscle. For example, it has been demonstrated that differences exist in the rate at which motor units are capable of firing (Gydikov & Kosarov, 1973; 1974). Two types of motor units have been identified: tonic and phasic motor units. The **tonic motor units,** which are driven by smaller motoneurons, generate smaller action potentials at a progressively lower rate as muscle force increases. By contrast, the larger **phasic motor units** are capable of generating larger amounts of force because they are served by larger motoneurons. They are therefore capable of producing large action potentials at rates that increase linearly as the amount of force applied to any set of muscles increases.

> The amount of force produced in a muscle can be raised by increasing the rate at which each individual motor unit is firing.

Once all available motor units are recruited, a second component of the rate-coding mechanism can be exploited to increase the amount of force generated within the muscle. The rate at which each individual motoneuron is fired is increased by manipulating the rate at which the motoneurons send nervous impulses to the muscles being contracted. As the interval between successive firings of individual motor neurons becomes shorter, the forces generated by each impulse begin to accumulate faster than the muscle's individual twitch contraction time. This rapid summation of nerve impulses has the net effect of producing increased levels of force within the already contracting muscles.

How are these differences in motor unit discharge rates likely to influence how movements are actually controlled? We will probably rely on the larger, phasic motor units to generate large amounts of force very quickly, whereas the smaller, tonic motor units will be more important contributors in movements that require lower but more finely graded levels of force. Given that the smaller motor units have also been shown to be more resistant to fatigue than the larger units, they are also likely to be used to help us sustain the necessary levels of muscular force during endurance activities.

Musculoskeletal Contributions to Force

As important as the many motor units are in grading the forces produced by the various muscle response synergies, other factors have also been shown to influence the level of force generated by a given muscle group. Two very important examples of these factors are the anatomical and mechanical forces acting on the body. These types of forces may be created by the way the musculoskeletal system is organized, by gravitational and reactive forces acting on the body as we stand and move in space, and by forces associated with a limb's changing moment of inertia. We will begin by describing how the anatomical position of a limb and the action to be performed influence the amount of force produced by the muscles involved.

Anatomical Limb Position.   It has now become clear that a given level of neural innervation does not result in a fixed level of force being produced by a muscle. Nor, for that matter, does it result in a fixed movement pattern. Instead, the amount of force any given muscle is able to generate varies as a function of the limb's anatomical position and/or the length of the muscle prior to innervation. Moreover, the velocity with which the muscle then shortens or lengthens also influences the amount of force it is capable of generating. For example, a limb that is in a flexed position prior to innervation can produce more force than one that is being held in an extended position. Similarly, a muscle moving at a greater velocity, whether it is shortening or lengthening, produces less force.

> The position of the limb and/or the length of the muscle prior to innervation affect the amount of muscle force produced.

The additional variability that arises as a function of the limb's anatomical position and muscle length prior to innervation clearly poses problems for hierarchical theories of motor control that assume that higher centers within the CNS prescribe the amount of activation for each individual muscle involved in a given movement. Turvey, Fitch, and Tuller (1982) have argued that this address-specific feature not only makes the unrealistic demand that the CNS regulate the contractile states of every muscle throughout the movement but also ignores other sources of potential variability that emerge as a function of the changing context.

Mechanical Properties of the Skeleton.   In addition to the influence that anatomical limb position exerts on the level of force a muscle can produce, a second influence is mechanical in origin. One has only to look at the body's skeleton to see that the bones form a chain linked by a variety of joints permitting different types of movements. The number of movements possible at any individual joint, in turn, determines the number of degrees of freedom available to us. Although certain joints (e.g., the knee and elbow) possess as few as one functional degree of freedom, others (e.g., the shoulder and hip) provide as many as three. As the total number of joints involved in an action increases, so too does the number of degrees of freedom that must be organized for efficient movement. This factor helps explain why movements involving multi-limb coordination are much more difficult to learn and/or control than single-limb movements.

Because of the way the bony skeleton is rigidly linked, we can also expect that any movement in one part of the chain will affect another, often quite distal to the joint being moved. This distal movement has the effect of generating kinetic energy that also influences the overall shape of the movement being produced. This is evident when we observe someone preparing to kick a stationary ball. As the hip joint is extended during the backswing and then flexed during the kicking phase, the lower leg and foot continue to accelerate as the kinetic energy generated by the hip's action is distributed throughout the length of the kicking leg.

> **Movement in one part of the chain will affect another, often quite distal to the joint being moved.**

A similar distribution of kinetic energy is evident during the swing phase of locomotion. In this latter situation, the activation of the flexor/extensor muscles at the hip joint produces angular acceleration of the thigh, which in turn leads to greater acceleration in the more distal segments of the moving limb.

Subconscious Control of Movement

In addition to the many conscious modifications we are able to make to movements in progress, certain neuronal connections within the spinal system contribute to the modification of movements in progress by providing sensory information at a subconscious level. The influence of some of these reflexive loops is limited to local control of muscle force, but others are capable of influencing force levels in muscle groups quite distant from those originally stimulated. These longer reflex loops are therefore capable of modifying movements to a much larger extent than the shorter reflex loops that are confined to single segments within the spinal cord. In what kinds of movement situations are we most likely to involve these different types of reflex circuits? The short reflex loops are most often called into play when minute adjustments in muscle length are needed. These adjustments are necessary when misalignment exists between intended muscle length and actual muscle length. This misalignment is most likely to occur in situations where unexpected forces are applied to the limb or the muscle begins to fatigue. Both situations can lead to an involuntary and undesirable lengthening of the muscles involved in the action.

Short-Loop Reflexive Adjustments.   Now that we have a better idea when these various reflex loops might be called on to assist us in modifying the action plan being executed, lct us look more closely at how these different types of reflex loops are organized and then activated during movement control. Two important examples of short reflex loops are the stretch reflex and the gamma reflex loop.

> Short-loop reflexes are limited to the local control of muscle force.

Stretch reflex. As Figure 3.4 illustrates, the stretch reflex comprises a sensory receptor (in this case the muscle spindle), which is responsible for monitoring changes in muscle length; an afferent sensory neuron, which relays the sensory information arising in the spindle to the spinal cord; and an alpha motoneuron, which then closes the loop by acting on the

FIGURE 3.4   Pathways involved in a stretch reflex. Excitation is indicated by +; inhibition is indicated by −. A stretch reflex is triggered when the length of the extrafusal muscle changes.

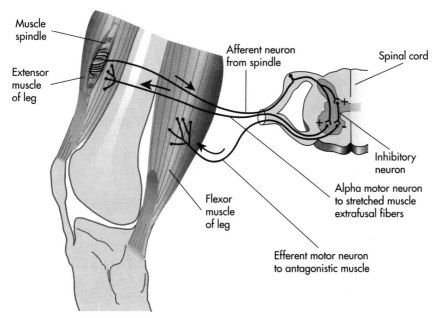

From *Human Anatomy and Physiology,* Second Edition,
by Alexander Spence and Elliott Mason. Copyright © 1983
by The Benjamin / Cummings Publishing Company. Reprinted by permission.

incoming sensory information—specifically by causing the extrafusal muscle fibers it innervates to contract.

The stretch reflex is triggered when the length of an extrafusal muscle is altered, causing the sensory endings within the muscle spindle to be mechanically deformed. Once deformed, these sensory endings fire, sending nerve impulses into the spinal cord via an afferent sensory neuron located just outside the spinal cord. As soon as these impulses reach the spinal cord, they are transferred to alpha motoneurons that innervate the very same muscle that houses the activated muscle spindles. Stimulation of the muscle spindle ceases when the muscle contracts, because the spindle fibers, which lie parallel to the extrafusal fibers, return to their original length. It is through the operation of this reflex that we are able to alter continually the tone of a muscle and/or make subtle adjustments in muscle length during movement. These latter adjustments may be in response to external factors producing unexpected loads or forces on the moving limbs.

Consider, for example, what happens when an additional load is added to an already loaded limb being held in a given position in space (Figure 3.5). The muscles of the limb are set at a given length, and alpha motoneurons are firing in order to maintain the desired limb position in spite of the load and gravity's influence. Now an additional load is added to the end of the limb, causing the muscles to lengthen as the limb drops. This stretching of the extrafusal muscle fibers results in almost simultaneous stretching of the muscle spindle, which then fires and sends signals to the spinal cord and alpha motoneurons that serve the same muscle. The firing rate of these alpha motoneurons is subsequently increased, causing the muscles in the dropping limb to be further contracted, and the limb is restored to its previous position.

Seeing the limb begin to fall would also lead to increased contraction in the falling limb, but initiating the correction *consciously* would involve considerably longer delays because of additional processing at a cortical level. In fact, Dewhurst (1967) has demonstrated that whereas corrections to limb position in similar movement situations are possible within 30 to 50 milliseconds using the stretch reflex, visually based corrections involve corrective delays on the order of 150 to 200 milliseconds. Given that the rapid correction of error in movement is desirable in a variety of movement situations, it is important that these reflexive adjustments be available to us.

Gamma reflex loop. Muscle spindles also play an important role in the ongoing control and modification of movement by virtue of their involvement in a spinal reflex loop known as the **gamma reflex loop.**

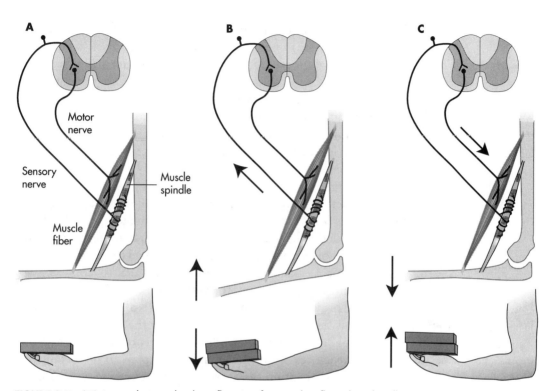

FIGURE 3.5 (A) A muscle is under the influence of a stretch reflex when the elbow joint is flexed and is steadily maintaining a load against gravity. (B) A sudden increase in the load lengthens the extrafusal muscle and results in muscle spindle firing and the transmission of sensory impulses to the spinal cord. (C) Alpha motoneurons that inner- vate the lengthened extrafusal muscle are excited, sending impulses back to the muscle and causing it to contract. The elbow joint is returned to its original position.

Recall that information conveyed by the two major motor pathway sys- tems synapses with both alpha and gamma motoneurons once it reaches the spinal cord. Whereas the alpha motoneuron sends the information it receives to the muscles involved in the pending movement, the gamma motoneuron sends the same information to the muscle spindle, which can be stimulated to begin firing. What could be the purpose of sending movement-related information via this second route? One early suggestion advanced by Merton (1953) was that this loop served as an alternative method of activating the muscles involved in a movement. This hypothesis has since been rejected in favor of the idea that the gamma loop assists in the control of limb movements. This is made possible by the fact that the gamma motoneurons can also innervate the muscle spindle at its polar ends.

> The gamma reflex loop appears to assist in the control of limb movements.

The independent innervation of the muscle spindle by the gamma motoneuron is thought to be very important during muscle contraction when the intrafusal fibers of the spindle would normally be slack. Gamma activation of the spindle results in the stretching of the intrafusal fibers even though the extrafusal muscle fibers are contracting. How might this gamma activity assist us during the moment-to-moment control of movement? Because it "takes up the slack" in the spindle caused by muscle contraction, minute changes in the length of the muscle can be detected and corrected more quickly.

Long-Loop Reflexive Adjustments.   For larger adjustments in limb and overall body position, it is necessary to involve the longer reflex loops that extend beyond single segments within the spinal cord. The pathways involved in these neural circuits travel to the more distant subcortical and cortical levels of the CNS to connect with structures such as the motor cortex and cerebellum within the larger projection system. As you will recall, it is the primary responsibility of this subsystem to add the final details to the general action plan. It is perhaps not surprising, then, that certain structures within this system also play an important role in the modification of movements in progress. Several studies have indicated that long-loop reflexes operate to restore our limbs to their original positions in response to changes in the environment that lead to undesirable changes in muscle length. These changes may be prompted by contact with objects or other persons during many game situations, causing a momentary loss in balance or alterations in the type of surface on which we are standing or moving (Nashner, 1976). These long-loop responses can also be used to stabilize our limbs in a variety of different postures and movements.

> Long-loop reflexes are used to make larger adjustments in limb and overall body position.

Solving the Motor Problem

The relationship between the brain and spinal system has been appropriately described by Turvey, Fitch, and Tuller (1982) as one wherein the two entities "relate between themselves as experts, cooperating on a problem" (p. 251). In this case, the problem to be resolved is how best to organize the many degrees of freedom available within the human system to accomplish a given movement task. As we are all too aware from our own early movement experiences, this is by no means easy. In fact, a considerable amount of practice is needed for us to learn to work with, rather than against, the many internal and external forces that act on our body as we move.

With repeated opportunities to experiment with different muscle activation patterns and their resulting torques, we learn to constrain and/or release available degrees of freedom, depending on the skill being practiced. In the case of learning to hit a baseball or softball, for example, we must learn to release, or free, a number of degrees of freedom, particularly in the trunk and lower body in order to accomplish a smooth swinging action. On the other hand, to be successful in a sport such as pistol shooting, we must constrain the joints of the shooting arm to act as a single degree of freedom in order to reduce the amount of pistol movement during the aiming phase of the movement. Newell and colleagues (Newell, Kugler, van Emmerik, & McDonald, 1989) stress the importance of developing "search strategies" that can be used to explore the dynamics of an action an individual is attempting to coordinate and control. These search strategies are intended to guide the learner in the perceptual exploration of what dynamic systems theorists commonly refer to as the "perceptual–motor workspace." This repeated perceptual exploration is thought to be central to the development of an appropriate solution to the motor problem at hand.

Contrary to hierarchical theories of motor control in which the ongoing control and modification of movement is the sole responsibility of a higher cortical executive, more recent theories acknowledge the self-organizing capabilities of the CNS and the dynamic interplay of other forces external to the nervous system (the musculoskeletal system and the environment). The purpose of this section of the chapter has been to demonstrate how each of these additional forces contributes to the evolving movement pattern.

ACTION PLANNING FOR STABLE AND VARIABLE ENVIRONMENTS

An important factor influencing the flow of information through the various task systems within the CNS is how the environment interacts with the performer. To illustrate this point, let us try to visualize ourselves dribbling a soccer ball toward a goal on an empty field or perhaps walking through an empty corridor. Now imagine adding a number of additional players or pedestrians to each of those scenes. Will this change

> The level of motor control required varies according to whether the environment is stable or variable.

in the environmental context affect how we plan and ultimately control our actions? It certainly will, given that the first two movement scenes are far less complex than the latter two. The first two scenes described are examples of highly predictable and **stable environments**. This type of environment reduces the demands placed on motor control by allowing us, among other things, to proceed at a self-determined speed.

Adding more players or pedestrians to these same two movement situations renders them much less predictable and therefore more **variable.** As a result, the level of motor control that is required increases. Our movements are now largely determined by the speed of others rather than by our own internal timing mechanisms, and we must continually adjust our movements as the constraints imposed by the environment change. Our increasing reliance on sensory feedback to guide our movements becomes evident in these variable environments. As we will see in later chapters, the characteristics of the environment in which a motor skill will ultimately be performed influence the type of instructional strategies used during the early stages of learning. It is therefore extremely important that physical educators and therapists carefully consider whether the environment in which the skill will ultimately be performed is stable or variable when they plan physical education lessons for athletes and treatment programs for patients.

DISORDERS OF THE MOTOR SYSTEM THAT AFFECT MOTOR CONTROL

All observable movement behavior, even in its simplest form, depends on the exquisite coordination of many complex neurological and mechanical processes. Any damage to the CNS can therefore be expected to interfere with a variety of important motor control functions. This final section of the chapter is devoted to a brief discussion of various neurological disorders that have been demonstrated to affect adversely the efficient functioning of the motor system.

The release phenomenon is the dissociation of the cortex from the spinal system, resulting in reflexive, stereotypical movement patterns.

Lesions and/or diseases that affect any of the neural task systems involved in the planning of action (such as the association cortex and the projection system) will lead to the most severe motor deficits and may even affect our ability to initiate movements. Damage at this level of the neurological system can also be expected to have a negative influence on spinal system operations responsible for coordination of the musculoskeletal system. As a consequence of this dissociation, movements become more reflexive and stereotypical in form. Previously learned movements are also affected, and many become highly disorganized or even impossible to perform. This process of dissociation has often been referred to as the **release phenomenon.**

A variety of motor deficits are also observed when damage occurs to either the basal ganglia or the cerebellum, two important components of the larger projection system. As you will recall, these two areas within the projection system are responsible for adding the specific details necessary to customize the more general action plan for a particular movement context. Let us first look at the types of motor deficits that emerge as a result of basal ganglia dysfunction.

Basal Ganglia Disorders

In general, any damage to the various nuclei that compose the basal ganglia results in movement disorders of various magnitudes. Perhaps the best-known disease related to the basal ganglia is **parkinsonism,** or Parkinson's disease. This chronic and progressive neurological disorder primarily affects older adults and is caused by the premature death of brain cells within the BG called the substantia nigra. These cells produce a chemical called dopamine that is responsible for sending correct signals to the muscle response synergies involved in initiating movements. Patients with this disease demonstrate various degrees of abnormal gait and posture, increased tremor (particularly at rest), and rigidity. As the disease progresses, both the initiation and the scaling of movements become increasingly difficult. Postural reactions and movements that are normally produced automatically must now be consciously controlled, increasing the time it takes to initiate and complete a particular activity.

Cerebellar Disorders

Serious deficits in motor control are also evident as a result of trauma to the cerebellum. In particular, movements that demand the complex coordination of multiple muscle response synergies are severely degraded. Despite their understanding of a movement's goal, patients with cerebellar lesions are unable to apply the movement dynamics necessary to implement planned actions. This inability is often reflected in a tendency to overshoot targets of interest (dysmetria) because of an inappropriate application of force or in failure to adapt a particular action to a changing environmental situation. Individuals with cerebellar dysfunction also tend to appear unsteady, or even clumsy, particularly when turning to change direction. Complex, sequential movements such as those required to button a shirt are also particularly difficult. Given that the cerebellum is primarily responsible for the coordination and regulation of action, it is not surprising that motor control is affected in this way.

Disorders in Descending Pathways

Lesions that affect either the corticospinal or the extrapyramidal pathways usually result in disturbances of posture and gait, the severity of the disturbance being determined by where in the pathway the lesion occurs. These disturbances produce the "scissors-like" gait patterns associated with spastic diplegia and the exaggerated forward lean that Parkinson's patients exhibit while walking. Individuals who have experienced a stroke resulting in paralysis of one side of the body can also be expected to exhibit abnormal gait patterns.

SUMMARY

The purpose of this chapter has been to provide the reader with a general understanding of both the cognitive processes involved in the planning and execution of movement and some of the neurological areas and/or structures that appear to play an important role in the planning and execution of action. For the purposes of the discussion, we assumed that a set of functional neuromotor task systems, distributed throughout the CNS, work cooperatively to produce coordinated action in response to an internally generated goal and/or to changes occurring in the environment.

The primary neuromotor task systems believed to contribute to the planning and execution of goal-directed actions were identified as the limbic system, which drives our desire to act; the association cortex, which is involved in the early development of the "best" perceived plan of action; the projection system, which provides the specific movement dynamics for the action plan; and the spinal system, which is ultimately responsible for the spatial and temporal aspects of execution.

During the planning process, communication among the various neural task systems is made possible by a rich network of feedback loops that also help the performer determine whether the action being planned or executed matches the original goal. The coordinated movements that emerge are ultimately produced by muscle response synergies that comprise groups of muscles constrained to act as functional units of action. This type of organization greatly simplifies the planning process and also provides for greater flexibility of action.

The flow of information through the CNS is strongly influenced by the nature of the environmental context in which the action is to occur.

Whereas stable environments impose lower demands in terms of the level of motor control required to plan and execute the prescribed movements, acting in more unpredictable or variable environments requires greater motor control. Variable environments also lead to increased dependence on sensory feedback to guide the action.

The moment-to-moment control of movement is made possible by the activity of a variety of spinal system mechanisms that link the spinal cord with the muscles involved in the action (the stretch reflex and the gamma reflex loop) and with other systems within the CNS itself (e.g., long-loop reflexes). In addition to these mechanisms, the anatomical and mechanical properties of the human system can be exploited to minimize the level of control required of the CNS. These properties determine not only the amount of force one can generate in a given movement but also the efficiency with which it can be completed.

As learning progresses, the relationship between the performer and the environment is continually redefined until the observable behavior perfectly matches the goal of the movement and the constraints of the surrounding environment. A number of theorists aligned with the dynamic systems approach to motor control believe that this redefining of the performer–environment relationship is achieved through repeated experimentation and exploration of the "perceptual–motor workspace."

IMPORTANT TERMINOLOGY

After completing this chapter, readers should be familiar with the following terms and concepts.

alpha–gamma coactivation	neuromuscular junction
alpha motoneuron	parkinsonism
association cortex	phasic motor unit
central pattern generators	projection system
efferent copy	pyramidal tract
excitation–contraction coupling	rate coding
extrapyramidal system	reciprocal inhibition
fusimotor neuron	release phenomenon
gamma motoneuron	size principle
gamma reflex loop	skeletal muscular system
interneuron	skeletomotor neuron
limbic system	spinal system
motor pathways	stable environment
motor unit	tonic motor unit
muscle spindle	variable environment

SUGGESTED FURTHER READING

Brooks, V.B. (1986). *The neural basis of motor control*. New York: Oxford University Press. (Chapter 2 provides an excellent overview of the contribution of the CNS to the planning and execution of action plans.)

Enoka, R.M. (1994). *Neuromechanical basis of kinesiology*. 2d ed. Champaign, IL. (Chapters 6 and 7 are particularly relevant to the discussion of moment-to-moment control in this chapter.)

TEST YOUR UNDERSTANDING

1. Identify the functional neural task system involved in each of the following cognitive processes associated with the planning and execution of action.
   (a) Formulation of a general plan of action.
   (b) Control and regulation of movements in progress.
   (c) Application of movement dynamics to a general action plan.
   (d) Decision to act.

2. In what *two* important ways does the dynamic systems model of motor control differ from the hierarchical model of motor control?

3. Identify the factors that influence the quality of the general action plan developed in the association cortex.

4. Identify the specific functions that the basal ganglia appear to serve in the planning and execution of action.

5. Describe the role played by the "efferent copy" in the action planning process.

6. Identify the specific function(s) of the motor cortex in the control of movements.

7. Identify the two major pathways responsible for transmitting the dynamics of movement to the spinal system. How do the functions of these two pathways differ?

8. Describe two ways the decision-making process is simplified.

9. How does the type of environment in which an action is to be performed influence the way a particular movement is controlled? Provide practical examples to illustrate your answer.

10. In what way(s) are the following neurological disorders most likely to affect an individual's level of motor control?
    (a) Parkinson's disease.
    (b) Cerebellar dysfunction.
    (c) Lesions of the corticospinal or extrapyramidal pathways.

About the Quote

Brooks likens the many different "task systems" within the CNS to a company of players—that is, actors—who all contribute in some way to the success of a theater production. The functional "task systems" that Brooks describes in his text The Neural Basis of Motor Control *may involve almost all the areas within the CNS during various phases of a motor action or may be limited to activity in just a few areas of the brain when the individual is assuming certain postures or performing simple, well-learned movements.*

Although the discussion in his text is framed very much in terms of a hierarchy of control, Brooks believes that the higher, middle, and lower levels of control do not operate as a rigid hierarchy with information moving only in a top-down direction. Rather, sophisticated networks of internal feedback loops linking the various levels allow for rich communication. Moreover, plans for action do not reside in a particular set of nuclei but are distributed throughout the brain. This text will be of great interest to readers who want to know more about the contributions of the various levels of the CNS to the control and learning of movement-based skills.

CHAPTER 4
SENSORY CONTRIBUTIONS TO ACTION

CHAPTER OBJECTIVES

■ Understand and be able to identify the general properties of sensory receptors and afferent pathways and the processes by which they assist the various subsystems within the CNS to derive meaning from the many different types of sensations.

■ Be able to identify and describe the relative contributions of the various receptors that are associated with somesthesia—bodily sensations of touch, pain, temperature, and limb position.

■ Be able to describe how the various types of somatic sensations are relayed to the brain.

■ Understand how knowledge about the processes underlying the reception, transmission, and interpretation of sensory information can be applied to practical settings.

■ Be able to identify the various afferent sources of kinesthetic sensations and explain how they can be exploited by the practitioner teaching different types of movement skills.

■ Understand and be able to describe the multiple roles played by sensory feedback in both the planning and the moment-to-moment control of movement.

■ Understand and be able to identify the various sources of error in the performance of movement skills.

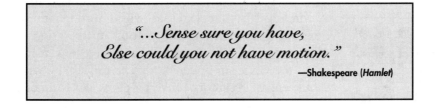

"...Sense sure you have,
Else could you not have motion."
—Shakespeare (*Hamlet*)

Now that we have reviewed the cognitive and neurological processes involved in the planning, execution, and moment-to-moment control of action, it is time to turn our attention to a more detailed discussion of the many factors, both internal and external, that influence these processes. The general focus of the next two chapters will be to describe the different types of sensory information available to us and the roles they play in the planning and execution of action.

Three sensory systems, in particular, provide us with a sophisticated ensemble of information about different aspects of our environment and our position within it. Once integrated, this information provided by the somatosensory, visual, and auditory systems is used to guide the planning and execution of a variety of actions. Although each of these three systems is unique in structure and function, certain principles related to the reception and transmission of sensory information are

Sensory systems provide us with a sophisticated ensemble of information about the environment that can be used to guide the planning and execution of action.

common to all sensory systems. We will briefly consider these general principles before proceeding with a more comprehensive discussion of the specific mechanisms associated with two of the three sensory systems just identified (the somatosensory and visual systems).

GENERAL PROPERTIES OF SENSORY RECEPTORS AND AFFERENT PATHWAYS

Sensory receptors that monitor the external environment and continually apprise us of our position in space are located throughout the body. They are found in the retina of the eye, in various layers of the skin, and in other regions such as the joints, muscles and inner ear. During the course of our discussion in the next two chapters, we will discover that different types of sensory receptors contribute specific information about the environment that is added to a larger ensemble of sensory information garnered from other sensory systems.

Sensory receptors convert various forms of environmental energy into electrical impulses by a process called transduction.

These sense organs, or sensory receptors, also serve as our "windows" to the external world through their ability to extract environmental information in its various forms (i.e., light, sound waves, and touch) and then convert it into a form that the CNS can understand. The process by which the various sensory receptors convert a particular form of energy into another form is referred to as **transduction**. In the case of the CNS, all environmental information is transduced into electrical impulses.

Three general properties of sensory receptors and their associated afferent pathways help the various subsystems within the CNS derive meaning from the various forms of energy available in the environment. These properties are adequate stimulation, intensity coding, and sensory adaptation. A discussion of each of these properties will be the focus of the next section.

Adequate Stimulation

How do we know that a certain event has occurred in the environment? For example, how do we know that someone is tapping us on the shoulder or waving at us from across a room? A considerable number of sensory receptors that are designed to respond to particular kinds of sensory stimulation assist us in registering this information as it actually occurs. For example, sensory receptors located in the retina respond to changing patterns of light entering the eye, and sound waves that enter the inner ear stimulate specialized receptors for auditory sensations.

Although it is possible for other forms of energy to stimulate sensory receptors (for instance, high levels of pressure applied to the eyeball result in a sensation of light), they are especially sensitive to particular kinds of sensory input. This property of sensory receptors is often called **adequate stimulation** and is exhibited when a particular sensory event or stimulus raises a receptor's resting level high enough to generate sensory impulses (Eyzaguirre & Fidone, 1975). In addition to informing the CNS that a particular sensory event has occurred, this characteristic of sensory receptors contributes to our ability to distinguish among the many types of environmental input available to us.

> Adequate stimulation is the process by which sensory receptors inform the CNS that a particular sensory event has occurred.

Intensity Coding

Not only do the sensory receptors and the afferent pathways that carry the generated impulse into the CNS provide us with information about *when* an environmental "event" or stimulus occurred, but they also convey information about the *intensity* with which the event occurred. This second piece of information is carried in the form of an **intensity code** that begins at the level of the sensory receptors. This property of sensory receptors enables us to discriminate, for example, between sensations associated with a light tap and those resulting from a hard push or a slap on the back.

The rate at which a particular sensory receptor or group of receptors is able to generate signals that are great enough to trigger an electrical impulse in the nearby sensory neuron largely determines how intensely we ultimately perceive a given stimulus to be. For example, a strong stimulus (e.g., a hard push) causes the stimulated receptors to fire at a much higher frequency than they would if a much less intense stimulus (e.g., a light tap) were applied to the skin's surface. This mechanism is referred to as **temporal summation.** Given that a stronger stimulus such as a hard slap also tends to affect a larger surface area, we can expect that a greater number of sensory receptors will also be stimulated. In fact, the number of sensory receptors that fire simultaneously provides another valuable clue to nature and intensity of the stimulus. This second mechanism is called **spatial summation.**

> The intensity code of a sensory event is conveyed to the CNS via temporal and spatial summation.

Sensory Adaptation

Consider for a moment how you feel when you first dive into a mountain lake or outdoor pool. The first overwhelming sensation is probably one of being extremely cold as the water comes in contact with the thousands of cutaneous receptors lying close to the surface of the skin. Though it is often unpleasant initially, the sensation of coldness usually lasts for only a short time. Similarly, you can feel a pair of glasses pressing against your skin for a while after you put them on, but it is not long before the sensation subsides. In fact, some people become quite disturbed when they are unable to locate a pair of glasses they were wearing earlier, only to be told by a friend that their glasses are perched on top of their heads. Why is it that we do not continue to be aware of these different cutaneous sensations until they are removed? A third property associated with sensory receptors, **adaptation,** provides us with the answer to this question.

As Figure 4.1 illustrates, shortly after a particular stimulus has been registered by a sensory receptor, the level of firing observed is greatly reduced. As you can also see by comparing the firing patterns of the two different types of sensory receptors shown, the rate of adaptation is not the same for all sensory receptors in the body. For example, receptors that transmit sensations of touch and pressure adapt rapidly, whereas pain receptors and certain proprioceptors adapt very slowly. Unlike rapidly adapting receptors that often cease firing immediately after a stimulus

> A sensory receptor adapts to a stimulus by reducing its level of firing soon after it is applied.

FIGURE 4.1   The sensory adaptation rates of these two sensory receptors are not the same as indicated by the different firing patterns.

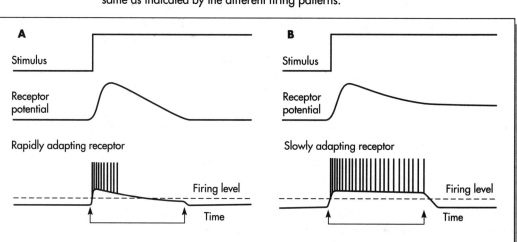

has been applied, slowly adapting receptors continue to respond throughout the duration of a sensory event. As we will see in a later discussion, these different adaptation rates also determine the type of information provided to the CNS.

THE TRANSMISSION AND INTEGRATION OF SENSORY INPUT

Once the different types of sensory inputs have been converted to electrical impulses at the level of the sensory receptor, they travel via specialized pathways toward the cortex, where they are further analyzed and integrated with other sensory inputs. Before reaching the cortex, however, all sensory information except that provided by olfaction (smell) passes through an important group of nuclei located in an area of the brain called the **diencephalon.** It is within this group of more than 30 nuclei, collectively called the **thalamus,** that neurophysiologists consider the initial stages of sensory integration and perceptual awareness to begin. The thalamus achieves these functions by "gating out" irrelevant sensory inputs and directing those that are relevant to an impending or ongoing action toward specific sensory areas within the cortex.

> The initial stages of sensory integration and perceptual awareness occur at the level of thalamus.

In addition to relaying sensory information directly to the cortex, the thalamus has also been shown to influence the nature of our emotional responses to sensory experiences. This function is made possible by its neural connections with the limbic system, whose functions we discussed in Chapter 3. Perhaps the best way to demonstrate how the thalamus influences our emotional responses to certain sensory events is to describe what happens when lesions form in the thalamus and disrupt its normal function.

Patients with a disorder known as **thalamic syndrome,** for example, experience sensations that are grossly exaggerated, distorted, and/or very unpleasant. Not only are sounds that were once pleasing to the ear perceived as extremely annoying, but even light touch induces painful burning sensations. In addition to the sensory problems experienced, patients with thalamic syndrome often suffer partial or complete paralysis of one side of the body. This is because certain nuclei within the thalamus connect with motor tracts leaving the cortex and the basal ganglia, which, as we now know, play an important role in the planning of movements.

The sensory pathways carrying general sensory information about touch, temperature, pain, and proprioception finally terminate in specific

Recognition of the source and intensity of sensations is possible once the sensory information reaches specific primary sensory areas.

primary sensory areas located in different regions of the cortex. It is at this point that we become consciously aware of the many sensations that have impinged upon us. For example, once the various somatosensory inputs reach their primary sensory areas in the parietal lobe, we are able to recognize the source and intensity of sensations associated with pain and temperature, to discriminate between simple touch and light pressure applied to the skin, and to sense consciously the position of our limbs and their movement through space. Similarly, visual information reaching the primary visual area located in the occipital lobe enables us to detect brightness, light and shade, color, and the shapes of objects.

Our final perception of what is occurring in the environment around us is achieved after all of these sensations are integrated and then interpreted by the **association areas** that lie adjacent to the various primary sensory areas associated with the different types of sensory input. With the assistance of memory, objects seen or felt can now be interpreted in a meaningful way, as can the sounds of a cascading waterfall. As we might expect, then, any damage to these interpretive areas of the cortex is likely to impair our perceptual abilities severely.

The meaningfulness of a sensory event is known once the sensory inputs reach their association areas.

Clinical observations have shown that damage to any one of these association areas makes it impossible to recognize familiar objects using one or more of the sensory modalities available to us. This disorder, which is called **agnosia,** may affect our ability to recognize familiar faces, to recognize the sound of a ringing telephone, and/or to identify known objects such as keys or utensils by handling them. Fortunately, an individual who suffers from agnosia caused by damage to the association area of one sensory system is able to compensate for the disorder by using other sensory modalities to derive meaning. For example, a person who has sustained damage to the association area that functions in the interpretation of auditory stimuli can learn to rely on other senses, such as vision. Visual devices can be installed that are activated when the doorbell rings or the oven timer sounds. In this way, an individual is able to function more effectively, at least, at home.

SOMATOSENSATION

Now that we have identified some of the important characteristics of sensory receptors and some general principles associated with sensory transmission, we can begin to describe the two most important sensory systems that influence our perceptions and subsequent actions. The first of these two systems, the somatosensory system, is described in this chapter. In the chapter that follows, we will discuss the visual system and its role in the control of action.

> The term *somesthesia* means sensations of the body.

The receptors associated with **somesthesia**—bodily sensations of touch, pain, temperature, and limb position—are located in the skin, muscles, tendons, and joints and in the vestibular apparatus of the inner ear. Collectively, they provide us with information we can use in a movement situation to distinguish between fine and gross tactile sensations, to keep track of the orientation of multiple body parts as they move in space, and to distinguish among different amounts of force applied to an object we are throwing at a target. These somatosensory receptors can be further subdivided into **cutaneous receptors** and **proprioceptors**. We will begin our discussion by identifying the various kinds of cutaneous receptors.

> Somatosensory receptors can be divided into two categories: cutaneous receptors and proprioceptors.

Cutaneous Receptors

The skin contains a myriad of receptors that differ in structure, function, and distribution density. Sensations of touch and pressure are mediated by various types of receptors located in different layers of skin. Each receptor is stimulated by physical deformation of the receptor itself or of the area surrounding it. Although certain of these **mechanoreceptors** (e.g., free nerve endings, Merkel's disks, and Meissner's corpuscles) respond immediately to light touch and pressure, others (e.g., pacinian corpuscles) require stronger stimuli in order to respond.

> The distribution and density of cutaneous receptors determine the level of sensitivity in that area.

The distribution of cutaneous receptors is interesting: Disproportionately greater numbers are evident in the lips, thumbs, and fingers than in the trunk and leg. This makes the lips and fingers ideally suited for performing finely graded movements such as pronouncing words and communicating through signing, respectively.

Proprioceptors

Specialized mechanoreceptors located in the muscles, tendons, and joints and in the vestibular apparatus of the inner ear provide us with uninterrupted knowledge about the position of body parts relative to each other and the general orientation of our body in space. The dancers and gymnasts use the sensory information provided by these receptors to sense, among other things, the changing and relative positions of their

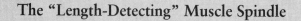

HIGHLIGHT

The "Length-Detecting" Muscle Spindle

In order to understand how the muscle spindle can rapidly detect changes in muscle length, it is important to consider the nature of its physical structure and how it is aligned with respect to the fibers of the extrafusal muscle. As the accompanying figure illustrates, the elongated structure of this proprioceptor, which resembles a spindle, lies in parallel with the extrafusal muscle fibers and actually attaches directly to the muscle sheath. This arrangement ensures that any change in muscle length results in similar changes in the length of the muscle spindle.

A closer look inside the muscle spindle reveals the presence of two types of intrafusal muscle fibers: the **nuclear bag fibers** and **chain fibers.** A typical muscle spindle contains two nuclear chain fibers for every four or five

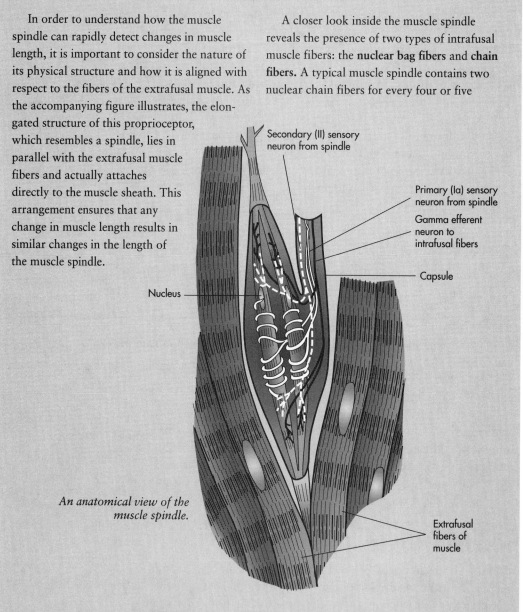

Secondary (II) sensory neuron from spindle

Primary (Ia) sensory neuron from spindle

Gamma efferent neuron to intrafusal fibers

Capsule

Nucleus

An anatomical view of the muscle spindle.

Extrafusal fibers of muscle

From *Human Anatomy and Physiology,* Second Edition, by Alexander Spence and Elliott Mason. Copyright (c) 1983 by The Benjamin / Cummings Publishing Company. Reprinted by permission.

nuclear bag fibers. In addition to two types of muscle fibers, each muscle spindle also contains two different types of sensory endings: group Ia and group II afferents. It is by means of one or both of these sensory endings that the spindle is able to detect any changes that occur in the length of the extrafusal muscle. As you can see in the figure, the larger Ia afferent, also called the **primary** spindle afferent, wraps its sensory endings around both the bag and chain fibers, whereas the group II nerve fibers, or **secondary** endings, attach almost exclusively to the nuclear chain fibers.

Exactly how does this small muscle receptor signal the changing length of a muscle? During the actual stretching of a muscle, whether it be passively manipulated or the result of increasing muscle fatigue, the intrafusal muscle fibers of the spindle are also stretched, causing both sensory endings to be deformed. This deformation of both endings gives rise to an afferent signal that is carried over the two sensory endings into the spinal cord and eventually to the higher levels of the CNS. Although both sensory endings fire during this initial stretch, the Ia afferents fire more rapidly than the type II endings.

These differences in firing patterns between the two different types of afferents have been attributed to the different mechanical properties of the bag and chain intrafusal fibers. The central area (equatorial region) of the bag fiber has a low threshold for stretch, whereas the chain fiber is stiffer and resists being stretched. Given that the Ia afferents wrap around the more compliant bag fibers, it is not surprising that these endings are primarily responsible for informing us about the speed with which our limbs are accelerating and/or moving through space as we execute a forehand stroke in tennis, swing a golf club, or begin to lift an object from the floor. In contrast, the II afferents, which originate on the stiffer chain fibers, do not begin firing until some time after the muscle has begun changing in length.

limbs in space throughout a routine. The baseball pitcher can be apprised of how quickly his throwing limb is moving through the wind-up phase of the pitch. In the absence of vision, these proprioceptors become even more critical for even the most fundamental postures and movements. A good understanding of their respective functions is therefore warranted.

Muscle Spindles. Muscle spindles, located within all somatic muscles, are considered the most important proprioceptive sense organs. Not only are they essential for the awareness of limb position and movement, but they are also key contributors to fine motor control. This dual sensory and motor function is made possible by the fact that the muscle spindle has both sensory and motor connections

> Proprioceptors provide us with uninterrupted knowledge about the general position of the body in space prior to and during movements.

with the CNS (see the accompanying Highlight). It is also interesting to note that a greater number of muscle spindles are found in muscles of the fingers that control fine joint movements than in muscles that control larger trunk movements.

The changing firing patterns of the two important sensory endings that originate in the spindle (Ia and II afferents) provide valuable information to the various subsystems within the CNS concerning the rate of change in muscle length and absolute muscle length. They also contribute to the automatic regulation of muscle length at the spinal cord level. Nervous impulses transmitted via these sensory pathways enter the spinal cord, where they synapse with alpha motoneurons that innervate the very same muscle being stretched. These **homonymous** motoneurons fire, causing contraction of the extrafusal muscle and simultaneous shortening of the intrafusal muscle spindle fibers. Once the stretch is released from the spindle, the afferent endings cease firing. To illustrate how the muscle spindle contributes to the automatic regulation of muscle length, let us consider the sequence of events associated with a monosynaptic stretch reflex such as the patellar tendon reflex (Figure 4.2).

> Muscle spindles signal the absolute length of muscles and the rate of change of muscle length during movement.

When a physician or therapist taps the skin surface above the patellar tendon, a reflex chain of events results in the leg rapidly extending from a flexed position. This external application of force stretches, or lengthens, the muscle fibers of the quadriceps beyond their current resting position. This stretching of the extrafusal muscle results in deformation of the sensory endings attached to the intrafusal muscles of the muscle spindle contained within the muscle. Deformation of the sensory endings causes the Ia afferent to fire and send a nervous impulse into the spinal cord.

> Muscle spindles contribute to the automatic regulation of muscle length via the stretch reflex loop.

Upon entering the spinal cord, the Ia afferent synapses with an excitatory alpha motoneuron, which sends a signal back to the same quadriceps muscle that has been stretched. The reflex loop is closed as contraction of the quadriceps muscle causes extension of the lower leg and shortening of the intrafusal fibers of the muscle spindle, leading to a cessation of firing. From a clinical perspective, triggering a stretch reflex provides useful information about the integrity of the sensory and motor pathways involved, as well as the level of muscle tone. Other reflexes that are typically examined include the jaw, biceps, triceps, hamstring, and ankle.

Golgi Tendon Organs.   A second important type of muscle receptor is situated at the musculotendinous junctions of skeletal muscle (Figure 4.3).

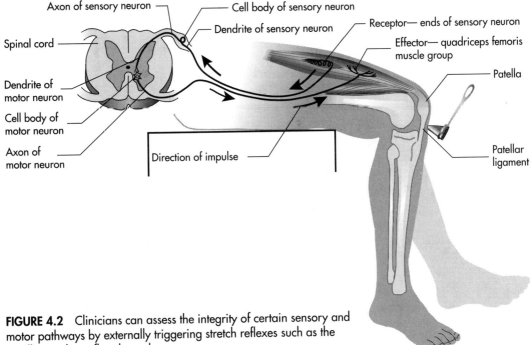

FIGURE 4.2 Clinicians can assess the integrity of certain sensory and motor pathways by externally triggering stretch reflexes such as the patellar tendon reflex shown here.

These mechanoreceptors are called **Golgi tendon organs** (or tendon organs), and their afferent fibers are called Ib nerve fibers. Each skeletal muscle contains a large number of tendon organs (about one to every ten extrafusal muscle fibers), which are arranged in series with the extrafusal muscle fibers. The mechanical arrangement of tendon organs results in stretching of the sensory endings of the Ib afferent during either active contraction or passive lengthening of the muscle.

Although tendon organs are firing during passive lengthening of the muscle, the frequency with which their sensory afferents fire is considerably lower at any given muscle length than that of the muscle spindle. Also, because of its higher threshold level, the tendon organ is not activated when the muscle is stretched close to its resting length. This lack of tendon organ activity provides further support for the idea that the more length-sensitive muscle spindle is responsible for signaling changes in muscle length.

The story is somewhat different, however, during isotonic and isometric contractions of the extrafusal muscle. While the stretch imposed on the muscle spindle is released as the extrafusal muscle shortens, causing the muscle spindle to stop firing, the tendon organ continues to be stretched, and its firing rate actually increases throughout the contraction.

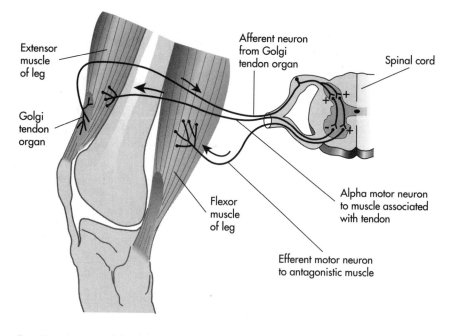

From *Human Anatomy and Physiology,* Second Edition,
by Alexander Spence and Elliott Mason. Copyright (c) 1983
by The Benjamin / Cummings Publishing Company. Reprinted by permission.

FIGURE 4.3 Pathways involved in a tendon reflex. Excitation is indicated by +; inhibition by −.

> The dynamic code of the GTO signals the rate of change in tension during contraction and relaxation of a muscle.

The **dynamic code** of the tendon organ signals the rate of tension increase during contraction and the rate of tension decline during relaxation. Similarly, in isometric conditions (in which tension is increased without a change in muscle length), the firing rate of the tendon organ increases markedly while the II endings in the muscle spindles continue to fire at an even rate, signaling **static** muscle length only. The firing pattern of tendon organs during muscle contraction indicates that their primary role is to monitor the rate of change in tension in a contracting muscle, while signaling the amount of tension present in an isometrically contracting muscle.

> The GTO plays a protective role by indirectly inhibiting the alpha motoneurons of the contracting muscle.

Tendon organs also serve a protective role, preventing muscles from being overloaded. This is achieved by indirect inhibition of the motoneurons that are responsible for exciting the muscles involved in the action. Afferent impulses transmitted via Ib afferents reach the spinal cord and synapse with inhibitory interneurons. These inhibitory interneurons then synapse with alpha motoneurons and actually prevent them from firing. As a result, all or part of the muscle in which the activated tendon organs are located stops contracting.

It is clear that these types of muscle receptors serve important, and often complementary, functions in the automatic regulation of muscle length and tension. While the muscle spindle monitors the movement-related changes in muscle length, the tendon organ monitors the changes in muscle tension, whether the length of the muscle changes or not. During the performance of a movement, the spinal system can use this information to make rapid corrections without the need to involve other subsystems within the CNS.

Joint Receptors.   The joint capsules and ligaments of all synovial joints in the skeletal system are well supplied with proprioceptors. These receptors signal mechanical changes in the capsule and ligaments, including changes associated with painful stimuli. Four types of sensory endings, each with a different structure and physiological responsiveness, have been identified. These are Golgi-type endings, ruffini or spray endings, free nerve endings, and puciniform endings.

Collectively, joint receptors provide us with important proprioceptive information related to both the static and the dynamic aspects of joint motion. In addition, free nerve endings respond to noxious stimuli that induce awareness of pain in the joint and surrounding areas. Although they were once believed to be the primary source of kinesthetic sensibility, recent research suggests a considerably smaller, if not negligible, role for joint receptors in the conscious awareness of limb position and movement. The role joint receptors may play in kinesthesis will be discussed in further detail later in this chapter.

> Joint receptors provide us with information related to the static and dynamic aspects of joint motion.

Vestibular Apparatus.   Another organ that contributes to the ensemble of sensory information we need to plan and execute action successfully is the vestibular apparatus Figure 4.4). This proprioceptor forms part of the membranous labyrinth of the inner ear. The vestibular labyrinth, as it is called, consists of two sac-like swellings, the **utricle** and **saccule,** and three **semicircular canals.** The sensory receptors of the vestibular apparatus are in the form of **hair cells,** which are highly sensitive to angular acceleration of the head. In contrast, receptors located in both utricle and saccule are more sensitive to static head positions and to changes in linear acceleration associated with movements of the head.

The vestibular apparatus, in conjunction with other somatosensory inputs, plays an important role in equilibrium, particularly in situations of **sensory conflict.** In these types of conditions, one or more senses may

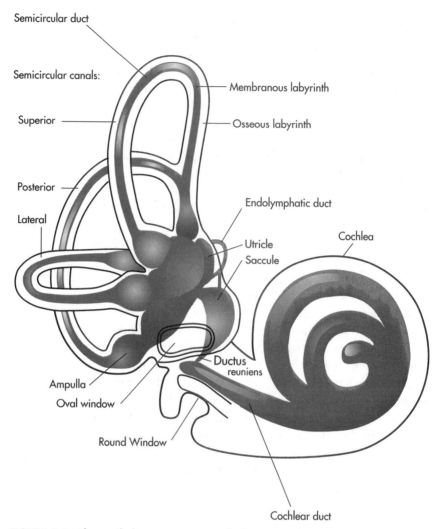

FIGURE 4.4 The vestibular apparatus signals changes in the acceleration of the head via three semicircular canals (superior, posterior, and lateral) and the utricle and saccule.

be providing inaccurate information about our orientation in space. For example, have you ever found yourself reaching for the brake in your car at a stop light because a vehicle next to you has begun to move? Despite the fact that your somatosensory inputs are telling you that you and your car are perfectly stationary, the visual system has tricked you into thinking that you are moving. This feeling of disorientation can be exacerbated by a moving or compliant surface; in this situation we must rely totally on the information provided by the vestibular appa-

> The vestibular apparatus signals the position and movements of the head in space.

ratus, because the somatosensory information provided at the ankles is no longer accurate. How fortunate we are to have multiple senses to help us maintain our balance in a variety of environmental conditions.

TRANSMISSION OF SOMATOSENSORY INPUT

Somatic sensation is relayed to the cerebral cortex via one of two major ascending systems: **dorsal column (DC)** and the **spinothalamic tract (ST)**. Both systems relay afferent information to the brain for arousal, perception, and motor control. These systems are similar in anatomical organization: Both involve three orders of neurons and three synapses in transmitting sensory input from the periphery to the cortex. The primary afferent, which is connected to the peripheral receptor, synapses with a second neuron in the spinal cord or lower brain, depending on the type of sensation. The second neuron then conveys information to the thalamus, where it synapses with the third and final neuron in an area of the thalamus called the ventroposterolateral (VPL) area.

From the thalamus, the third-order neuron then projects to the primary somatosensory areas in the cortex where perceptual processing begins. It is important to note that neurons within both ascending systems transmit somatosensory information that is modality and location specific. This rigid organization of input makes it possible for the cortex to differentiate between sensations of pressure and touch and, between sensations arising from the left leg and right hand.

Dorsal Column System (DC)

As Figure 4.5 illustrates, the dorsal column system (DC) contains axons of primary sensory afferents from joint, skin, and muscle receptors. The primary afferents enter the spinal cord and immediately divide into long and short branches. The short branches terminate in the spinal cord, but the longer branches continue upward, without interruption, to synapse in the medulla at the level of the brainstem. The second-order neurons leave the medulla and immediately **decussate,** or cross, the midline to the **contralateral** (opposite) side before reaching the VPL area of the thalamus. The third-order neurons then convey the afferent information **ipsilaterally** (on the same side), terminating in the **sensory projection area** of the somatosensory cortex.

> The DC pathway transmits sensory information that is important for the planning and execution of movements.

The nerve fibers of this system convey information about fine, discriminative sensations (e.g., light touch and vibrations), tactile pressure,

FIGURE 4.5 The dorsal column system pathways convey touch, pressure, and proprioceptive information to the cerebral cortex.

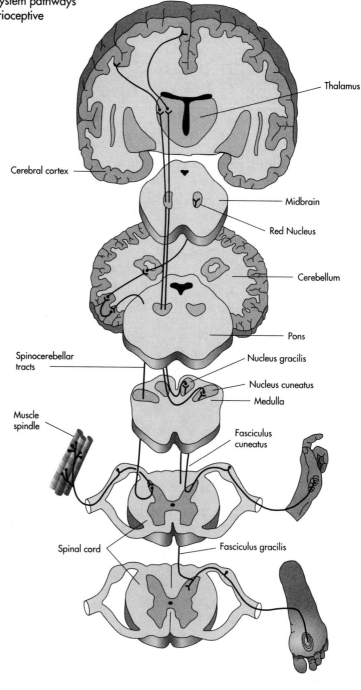

From *Human Anatomy and Physiology*, Second Edition, by Alexander Spence and Elliott Mason. Copyright (c) 1983 by The Benjamin / Cummings Publishing Company. Reprinted by permission.

and limb proprioception. The DC plays an important role in motor control because of its speed and fidelity of transmission. The heavily myelinated and wide-diameter axons within this system transmit at speeds of 80 to 100 meters per second. This characteristic facilitates rapid sampling of the environment, which enhances the accuracy of motor actions about to be executed and of those already in progress. The spinocerebellar tracts, of which there are four, also convey important proprioceptive information from the neuromucular receptors (such as muscle spindles) to the cerebellum. Unlike the DC system, these pathways do not synapse in either the thalamus or the cerebral cortex. As a result, the proprioceptive information conveyed by the spinocerebellar tracts does not lead to conscious perceptions of limb position, or kinesthesis. The afferent sources believed to contribute to kinesthesis will be discussed in more detail later in this chapter.

Spinothalamic Tract System (ST)

Primary sensory afferents from pain, temperature, and touch, receptors and some proprioceptors enter the spinal cord and immediately synapse with sensory neurons located in the dorsal horn of the spinal cord (Figure 4.6). Approximately 90% of the axons of these second-order neurons immediately decussate and form the fibers of the spinothalamic tract (ST), whereas the remaining 10% of the fibers do not decussate but ascend ipsilaterally to the somatosensory cortex. ST neurons then synapse with third-order neurons in the VPL of the thalamus before terminating in the somatosensory cortex.

> The ST pathway transmits sensory information the delivery of which can be delayed.

In contrast to the transmission properties associated with the DC system, neurons that make up the ST conduct slowly (1 to 40 meters per second) and are small in diameter; some are unmyelinated. Information related to pain and temperature appreciation and to crude touch is mediated by this system. Some proprioceptive information is also conveyed by the ST. The anterolateral system therefore transmits information that the brain can afford to receive after delay.

DISORDERS OF THE SOMATOSENSORY SYSTEM

Some level of sensory impairment usually accompanies disease or injury to the peripheral nerves or spinal cord, fractures, hemiplegia, multiple sclerosis, and cerebrovascular accidents. Normal aging also results in neurosensory changes that may lead to diminished sensory function.

FIGURE 4.6 The spinothalamic pathways convey pain and temperature information to the cerebral cortex.

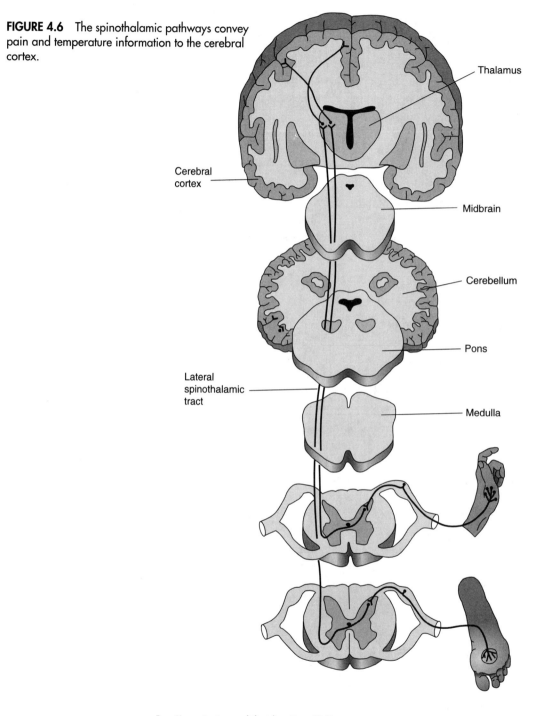

Thalamus

Cerebral cortex

Midbrain

Cerebellum

Pons

Lateral spinothalamic tract

Medulla

From *Human Anatomy and Physiology,* Second Edition, by Alexander Spence and Elliott Mason. Copyright (c) 1983 by The Benjamin / Cummings Publishing Company. Reprinted by permission.

Decreased acuity of many sensations that arise from cutaneous and proprioceptive sources occurs, or is considered likely to occur, during the normal aging process. The performance of many daily motor activities is often affected.

As one might expect, the nature of the sensory impairment depends on which of the two ascending systems is affected. For example, lesions occurring anywhere along the dorsal column system result in partial or complete loss of discriminative tactile sensibilities in areas of the body served by the affected region. Discrimination between two points simultaneously applied to the skin is often severely affected, as is the ability to discriminate between different textures. Some kinesthetic sensations are also lost, such as the ability to recognize the direction of limb movement in space without visual or tactile cues.

> The nature of the sensory impairment differs depending on which sensory pathway is affected.

In contrast, lesions of the spinothalamic system generally result in the loss of pain, temperature, and coarse tactile sensations, and the sensory deficits are usually felt on the side opposite that on which the lesion occurred. This is due to the early decussation of the nerve fibers composing this pathway in the spinal cord. Given the close relationship between sensory input and motor output, any reduction in somatosensory sensation is likely to affect the performance of many activities. For many physical therapists, this is an important consideration in designing treatment programs for their patients.

APPLICATION OF THEORY

Why is it important for practitioners to understand the seemingly intricate neuromotor processes underlying the reception, transmission, and processing of sensory information? Certainly, practitioners working in a clinical setting use their knowledge of how the human system receives, transmits, and finally gives meaning to sensory input as they devise and implement treatment programs. In view of the close relationship between sensory input and motor output, certain kinds of sensory disorders can be expected to influence motor performance negatively. For example, a patient who is experiencing decreased spatial awareness of a limb's position in space will surely find it difficult to perform a variety of movements that require accurate limb positioning. Any reduction in the level of sensory feedback available to us while we are planning motor actions can also be expected to compromise the quality of the movements produced. The more clinicians know about the healthy somatosensory system, the better equipped they are to make accurate diagnoses.

Similarly, the physical educator or coach who understands how sensory information is processed and integrated within the CNS can learn to use cutaneous and proprioceptive cues to facilitate motor skill learning. For example, an instructor can apply this information to impart a better understanding of how a particular motor pattern should feel. In teaching aquatic skills, the instructor can encourage the learner to focus on the "feel" of the water against the forearm throughout the pull phase of a particular stroke or on the contrast in temperature as the arm and fingers leave the water at the start of the recovery phase. Similarly, a child's attention can be directed to the pressure of the ball contacting the fingers as it returns from the floor during dribbling. These somatosensory cues can be used to supplement visual demonstrations of a skill and to guide the learner's performance during practice.

Focusing the learner's attention on the somatosensory aspects of a movement contributes much to the learner's awareness of where the limbs are in space throughout the movement. It also provides the learner with a better understanding of the level of effort required. These sensory impressions of the movement can then be incorporated into the knowledge base the learner is developing about the movement being learned. The more knowledge a performer has about a particular movement pattern, the better he or she will recall the skill at a later time. The detection and correction of errors in performance will also be enhanced if the learner is aware of the somatosensory aspects of the movement.

THE CONSCIOUS SENSATION OF MOVEMENT

Knowing exactly where our limbs are in space and how much muscular effort is required to perform a particular action is critical for successful performance in many sports and other activities that involve the intricate coordination of various body parts (gymnastics, diving, figure skating). Indeed, most activities that call for coordination of several body parts require that we understand these two important pieces of information. Fortunately, information about the position and movement of various body parts is available to us via peripheral receptors located within the skin, muscles, and joints throughout the body. In addition, there is evidence to suggest that internally generated commands associated with movement also provide us with valuable information about muscle force.

> Kinesthesis is the conscious sensation of movement and/or limb position.

The *conscious* sensation of movement and/or limb position that arises as a function of certain sensory activity is often called **kinesthesis**, a term derived from the Greek words *kines* ("to move") and *thesis* ("sensation"). We discussed the role of the proprioceptors in the subconscious control of action earlier in this chapter. Let us now consider whether these same proprioceptors provide information about movement control at a conscious perceptual level.

Afferent Sources of Kinesthesis

Let us begin by briefly reviewing the literature identifying various afferent sources of kinesthetic sensations. Both the type and the number of afferent sources believed to be involved in kinesthesis have changed over the past 90 years, as different research findings have emerged. Among the candidates still considered most likely to provide conscious sensation of limb position and other movement-related sensations are joint receptors, muscle spindles, Golgi tendon organs, and cutaneous receptors.

Joint Receptors.   Until quite recently, receptors in and around the joint were considered the primary afferent source of limb movement and position. The presence of slowly adapting receptors that continued to fire when a joint was maintained in a steady position, coupled with the finding that joint receptors sent signals to the higher cortical regions of the nervous system, seemed to establish a role for joint receptors in the conscious awareness of limb position. In addition, Adams (1977) proposed that these receptors performed two important feedback functions during movement. The first function was to regulate the dynamic aspects of limb movement; the second was to regulate static timing, or the sequence of action.

The conclusions of Adams and other theorists, however, were severely compromised by the results of neurophysiological experiments employing single unit recordings of joint receptors (Burgess & Clark, 1969; Clark & Burgess, 1975). Although joint receptors were shown to fire at the extreme range of joint rotation, they stopped firing when the limb was in mid-position, a finding clearly incompatible with the idea that joint receptors continuously signal limb position. Because kinesthetic sensations continued throughout the range of motion, it was clear that other afferent sources were also being used to signal joint position.

Muscle Spindles.   Despite the rejection, from 1960 to 1970, of muscle spindles as a possible afferent source of kinesthesis, they have since been shown to be the most important afferent source of kinesthesis available to us. A role for muscle spindle afferents in kinesthesis was finally confirmed by research conducted in three different areas: muscle vibration, tendon pulling, and elimination of joint and cutaneous signals.

Perhaps the most conclusive evidence was provided in a series of experiments using percutaneous vibration techniques (Goodwin, McCloskey, & Matthews, 1972; McCloskey, 1973). When high-frequency vibration was applied through the skin over a muscle or its tendon, causing the level of spindle firing to increase (particularly the Ia endings), the vibrated muscle contracted involuntarily. Surprisingly, the resulting **tonic vibration reflex** was accompanied by an illusion of limb movement in the direction that would normally stretch the vibrated muscle. The blindfolded subjects in these studies were requested to keep the nonvibrated arm aligned with the vibrated limb, thus revealing their perception of the vibrated limb's position in space. Despite the fact that the vibrated arm was actually extending, the subject did not begin to move the tracking arm from its original position until the vibrated arm had already moved several degrees from its starting position. Once the vibration was stopped, however, the subjects were able to realign their arms quite accurately. When allowed to view the position of their arms at some point during the movement, subjects would appear surprised at the actual position of their limbs. It is clear from this observation that the subjects' perception of limb position was being severely distorted by the vibration.

> Muscle spindles have been shown to be the most important source of kinethesis available to us.

Why would a subject experience a sensation of movement in a limb that was not moving? Brooks (1986) suggests that the brain is unable to distinguish between artificially induced sensory input and that which arises from actual changes in muscle length. In the absence of information suggesting otherwise, the brain simply adds the two types of input in estimating limb position. Depending on the original position of the limb and on the level of vibration, subjects report sensations ranging from mild hyperextension to broken limbs!

Further support for muscle spindle involvement in signaling joint position was provided by experiments in which surgically isolated tendons were stretched (McCloskey, Cross, Honner, & Potter, 1983; Moberg, 1983). As a consequence of having their tendons pulled, subjects experienced direct sensations of joint rotation rather than specific muscular sensations, which indicated that sensory stimulation of the muscle spindle was being directly referred to the joint and translated into position sense.

Advancements in prosthetic medicine during the 1960s, which enabled surgeons to replace diseased joints with artificial ones, also provided clinical evidence that further discredited the involvement of joint receptors while providing further support for muscle spindle involvement in kinesthesia. Patients who receive total hip replacements do not

Despite hip replacement surgery, Bo Jackson maintained a high level of kinesthetic awareness in his artificial hip joint.

suffer kinesthetic anesthesia and are able to detect small movements (5 degrees per second) of the artificial hip with little difficulty. Consider the difficulties Chicago White Sox player Bo Jackson would experience if he were unable to sense the position of his limbs during movements such as batting, a skill that requires heightened kinesthetic awareness. Jackson made history by returning to professional baseball, however briefly, after successful hip replacement surgery.

Golgi Tendon Organ.   The Golgi tendon organ (GTO) has also been identified as a possible source of kinesthesis, particularly because it is also located within skeletomotor muscle. As you will recall from our earlier discussion of this proprioceptor, the GTO conveys information about muscle tension, whereas the muscle spindle signals changes in muscle length. Despite the fact that tendon organs are excited when a muscle is vibrated or actively contracted, a kinesthetic role for the tendon organ has not been clearly established. The consensus among researchers, as summarized by Matthews (1981) in a comprehensive review of the issue, is that tendon organs may work cooperatively with other proprioceptors in the muscles and joints to signal other movement-related sensations, such as the forces acting on the body during movement.

Cutaneous Receptors. Although cutaneous receptors are inevitably excited as a result of movement in a nearby joint, the possibility that cutaneous afferents provide an important afferent source of kinesthesia has received little support on the basis of studies in which the skin was anesthetized (Clark, Matthews, & Muir, 1979). Kinesthetic sensation of joint movement was not significantly affected by eliminating cutaneous signals. The conclusion that cutaneous afferents do not contribute significantly to kinesthesis must be tempered, however, in light of other research involving anesthesia (Goodwin, McCloskey, & Matthews, 1972). In contrast to the limited effects on kinesthesis observed at the hip joint, kinesthetic judgment of limb position was significantly impaired after the elimination of cutaneous signals from the hand and fingers. These contradictory findings suggest that the kinesthetic contribution of cutaneous afferents varies across joints in the body, becoming increasingly more important in distal joints involved in the performance of more finely graded movements.

PRACTICAL APPLICATIONS

Movements that require us to maintain a given posture or consciously direct our limbs to a particular point in space in a controlled fashion depend on our ability to utilize kinesthetic information efficiently, particularly in the absence of vision. The application and ongoing adjustment of just the right amount of muscular force and effort are also critical for successful completion of a movement.

A teacher or therapist who encourages an individual to focus on the feelings associated with a particular movement is acknowledging the importance of proprioceptive and cutaneous information in the control and learning of movement. The knowledge that certain proprioceptors provide information that can be used to sense the movement and position of joints in space can be exploited by the instructor, particularly in the teaching of skills that demand an acute sense of spatial positioning and rapid error correction while they are being executed. For example, skills such as ballet dancing and gymnastics are well suited to the use of kinesthetic cues to guide learning.

In movement situations where visual input is absent or distorted, as it is in swimming and discus throwing, the performer is highly dependent on the kinesthetic cues provided by the cutaneous and intramuscular receptors. Just as the swimmer derives sensations of muscular force as the arm moves against the resistance created by the water, the discus thrower uses the kinesthetic sensations associated with the movements of the body and outstretched arm as he or she is rotating rapidly to optimize the release angle of the discus. Directing such performers' attention to the kinesthetic aspects of the performance should significantly enhance their immediate perception and ultimate memory of the skill.

It is interesting to note that coaches often employ devices that are designed to accentuate the kinesthetic feel associated with certain movements. Hand paddles or webbed gloves may be provided to swimmers. Weighted rings may be added to a baseball bat to give the batter a heightened "feel" of the bat's movements throughout the swing.

Can our ability to use kinesthetic information during movement be improved? This question was the focus of a series of studies conducted by Laszlo and Bairstow (1983). It was well known that kinesthetic perception improved with age, but little attention had been directed to investigating whether kinesthetic perception and memory could be improved with training. In addition to finding that children ranging in age from 6 to 8 years could be trained to improve their level of kinesthetic sensitivity, the authors also demonstrated that once kinesthetic awareness had been established, the ability to use the kinesthetic information was retained.

The knowledge derived from early muscle vibration studies has also been successfully applied in clinical settings to facilitate accurate diagnoses and improved rehabilitation. The tonic vibration reflex (TVR),

The kinesthetic "feel" of certain swimming movements can be heightened with the use of devices such as hand paddles or webbed gloves.

elicited by muscle vibration, has been used to evaluate muscle tone, the integrity of certain stretch reflexes, and higher cortical function. As Brooks (1986) reports, the TVR has also been used in the clinical setting to assist in the rehabilitation of hemiplegic patients who would otherwise ignore their affected limbs, to inhibit undesirable motor patterns resulting from spasticity, and to provide a valuable source of biofeedback for patients with reduced skin sensations.

THE ROLE OF FEEDBACK IN CONTROLLING ACTIONS

> It is important that the CNS receive an uninterrupted flow of sensory information if movements are to be performed effectively.

The important role played by sensory (afferent) information in both the planning and the moment-to-moment control of movement should now be evident. In fact, if we are to perform movements effectively, it is essential that the nervous system receive an uninterrupted flow of sensory information. The performer uses this sensory information in a variety of ways; we will consider three important uses here. Sensory information (1) provides us with information about the body's spatial position before, during, and after the action, (2) guides the planning and modification of action plans, and (3) helps us learn or relearn movement patterns.

Knowledge of Body Position

The first important function sensory feedback serves is to provide us with information about the position of our many body parts in relation to each other (proprioception) and about the orientation of the whole body to the surrounding environment (exproprioception). This information is useful to a batter trying to adopt the appropriate stance before the pitch and to the gymnast performing a difficult maneuver on a balance beam. In this latter movement situation, sensory information provided by the visual and proprioceptive senses enables the gymnast to monitor the changing positions of her limbs and body frequently throughout the routine. In this way, she can check the correctness of her movements and make minor adjustments in limb and body position to optimize her performance. Movement-related sensory feedback that is available after a movement has been completed can also serve an important error-correcting function. Knowing the final position of the limbs and/or body following a movement can often give us valuable information about the performance and provide clues to why the intended outcome was not achieved.

Sensory feedback provides information about the relative positions of the various parts of the body and about the body's orientation relative to other objects in space.

Planning and Modification of Action Plans

A related function of sensory feedback is to guide us in the action-planning process by helping us construct the plan of action that best suits the demands of the environment. The rich network of interconnecting pathways between the various neural task systems ensures that feedback from a variety of internal and external sources can be used to elaborate and/or modify an action plan throughout the planning process. Given sufficient time to execute the action plan, we can also use sensory feedback to make numerous minor adjustments to the movements to ensure their success.

To illustrate this point, consider a tennis player who is preparing to follow up an attempted deep forehand return to his opponent with a short, angled volley stroke. In this movement situation, the player uses the available visual and proprioceptive feedback to determine whether a volley stroke is, indeed, the most suitable action. If the player fails to strike the ball with sufficient force or observes the opponent speeding into the net immediately after his own stroke, it is likely that the player would consider altering that proposed course of action. This would not be possible, however, if the player were unable either to observe the movements of his opponent or to feel the impact associated with striking the ball.

Learning or Relearning of Movements

The third, and perhaps most important, function of sensory feedback is to facilitate the learning of new movement skills and the relearning of existing movement patterns that have become dysfunctional through trauma and/or disease. The novice performer attempting to learn how to hit a baseball uses the feedback derived from physically practicing the skill to make adjustments in subsequent attempts. This trial-and-error approach continues until the goal of hitting the ball is consistently achieved. Similarly, patients attempting to relearn how to walk after a stroke must depend on visual feedback to guide their legs through the action.

ERRORS IN PERFORMANCE

Despite the cooperative efforts of the various neural task systems and despite the availability of sensory feedback, various types of performance errors are inevitable. These errors may arise as a consequence of incorrectly evaluating the environmental display and thus developing an inappropriate plan of action; developing an appropriate plan of action but applying the wrong movement dynamics (e.g., force, velocity, timing); sensory conflict that results in a misperception; or many other unexpected factors that lead to inappropriate motor behavior.

Although these errors are sometimes unavoidable, the degree to which they affect performance is largely determined by how much time it takes to complete the movement and by the quality of the feedback mechanisms available to the performer. Movements that must be performed ballistically, such as firing a pistol, give the performer little opportunity to use the available sensory feedback to change the plan of action or modify the movement in progress. In contrast, movements that last for several seconds can be continuously modified on the basis of the feedback arising from the action itself and on the basis of changes observed to occur in the environment.

> The degree to which errors affect a performance depends on the time required to complete the movement and on the quality of the feedback.

The level to which the various feedback mechanisms are developed within the performer clearly determines the degree to which errors influence performance outcomes. Given that the quality of these mechanisms is strongly influenced by experience, it is to be expected that the performance of less skilled performers will be most affected by the types of errors we have described.

SUMMARY

Sensory receptors help the various subsystems in the CNS derive meaning from the external world. They not only tell us when a sensory event has occurred (adequate stimulation) but also code the intensity of that event by means of their temporal and/or spatial firing patterns. These same receptors are also able to block out redundant or irrelevant sensory information by reducing their firing levels shortly after an event occurs. This property of sensory receptors is called sensory adaptation.

Sensory information is conveyed by specialized afferent pathways to primary sensory areas distributed throughout the cortex. It is then further processed and integrated with sensory information from other senses. Before reaching the cortex, however, all sensory information (except that derived from smell) passes through the thalamus, which serves as a "sensory roundhouse." Our final perception of what is occurring in the environment is achieved once the integrated sensory information reaches the association areas of the cortex. This final perception forms the basis of future voluntary actions.

The cutaneous receptors and proprioceptors that make up the somatosensory system give rise to sensations of touch, pain, temperature, and limb position and movement. These sensations are conveyed to the cortex by one of two primary sensory pathways: the dorsal column system (DC) and the spinothalamic system (ST).

Disorders of the somatosensory system can be expected to compromise our ability to perform many activities of daily living because of the close relationship between sensory input and motor output. The treatment programs prescribed for patients are influenced by this relationship.

Somatosensory cues can be used in motor skill settings to enhance a learner's understanding of a skill's spatial requirements and of the amount of effort needed to accomplish the goal of the movement.

Muscle afferents, primarily muscle spindles, are the most important peripheral source of kinesthetic sensations related to joint movement and position in space. The primary (Ia) endings signal the dynamic and static aspects of limb position and perhaps velocity of limb movement, whereas the secondary (II) endings contribute to awareness of static limb position. Sensations of force associated with increased levels of tension in the muscle are believed to be provided by Golgi tendon organs, which are also located within skeletomotor muscle.

Cutaneous receptors contribute to kinesthesis primarily by supporting and enhancing signals generated by muscle receptors, and their contributions are more important in distal joints involved in fine movement control. Joint receptors, once considered the only afferent source of kinesthesis, probably play no major role in the conscious sensation of movement.

Sensory feedback has many functions in the control of action. We discussed three: knowledge of body position, the planning and modification of action, and the learning and relearning of movements. The degree to which the individual is able to utilize her or his internal sensory feedback mechanisms determines the magnitude of the errors made in the performance of any movement.

IMPORTANT TERMINOLOGY

After completing this chapter, readers should be familiar with the following terms and concepts.

adequate stimulation
adaptation
agnosia
association areas
chain fibers
contralateral
cultaneous receptors
decussate
diencephalon
dorsal column tract (DC)
dynamic code
Golgi tendon organ
hair cells
homonymous
intensity code
ipsilateral
kinesthesis

mechanoreceptors
nuclear bag fibers
proprioceptors
saccule
semicircular canals
sensory conflict
sensory projection area
somesthesia
spatial summation
spinothalamic tract (ST)
static code
temporal summation
thalamic syndrome
thalamus
tonic vibration reflex
transduction
utricle

SUGGESTED FURTHER READING

Gandevia, S.C., & Burke, D. 1992. Does the nervous system depend on kinesthetic information to control natural limb movements? *Behavioral and Brain Sciences, 15,* 614–632.

Jones, L.A. 1988. Motor illusions: What do they reveal about proprioception? *Psychological Bulletin,* 103, 1, 72–86.

TEST YOUR UNDERSTANDING

1. Identify the specific characteristic(s) of a sensory receptor that:
    (a) Help(s) us know when a particular sensory event occurred.
    (b) Assist(s) us in distinguishing between sensations of light touch and heavy pressure applied to the skin.
    (c) Prevent(s) us from becoming irritated by clothing against our skin.

2. Briefly describe the specific routes that electrical impulses follow from receptor to cortex for each of these somatosensory sensations:
    (a) Fine, discriminative touch.
    (b) Pain.
    (c) Proprioception.

3. Describe the disorder known as agnosia that is caused by damage to the association area in the cortex.

4. Identify the two categories into which somatosensory receptors have been divided. Briefly explain the sensory contribution that each category makes to perception and action.

5. Briefly describe the different types of sensory information provided to the CNS by the primary (Ia) afferent and the secondary (II) afferent in the muscle spindle.

6. Briefly explain how the muscle spindle contributes to the automatic regulation of muscle length during movement.

7. Describe the role of Golgi tendon organs during (a) isotonic and (b) isometric muscle contractions.

8. What type of information is provided to the CNS by the various types of joint receptors located throughout the body?

9. In what way does the information provided by the sensory receptors within the semicircular canals differ from that provided by receptors located in the utricle and saccule of the vestibular apparatus?

10. Explain how the nature of the sensory impairment differs depending on which of the two major ascending pathways is affected.

11. Briefly describe ways in which knowledge about the somatosensory system can be utilized in a practical setting. Provide examples to illustrate your answer.

12. Briefly explain what the term *kinesthesis* means.

13. Identify the afferent sources that contribute to the conscious perception of limb position and movement.

14. Discuss the various clinical and practical implications of the fact that certain proprioceptors can be used to sense the position of limbs in space.

15. Identify the various functions served by sensory feedback in the planning and execution of movements.

16. Identify the various factors that may lead to errors in performance.

About the Quote

Apparently, even Hamlet was aware of the importance of the various senses in the production and moment-to-moment control of movement!

C H A P T E R 5
VISION AND ACTION

CHAPTER OBJECTIVES

- Understand and be able to describe the different types of sensory information provided by the visual system in the control of movement.

- Understand and be able to explain how the visual system is functionally organized to receive and interpret incoming visual information.

- Be able to identify the functional differences between the two visual systems and their respective contributions to various aspects of motor control.

- Become familiar with the two contrasting theories of visual perception and the different underlying assumptions associated with each theory.

- Understand and be able to describe how vision is used as a feedforward mechanism in certain movement situations and as a feedback mechanism in others.

- Understand and be able to describe how vision can be used to predict time-to-contact with another object and/or person.

> *"What you see when you see a thing depends upon what the thing you see is. But what you see the thing as depends upon what you know about what you are seeing...."*
>
> —Fodor & Pylyshyn (1981) p. 189

Proprioception, though it is an important source of information for controlling and coordinating movement, is not the only means by which we successfully interact with our environment. As we will see in this chapter, the visual system is another important source of information for the control and learning of many motor skills. Not only do we use our eyes to monitor the position of other players on a basketball court or to determine when to strike a pitched ball, but we also rely on vision to help us perform more fundamental skills such as standing and walking.

According to Lee (1978), vision provides three very important types of sensory information in the control of movement. These are exteroception, proprioception, and exproprioception. First, vision provides **exteroceptive** information by informing us about the layout of surfaces and the relative positions of objects in the environment. The monitoring of events occurring in a given movement situation is also made possible by vision, which therefore guides us in the planning and execution of actions. Although we tend to think that information about the movement of body parts relative to each other derives from the mechanical receptors in muscles, joints, and the inner ear, vision has also been shown to serve a **proprioceptive** function.

> Vision provides three types of sensory information: exteroceptive, proprioceptive, and exproprioceptive.

As we will see when we discuss posture and balance, vision is an integral component of the control system used to maintain an upright stance because of its ability to extract important sensory information from the changing optic array. This third type of sensory information provided by vision is called **exproprioception.** Unlike proprioception, this type of information provides us with knowledge about the position of the body and its various parts relative to the surrounding environment. It therefore helps us to intercept moving objects, avoid obstacles in our path, and perform many other activities associated with daily life.

In this chapter we will once again adopt a multilevel discussion of vision and the many important contributions it makes to the planning and execution of movement. Our discussion will begin at the neuromotor processing level of analysis, where we will focus on describing how the visual system is functionally organized to receive and process incoming visual information. Then we will move to a psychological level of analysis and describe two theories of visual perception that view perception and action quite differently. Finally, we will consider the role of vision in the guidance of human action.

NEUROMOTOR PROCESSING OF VISION

Reception of Visual Input

Light enters the eye through the cornea and proceeds through the **pupil** and **lens** before reaching the **retina.** Light-sensitive receptors then convert the light waves to electrical impulses. This process of **transduction,** which we first discussed in Chapter 4 as it operates in the somatosensory system, prepares visual input for further processing in various subsystems within the CNS. Two types of photoreceptors, located in different parts of the retina and serving different functions, are responsible for this first stage of visual processing.

The receptors called **rod** cells tend to be heavily concentrated in the peripheral retina, nearest the lens. They are absent from the center of the retina (fovea). These rod cells, by virtue of their sensitivity to very low levels of illumination, act as our primary photoreceptors in conditions of poor lighting and for night vision. In contrast, the **cone** receptor cells are stimulated only at very high levels of illumination. They are therefore more suited for day vision. Cone receptors not only contain photopigments that enable us to see objects in fine detail (e.g., the seam of a baseball in flight and the variations of texture in an oil painting) but also allow us to detect colors. Unfortunately, colorblind individuals lack the types of cone cells that contain the photopigments necessary to detect red and green light and are therefore "blind" to these colors.

> Rod and cone cells transduce light waves into electrical impulses, preparing them for further processing in other subsystems.

Transmission to the Brain

After further processing in progressively deeper layers of the retina, electrical impulses leave the eye via the **optic nerve,** which transmits impulses directly to the brain. Just as somatosensory input received by receptors on one side of the body is transmitted via nerve pathways that eventually terminate in the opposite cortical hemisphere, impulses arising from the portions of the retina that serve the left visual field are sent to the right hemisphere of the brain, and impulses derived from viewing objects in the right visual field terminate in the left hemisphere. The point at which this crossing of nerve fibers takes place is called the **optic chiasm.** The partial crossing of optic nerve fibers at the optic chiasm is also a requirement for the binocular vision that enables us to see the world in three dimensions.

As Figure 5.1 illustrates, the greatest percentage of optic nerve fibers synapse in a specialized area of the **thalamus** known as the **lateral geniculate nucleus (LGN).** From here, visual impulses are relayed via optic radiations to the **primary visual cortex,** or **striate cortex.** This area is located in the most posterior portion of the occipital lobe. It is not until this stage in the transmission process that the spatial organization of a visual scene is detected. This ability is made possible through the functioning of specialized cells located in the primary visual cortex that enable us to identify such characteristics of objects as shading, brightness, and form.

> Two anatomically distinct pathways convey visual input to two separate areas in the brain.

A smaller percentage of impulses also travel via other nerve pathways and terminate in the **superior colliculus** located in the midbrain. In the superior colliculus, vision is integrated with other incoming sensory inputs from the somatosensory and auditory systems. This integration of the senses enables other sensory responses to be coordinated with movements of the head and eyes toward events occurring in the envi-

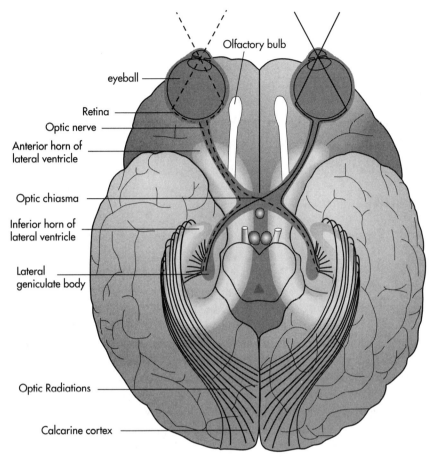

FIGURE 5.1   The anatomy of the visual system.

ronment. Although the superior colliculus is primarily involved in the reflex control and regulation of many eye and head movements, it also plays an important role in attention and visual perception.

Topographic Organization in the Visual System

The **topographic organization** of subcortical and cortical areas that was evident in the somatosensory system is once again observed in the visual system. Neurons in the visual system are arranged such that specific regions of the retina project to clearly defined areas within the thalamus and the visual cortex. The degree of representation is once again determined by the level of receptive sensitivity in the area of the body being represented. The foveal region of the retina permits the highest level

> The final interpretation of what has been seen occurs in the association areas of the visual cortex.

of visual acuity, and almost 50% of the representational area in the thalamus and visual cortex is devoted to the fovea. The much larger and less sensitive peripheral areas of the retina are significantly less well represented. Such a topographic arrangement of neurons provides us with a map of the retina that can be recreated in the visual cortex. The final interpretation of what has been seen occurs in the visual association areas of the visual cortex, giving rise to a perception of the external world.

In addition to the topographic representation of vision observed throughout the cortical pathway, the superior colliculus also contains maps of the various parts of the body and ear surface. Unlike the somatosensory system, however, the level of representation in the superior colliculus is determined not by the sensitivity of the given body part but rather by the proximity of the body part to the eye. The closer the body part is to the eye, the larger its representational area.

TWO VISUAL SYSTEMS?

The existence of two structurally distinct visual pathways that terminate in different areas of the brain has prompted several researchers to advance the idea of two separate visual systems that are functionally different from each other. The terms **focal** and **ambient** are generally used to describe these two systems. The focal system, which is served by the fovea of the eye and where visual acuity is high, is thought to be responsible for identifying objects primarily in the center of the visual field. The fact that identifying objects requires conscious thought also suggests that the visual pathway that terminates in the primary visual cortex is responsible for this type of visual processing. Unlike the focal system, the ambient system is used for detecting space around the body while providing information about where objects are located in space. The major advantage of ambient vision is that it is served by the whole retina and so is not degraded in conditions of poor lighting. It is this second system that helps us navigate through space at night.

Empirical evidence supporting the existence of two visual systems has been provided in controlled animal studies and case study reports of patients with damage to the visual cortex. In one such case study, Weiskrantz and colleagues (Weiskrantz, Warrington, Sanders, & Marshall, 1974) observed patients in whom partial destruction of the visual cortex caused blindness in certain areas of the visual field. Their report indicated that even though patients were unable to identify an object presented in the affected part of their visual field, they were able to point to it accurately. Patients were also able to orient their eyes toward the object when asked to guess where it was presented in space. It appears that patients were able to use their functioning ambient system to *locate* the object even though damage to the area of the brain responsible for focal vision prevented them from being able to *identify* it.

Two Visual Systems and Motor Control

How do these two systems contribute to the various aspects of motor control? Although the two visual systems serve different functions, it is likely that both systems operate in parallel in most movement situations. The focal system helps us identify objects in space, and the ambient system is used to locate objects in space at a subconscious level. This parallel operation of the two visual systems is particularly useful in situations such as downhill skiing and even just walking along a busy street. In both of these situations, it is important to orient the body with respect to objects in the peripheral field of vision in order to avoid potential collisions, but there is no need to identify the particular object.

> The focal visual system identifies objects; the ambient system locates objects in space.

The focal system operates concurrently to identify important changes in terrain or objects in the center of the visual field that may

Whereas the focal system assists us in identifying objects in space, the ambient system is used to locate objects in space at a subconscious level. This second system is particularly useful in helping us avoid collisions with others when walking on a busy street.

pose a more immediate problem. In this way, one system can be used to attend to one type of visual input while the other system guides the orientation of our body as we move through the complex environment. Indeed, the parallel organization evident in the visual system is often cited by theorists as evidence for the distributed model of motor control described in the first chapter of this section.

PSYCHOLOGICAL STUDIES OF PERCEPTION AND ACTION

Contrasting Theories of Visual Perception

Now that we have outlined the neuromotor processes of vision, let us turn to the psychological level of analysis and begin to explore how our perceptions of the external world can be used to plan and guide our actions in a variety of movement contexts. Unfortunately, considerable disagreement exists among researchers striving to understand the relationship between perception and action. The primary issue dividing researchers is related to whether or not inferential, or cognitive, processes are necessary for perception. This section is devoted to a discussion of this controversial issue and how it has influenced the way the perception–action relationship has been investigated by the different groups of researchers.

At present, two seemingly different theories of visual perception are being put forward to explain how perception is coupled to action. These may be described as the **cognitive** or **indirect** (Shallice, 1964; Sharp & Whiting, 1974; Smyth & Marriott, 1982) and the **ecological** or **direct** (Gibson, 1979; Michaels & Carello, 1981) theories of visual perception. Central to cognitive theories of perception is the assumption that information received from the environment is not perceived as meaningful by the performer until a series of inferential processes have been completed internally. These cognitive processes are considered necessary to elaborate the flat, two-dimensional visual image falling on the retina and to determine its potential relevance by making a comparison with existing mental representations. The assumption of cognitive theories that perception is indirect would certainly appear reasonable in light of our discussion of the neuromotor processing aspects of vision. Recall that identification of a visual scene did not occur until the incoming visual information reached the level of the occipital cortex.

Central to traditional theories of visual perception is the idea that information received from the environment is not immediately meaningful.

Ecological theorists argue that visual information can be directly extracted from the environment.

In contrast to this indirect view, proponents of the direct, or ecological theory, of perception argue that visual information can be directly extracted from the environment without the need for any intervening cognitive processes to render it meaningful. Cognitive mediation is considered unnecessary because of the direct relationship between perception and action. The assumptions governing this theory were founded on the early work of J.J. Gibson (1966; 1979), who argued that the optic array alone provides the observer with all the visual information necessary to guide action. Moreover, this visual information can be directly extracted from the environment with no need for any mediating processes.

> The movement context appears to influence strongly whether our perception of sensory events is direct or indirect.

The indirect and direct theories of perception differ both in their theoretical assumptions and in the types of investigative procedures and experimental settings that have been used to test them. The proponents of the indirect view have chosen to conduct experiments in carefully controlled laboratory settings, whereas advocates of the direct perception theory have attempted to study the relationship between perception and action in more natural movement settings.

As appealing as the direct perception theory of visual perception appears because of its inherent parsimony, it is not devoid of shortcomings. These were recently addressed in an excellent review article (Williams, Davids, Burwitz, & Williams, 1992). One of the more important shortcomings is the use of realistic skills, which actually makes it more difficult to determine exactly what type of perceptual mechanisms are being used to guide action. In fact, Williams and colleagues suggest that in natural conditions, subjects have the opportunity to estimate "time-to-contact information by both direct and computational methods" (p. 176).

Whether our perception of sensory events is direct or indirect also appears to be strongly influenced by the movement context itself. For example, van Wieringen (1988) has suggested that direct perception strategies may be best suited to situations wherein a direct fit between perception and action exists. Examples of such movement situations include those in which we are maintaining an upright posture, locomoting through space, or attempting to intercept a moving object in a stable, nonchanging environment. In contrast, actions performed in more variable movement environments that are governed by a set of abstract rules appear to demand additional cognitive processing. These additional cognitive processes are thought necessary in order to compare what is seen with what is known about the rules of the game. Williams argues that during the course of a game of soccer, for example,

Direct perception theories cannot explain actions performed in sports environments that are governed by abstract rules. In these situations, there is no longer a direct fit between the perception and the action.

simply seeing a ball approaching at head height does not provide enough information on which to base subsequent action. In this situation, the player must refer to the rules of the game before knowing what action is appropriate. As those familiar with the rules of soccer know, it is not legal for a player, other than the goalkeeper standing in the penalty area, to intercept the ball with his or her hands. Given that these rules governing action cannot be discerned simply by watching the approaching ball, the player must use additional cognitive processing to guide action.

Direct perception explanations also appear to be inadequate to explain actions that occur in time-constrained movement contexts. In these contexts, a performer attempts to extract advance cues by watching an opponent's movements just before or shortly after movement begins. Indirect perception theorists argue that performers first derive meaning from these advance cues by referring to an existing knowledge base stored in memory and then act accordingly. The very speed with which the visual scene is unfolding would seem to limit the use of the optic array alone to guide action.

Even though the direct perception theory of visual perception cannot adequately describe how perception and action are coupled in certain movement situations, this alternative approach has challenged researchers to study perception and action in more natural movement settings where the perceptual processes are directly coupled to action. Ecological theorists have also helped us to understand other forms of human action (such as jumping, locomotion, and stairclimbing) that have been largely ignored in cognitive theories of perception and action.

> Direct perception theories may be best suited to describing how vision is used in movement contexts where there is a direct fit between perception and action.

Perhaps the best compromise between the two theories is offered by Williams and colleagues (1992) in the concluding section of their review article. They suggest that an ecological theory of visual perception may be best suited to describing how vision is used during the visual control of gait and the performance of interceptive actions such as catching and striking objects. Conversely, in movement situations where meaning is not readily apparent from the visual scene, or where decisions to act must be made on the basis of advance visual cues, it may be necessary to refer to a computational, or indirect, view of perception. Examples of movement contexts in which indirect theories of perception seem better able to account for the relationship between perception and action include rule-bound sporting environments, time-constrained movement contexts, and the appreciation and/or expression of movement aesthetics typical of many dance and mime performances.

VISUAL GUIDANCE OF ACTION

Posture and Locomotion

A balanced and upright posture can be achieved using a variety of sensory inputs. These include cutaneous and proprioceptive inputs from the feet and ankle joints, vestibular input, and of course, vision. Among adults, vision is generally used to supplement the information provided by proprioceptors to maintain an upright posture. Not so for children, however, who tend to rely more on visual inputs when first learning to stand. This preference for visual input at an early age is believed to be due to the infant's inability to integrate the various proprioceptive inputs

> In children, vision plays a greater role in maintaining upright stance than it does in adults.

necessary for successful balance control. The infant's visual system tends to be more advanced developmentally and therefore more reliable. Continued experience with tasks requiring postural control, however, eventually enables the growing child to take full advantage of the multiple sensory inputs available and rely less on visual cues.

An important proprioceptive role for vision in the control of balance has been demonstrated by Lee and colleagues (Lee & Aronson, 1974; Lee & Lishman, 1975) in their innovative series of "moving wall" experiments. The researchers were able to manipulate visually the environment in which they placed their subjects by constructing a three-sided room that was suspended slightly above a stable floor surface. Movement of the wall in a forward or backward direction produced an optic flow field and provided visual information that convinced the subject that he or she was swaying in the opposite direction. Despite the fact that the information coming from the mechanical proprioceptors was in conflict with the visual information, subjects attempted to correct their perceived postural sway with varying levels of gusto. The loss of upright posture was most visible among infants, who had not yet acquired the adult degree of fine tuning in the mechanical proprioceptors. The findings of these studies suggest that vision plays a major role in maintaining upright posture because it provides us with a higher level of proprioceptive sensitivity than do the mechanical proprioceptors.

The role played by vision in controlling locomotion clearly varies as a function of the movement situation. When the surface is smooth, the locomotor pattern appears to be largely controlled by the spinal system (Chapter 3). Similarly, running in daylight conditions poses little problem, given our ability to use the visual system to monitor and anticipate changes in the environment. We are also able to use vision in these lighted conditions to tell us what direction we are traveling in, to avoid colliding with objects in our path, and to identify the type of terrain ahead. In addition to providing us with important exproprioceptive information in these movement situations, vision also serves an important **feedforward** function by preparing the motor system in advance of the actual movement.

> Vision serves an important feedforward function by preparing the motor system in advance of the actual movement.

Our ability to use vision in this way is particularly important when we are moving over irregular terrain. In this movement situation, proper footing is achieved by visually regulating step length, primarily by varying the vertical impulse applied to the ground during the stance phase of the step cycle. This temporal regulation of the step cycle occurs before the foot strikes the ground, ensuring a secure footing once it does so (Warren, Young, & Lee, 1986). A feedforward role for vision has also

The feedforward role played by vision enables this runner to prepare the movement system in advance of her performance, ensuring a secure footing when the foot strikes the ground.

been demonstrated in situations where we are required either to change directions on the basis of visual cues while walking or to step over obstacles placed in our path (Patla, Prentice, Robinson, & Neufeld, 1991).

Visual feedforward is also evident in locomotor activities that require a change in the dynamics of posture at a certain point in space. The performer must not only judge the distance involved but also predict, on the basis of the speed at which she or he is moving, when to begin altering body position. Thus these activities comprise both a spatial and a temporal component. In long jumping, for example, the athlete must strike a take-off board at a predetermined point in space while running at maximum speed. As soon as the board is contacted, the performer must forcefully project his or her body upward, adopting a position that will maximize distance through the air.

Contrary to the opinion of many coaches, however, who argue that successful striking of the board is achieved by developing a standardized approach run, the filming of highly skilled athletes suggests the use of a different strategy—one that employs vision to estimate time to contact, particularly during the final strides before the board. Lee, Lishman, and Thomson (1982) filmed the approach runs of three highly skilled female athletes. The temporal regulation of stride length via vision was particularly evident when the early phase of the approach run was compared to

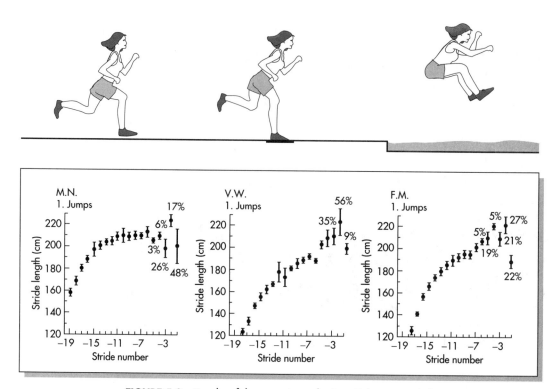

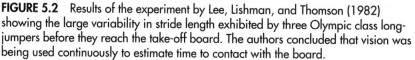

FIGURE 5.2   Results of the experiment by Lee, Lishman, and Thomson (1982) showing the large variability in stride length exhibited by three Olympic class long-jumpers before they reach the take-off board. The authors concluded that vision was being used continuously to estimate time to contact with the board.

the last few strides before contacting the take-off board. As Figure 5.2 demonstrates, stride length began to vary quite dramatically during the final three strides as the performer attempted to compensate for the inconsistencies in stride length that occurred during the early phase of the approach run. These results provided support for the idea that the athletes were using vision to adjust the flight time of the final few strides in order to zero in on the take-off board. The findings of Lee et al. have since been supported by Hay (1988), who studied a larger number of highly skilled male and female long-jumpers, and by Meeuwsen and Magill (1987), who observed similar variability in foot placement among female collegiate gymnasts approaching the vault.

Vision also enables us to prepare the appropriate muscle synergies in advance of a landing to absorb the shock of impact and prevent injury to our joints and muscles. This feedforward role for vision is particularly important for gymnasts attempting to perform difficult dismounts from various apparatus and for parachute jumpers, who are traveling at very high speeds just before contacting the ground.

In a recent laboratory experiment, Sidaway, McNitt-Gray, and Davis (1989) demonstrated how vision can be used to prepare the motor system in advance of a landing during a jumping activity. The authors recorded the level of EMG activity in the rectus femoris muscle of a group of subjects required to jump from a platform set at three different heights (0.72 m, 1.04 m, and 1.59 m) above a force plate. The research question of interest was whether the subjects used a computation process based on such parameters as distance to the floor, velocity, and acceleration, or simply used the readily available visual information to predict time to contact. A comparison of the EMG data with the force plate trace indicating foot contact provided support for the idea that subjects were using vision to determine exactly when the muscles should be activated in preparation for landing from the different heights.

Anticipation Timing

Many motor activities require that we not only regulate the movements of our body as we locomote through space but also make our movements coincide with those of an object or another person. Consider, for example, the timing sequence involved in an outfielder's attempt to catch a fly ball in a game of baseball or softball. As soon as the ball leaves the bat, the outfielder visually locates the ball and begins to move the whole body to the position in space where the ball is predicted to be at a given time. As the fielder continues to move, the catching hand is oriented to coincide with the path of the ball, and the fingers begin to close in anticipation of the ball's contact with the glove.

> In anticipation timing skills, vision is used to make the movements of the body and/or its parts coincide with those of an object or other person.

In order for the catch to be successful, the outfielder must complete this sequence of movements *before* the ball reaches the catching hand. In fact, a cinematographical study of one-handed catching conducted by Alderson and colleagues (Alderson, Sully, & Sully, 1974) has shown that orientation of the catching hand must begin between 150 and 200 milliseconds before the ball contacts the palm, and that closure of the fingers around the ball must begin as early as 50 milliseconds before ball contact, if the catch is to be successful. This study also demonstrated a smaller margin for error with respect to the timing of these movements when the velocity of the ball was greater.

The precision with which the outfielder executes this sequence of movements also demands a precise visual assessment of the ball's flight characteristics. Once the player's eyes locate the ball in space, its flight must be monitored long enough to predict where the ball will be at any given time. Continuous monitoring of the ball's entire flight is not necessary for successful timing of the catch, but good vision of the ball becomes critical in the final 200 to 300 milliseconds. In fact, a number of catching studies (Fischman & Schneider, 1985; Smyth & Marriott, 1982; Whiting, Gill, & Stephenson, 1970) have demonstrated the importance of seeing the ball and/or the catching hand during the final moments of the ball's flight. According to indirect theories of visual perception, the predictive information provided by the visual system early in the ball's flight ensures that the outfielder's movements to intercept the ball begin well before its arrival.

A second coincident timing skill in which vision plays an important role is that of hitting. Although studies have shown that even professional baseball players are unable to keep their eyes on the ball until it hits their bat, sight of the ball early in its trajectory enables the batter to predict the ball's location as it crosses the plate (Bahill & La Ritz, 1984). Hubbard and Seng (1954) have also shown that batters use vision to synchronize the timing of their forward step with the release of the ball from the pitcher's hand and that they regulate the duration of their step as a function of the ball's speed. This use of vision enables skilled batters to keep the duration of their batting swing relatively constant from pitch to pitch.

More recently, a group of researchers at the Free University in Amsterdam (Bootsma & van Wieringen, 1990) investigated the role of vision in timing a forehand stroke in table tennis. Although they too found that highly skilled players demonstrated a high degree of temporal consistency and accuracy at the moment of ball–paddle contact, it was not due to the players' adopting a standardized movement pattern. Instead, their ability to compensate for variability occurring in one movement parameter (time at which the stroke was initiated) by adjusting a second movement parameter (speed with which the bat was swung) as the ball approached the bat, differentiated their performance from that of their novice counterparts. The authors concluded that the players were continuously using the visual information present in the visual display to guide their actions prior to ball–bat contact.

Time-to-Contact Information

Just how are we able to use vision to regulate our actions temporally in each of the movement situations discussed? According to traditional, or indirect, theories of visual perception, our ability to alter the position of our body at a given point in space and to intercept a moving object depends on our ability to process a number of movement variables (e.g.,

Bootsma and van Wieringen (1990) demonstrated that the high degree of movement consistency and accuracy achieved by skilled table tennis players was not due to the players' adopting a standardized movement pattern.

distance, velocity, and acceleration) during the early stages of execution. This early processing of visual information involves taking discrete retinal "snapshots" of the visual array that form the basis for predicting when the body or an object will arrive at a certain location. How accurately the performer is able to predict where an object or the body will be at a given time is largely determined by his or her existing knowledge of the movement situation and by the speed with which an appropriate action plan can be retrieved from memory and then executed.

The advocates of direct perception theories offer an alternative interpretation. They argue that time-to-contact information can be gleaned directly from the changing optic array, eliminating the need for the performer to compute other flight-related variables that would appear to make the predictive process much more complex. For example, Lee and Young (1985) believe that computing time to contact from such variables as distance and velocity introduces multiple sources of error that would not exist if contact point were directly perceived (p. 7). According to these and other authors, a single optic variable provides us with an estimate of time to contact.

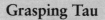

Grasping Tau

Perhaps the strongest empirical evidence supporting the use of the optical variable tau to predict time-to-contact information has been provided by a group of creative researchers at the Free University in The Netherlands (Savelsbergh, Whiting, & Bootsma, 1991). During the course of two experiments, subjects were required to catch different-sized balls suspended from an aluminum pendulum (see the figure) that was released from an electromagnet. The unique feature of these experiments was that the size of the approaching ball could be altered during its flight. How was this possible? A luminous balloon was used to form a "skin" around the enclosed ball that could be inflated prior to its release and then progressively deflated, by as much as 2 centimeters in diameter, during flight. In fact, the deflation of the ball was so subtle that it was not perceptually noticeable to the subjects.

The authors hypothesized that if performers rely on time-to-contact information to time

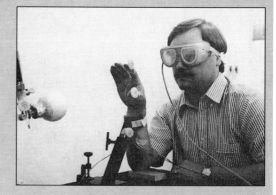

The experimental setup.

their actions, they would be able to adjust their hand movements to accommodate the changing ball size. The variables measured included the time at which the grasping movement was initiated after release of the ball pendulum and the time elapsed beween the initiation of the grasp and the moment of ball–hand contact.

This optic variable, referred to as **tau,** has been mathematically defined by Lee (1976, 1980) as the inverse of the rate of dilation of an image on the retina. Simply put, the faster an approaching object fills the visual field, the faster the object will contact a particular point in space (e.g., a ball contacting a bat or a vehicle contacting another vehicle). Performers can therefore use tau to time their actions simply by determining how quickly the size of an approaching object fills the visual field. This explanation has been invoked to interpret the experimental findings of many of the studies discussed in the previous section. Unfortunately, as easily as many experimental findings can be used to support this alternative explanation, many of the results can be explained just as well in

> **Tau is an optical variable used to predict time to contact.**

As the results show (see the figure below), subjects were clearly adjusting the timing of their grasping movements right up to the moment that the deflating ball contacted the hand. On the basis of this finding, in particular, the authors concluded that the subjects were using the optical expansion rate of the oncoming ball to time their grasping movements, particularly in the final 200 milliseconds before ball contact.

The hand aperture was affected by the nonveridical, or illusory, visual information, particularly during the final moments before the ball contacted the hand. (L = large; B = deflating; S = small.

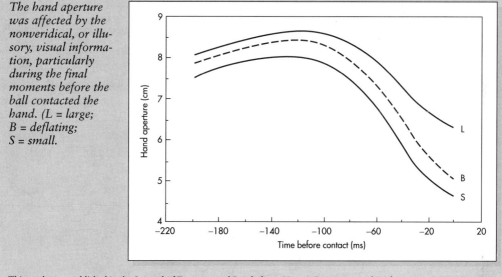

This study was published in the *Journal of Experimental Psychology: Human Perception and Performance,* 17 (2), 315–322.

terms of the performers' using a computational process to predict time to contact. Future research will need to focus on devising experimental situations and methods of testing that clearly demonstrate the use of one strategy rather than the other.

Visual Dominance

Although the foregoing discussion might lead us to conclude that vision always contributes significantly and positively in a wide variety of movement situations, there are times when our reliance on vision leads to errors in performance. In situations of **sensory conflict,** for example, our preference for visual

> In situations of sensory conflict, our preference for vision can result in slowed or incorrect responses.

information can often result in slowed or even incorrect responses. Even when contradictory sensory input is available from receptors in the skin, muscles, joints, and inner ear, we still tend to rely on vision to guide the action. For example, have you ever found yourself quickly reaching for the brake in the car while you waited at a traffic light only to realize it was the neighboring car, not yours, that was moving? In this situation, seeing movement in the periphery has convinced you that you are the one moving, even though other sensory inputs suggest otherwise. The "moving wall" experiments discussed earlier in this section also demonstrate how easily postural stability can be influenced by manipulating vision alone.

The predominance of vision over other sensory systems has also been demonstrated to affect performance negatively in movement situations that require rapid responses. For example, Jordan (1972) studied a group of elite fencers and found that they actually responded much faster to an opponent's advancing blade when deprived of any visual information! In the absence of vision, the athletes were utilizing the faster somatosensory cues provided by cutaneous receptors and proprioceptors. When vision of the blade was restored, however, they once again relied on visual input to guide their actions. And this once again resulted in a slowing of their responses.

DISORDERS OF THE VISUAL SYSTEM

Any damage to the eye or to visual pathways projecting into the midbrain or cortex will cause partial blindness in the visual field. Many individuals with higher cortical damage (particularly damage to the parietal lobe of the brain) may also experience a lack of awareness of the body's structure and of the relationship among body parts. This body scheme impairment can make it impossible for such patients to distinguish among body parts or imitate movements. In order to offset these problems, physical therapists often adopt a **sensorimotor approach.** This type of treatment may involve asking the patient to stimulate the ignored body part, perhaps by rubbing it with a rough cloth as the therapist either names or points to it.

> A sensorimotor approach is often used to offset a patient's inability to distinguish among body parts or imitate movements.

Visual deficits are also a common form of sensory loss among hemiplegic (stroke) patients. These deficits may result in poor visual acuity, partial blindness, or eye movement disorders. Visual–perceptual dysfunction may also be evident when damage occurs to the higher cortical areas responsible for recognizing and attaching meaning to visual input.

Total failure to appreciate incoming visual information caused by damage to the cortex ultimately results in cortical blindness. For those hemiparetic patients who do not suffer from any visual impairment, vision can be used to assist them in the temporal sequencing of muscular activity. How is this possible? Lee, Lough, and Lough (1984) hypothesized that vision provides extrinsic timing information that can serve as a substitute for the information derived from such intrinsic sources as joints and muscle receptors.

In order to test their hypothesis, Lee et al. studied the ability of four left-hemisphere stroke patients to reach for a stationary soccer ball and intercept a soccer ball moving down an inclined track toward them with one or two hands. When they compared the quality of movement in the affected arm when the ball was stationary with the quality of arm movement when the ball was moving, the authors found significant differences in performance. Not only did the patients reach for the moving ball more smoothly, but they were also able to reach for it more quickly. These results would appear to provide support for the authors' original idea that vision can be used to drive the motor system when intrinsic sources of sensory information are disrupted. Findings such as these have important implications for the physical therapist's work with hemiparetic patients during the recovery phase.

> Vision can be used to drive the motor system when intrinsic sources of sensory input are disrupted.

SUMMARY

Vision plays a multifaceted role in the guidance of human actions. It not only provides important feedback information for evaluating and modifying actions but it can also be used to anticipate, and therefore accommodate to, changes occurring in the environment. This feedforward function of vision guides us in a variety of postural and locomotor activities as well as in those that involve interaction with objects or other persons.

The existence of two distinct visual pathways that terminate in different areas of the brain suggests that there are two visual systems serving different functions. The focal system is thought to be responsible for identifying objects in the visual field, and the ambient visual system helps us detect the space around us and other objects in space. These two visual systems appear to operate in parallel in most movement situations.

Two very different theories of visual perception have been advanced to account for the relationship between perception and action. Cognitive, or indirect, theories assume that a number of inferential processes are necessary to render incoming visual information meaningful to the performer, whereas direct, or ecological theories, maintain that seeing is knowing. That is, visual information can be directly extracted from the optic array without the need for any mediating processes. Neither theory has been shown to account for the relationship between perception and action in all movement situations.

The optical variable tau has been shown to guide performance in movement situations that require high levels of spatial and temporal accuracy. According to the ecological theory of visual perception, this variable is directly extracted from the optic array and then used to provide important time-to-contact information. Research findings suggest that it is used to regulate stride length temporally, to prepare muscle response synergies in advance of a landing, and to intercept objects moving at constant or accelerating velocities.

Finally, our overreliance on vision to guide actions can often lead to slowed responses and/or errors in performance. Despite the availability of often contradictory sensory input from the various somatosensory receptors, the performer continues to rely on visual inputs to guide movement. Our susceptibility to making errors is greatest in situations of sensory conflict.

IMPORTANT TERMINOLOGY

After completing this chapter, readers should be familiar with the following terms and concepts.

ambient system	optic nerve
cognitive theory	primary visual cortex
cones	proprioceptionl
direct theory	pupil
ecological theory	retina
exproprioception	rods
exteroception	sensorimotor approach
feedforward	sensory conflict
focal system	striate cortex
indirect theory	superior colliculus
lateral geniculate nucleus (LGN)	tau
	thalamus
lens	topographic organization
optic chiasm	transduction

SUGGESTED FURTHER READING

Abernethy, B., & Burgess-Limerick, R. 1992. Visual information for the timing of skilled movements: A review. In *Approaches to the study of motor control and learning,* ed. J.J. Summers, pp. 343–384. New York, NY: Elsevier Science Publishing Co, Inc.

Williams, A.M., Davids, K., Burwitz, L., & Williams, J.G. 1992. Perception and action in sport. *Journal of Human Movement Studies,* 22, 147–204.

TEST YOUR UNDERSTANDING

1.   Briefly describe the three types of sensory information provided by the visual system in the control of movement. Provide an example to demonstrate your understanding of each type.

2.   Briefly explain why researchers believe there are two separate visual systems that serve different functions. Identify the two systems and describe their respective roles in motor control.

3.   In what way(s) does the ecological theory of visual perception differ from traditional theories?

4.   In what type of movement situations is vision most likely to serve a feedforward function? Explain your answer.

5.   Briefly describe how balance is affected in situations of sensory conflict. Why is balance affected in this way?

6.   Define the term *tau*. What role does tau appear to serve in the visual control of movement?

7.   Briefly describe the type of research evidence that suggests that vision can provide time-to-contact information.

8.   Why does our reliance on vision to guide action often lead to unsatisfactory motor performance?

9.   Explain why physical therapists use a sensorimotor approach to treating patients with damage to the visual areas in the cortex.

About the Quote

This quote is intended to identify an important flaw in the ecological theory of perception first described by Gibson (1979). Fodor and Pylyshyn argue that theories of visual perception that dispense with mental representations fail to explain how we know what we see is meaningful or how it guides our subsequent actions. They use the example of a lost sailor adrift on a foggy evening who sees an identifiable star as the sky clears. The authors reason that if the sailor knows the star is at the celestial north pole, then he will have derived important information about his location. If the sailor has no pre-existing knowledge about astronomy, however, he will remain lost at sea because he has derived no meaningful information from the position of the star. According to Fodor and Pylyshyn, simply seeing the star as a star is not enough unless the star is seen as the pole star. Seeing the star as a meaningful clue to location therefore requires that some type of pre-existing knowledge be stored in memory—a conclusion clearly at odds with ecological theories.

CHAPTER 6
THE NATURE OF MOTOR LEARNING

CHAPTER OBJECTIVES

■ Understand and be able to identify the variables that do and those that do not influence the learning of movement skills.

■ Become familiar with the theories that attempt to explain how movement skills are learned.

■ Become familiar with the various models describing performer-related changes evident during the various stages of the motor learning process.

■ Understand and be able to explain the relationship between the learning and the transfer of movement skills.

■ Become familiar with past and present theories intended to describe the transfer of learning.

■ Understand and be able to describe a number of practice, or training methods that a practitioner can use to promote better transfer of learning.

> *"...the problem of refining one's general knowledge and skills is not necessarily equivalent to the problem of learning inputs so that they can later be retrieved. Instead, growth involves learning from experiences in ways that facilitate subsequent transfer."*
>
> —Bransford et al. (1979)

Do you ever find yourself wondering how expert performers are able to control their body movements so effortlessly? Whether they are leaping across a stage, dribbling a basketball down court, or twisting and turning through a set of uneven parallel bars, these performers appear to direct very little attention to the mechanics of the performance. Their seemingly automatic behavior is in stark contrast to that of novice performers who are learning their first dance routine or the fundamental ball-handling skills necessary to play basketball. The movements of novice performers usually demand a considerable amount of physical and mental effort as they attempt to discover how the skill should be performed to achieve a certain movement goal.

There is no doubt that many thousands of hours of instruction and skill-specific practice separate novice and expert performers as they learn to "solve" the motor problem at hand. In observing the learning process, however, one is often struck by the variety of solutions that are found to achieve a particular movement goal. Despite the fact that a group of learners often observe the same model perform the skill, receive the same type of instruction, and are provided with similar opportunities to practice, very few of these individuals appear to learn and/or perform the skill in the same way. This is not surprising, however, when one considers how differently each performer is structured. Not only do they vary in physical parameters such as height, weight, limb length, muscle strength, and flexibility, but they also differ in cognitive and perceptual abilities.

The combined influence of the many performer-related differences that are evident, coupled with the changing constraints of the environment in which a given skill is first learned, ensures that the learning process remains challenging for both learner and instructor. We will begin exploring the many facets of the learning process by considering a number of theories that have been advanced to explain *how* the learning of motor skills is accomplished. Starting with this theory-based discussion will help us better understand *why* certain instructional strategies are used to foster learning in applied settings and why the learning environment is manipulated differently throughout the learning process. This discussion of the various learning-related theories will be followed by an account of *what* changes we can expect to observe in the learner at various points along the learning continuum. We can then use the knowledge gleaned from these descriptions to determine *when* to apply certain instructional strategies, or perhaps, alter the learning environment to speed up the learning process.

DEFINING MOTOR LEARNING

In the introduction to this chapter, the term *learning* was frequently used to differentiate novice from expert performers. Although everyone is aware that learning is a process by which a novice performer achieves increasingly higher levels of skilled performance, it is perhaps important to define what is specifically meant by the term **motor learning**. Three important and related aspects of the definition appear in a number of contemporary textbooks (Magill, 1993; Schmidt, 1991). First, motor learning is a set of internal processes that leads to a relatively permanent change in an individual's capability for skilled motor performance. Second, the learning process itself is not readily observable, and third, learning occurs as a function of practice and experience, not maturation, motivation, and/or training.

Learning Leads to Relatively Permanent Changes

Many of the neurological mechanisms we described in the first section of this book are altered to varying degrees each time we learn new skills. Indeed, research has demonstrated a number of learning-related **morphological** changes in the central nervous system. These include increased dendritic branching, an increase in the number of synaptic connections between neurons, and structural alterations to pathways entering and leaving certain areas and/or structures within the nervous system (Glickstein & Yeo, 1989). In addition to these structural changes, a number of functional changes can also be observed within the nervous system. These may lead to changes in the nature or prominence of the roles played by certain neurological subsystems as the control strategies used to coordinate movement are altered (Brooks, 1986). Research also suggests that certain reflexive pathways are altered as a function of learning (Fournier & Pierrot-Deseilligny, 1989; Wolpaw & Carp, 1990).

> Motor learning is a set of internal processes that lead to a relatively permanent change in the learner's capacity for skilled performance.

Learning Must Be Inferred

Although many changes occur within the nervous system infrastructure as a direct result of learning, we cannot actually see the learning process taking place. Instead, the fact that learning has occurred must be inferred from our repeated observations of an individual's performance. This is the strategy that the teacher of motor skills and the physical therapist use most often to determine whether a particular instructional or rehabilitation program has been successful. These observable changes in performance can be documented over time and used to determine how far along the learning continuum a learner has progressed. As we will see later in this chapter, several models have been developed that eloquently describe the changes in cognition and movement control throughout learning.

> The learning process is not readily observable and therefore must be inferred from repeated observations of performance.

Learning Is Promoted through Practice and Experience

The third aspect of the definition identifies the two most important factors that promote learning: practice and experience. Developmental, motivational, and training factors also contribute to changes in skill performance, but none of these factors provides evidence of learning. Moreover, motivation and training-related changes are often transient elements of performance. For example, if an individual completes a two-month fitness program designed to improve cardiovascular endurance, muscle strength, and overall flexibility, we expect to see discernible changes in performance. However, if this individual does not continue to maintain or increase his or her level of training, then performance can be expected to decline. This deterioration does not occur when a skill has been learned.

> Learning occurs as a function of practice and experience.

It will become clear in a later chapter, when we discuss how best to organize the practice environment, that it is not only the amount of practice that determines how well a skill is learned but also how that practice is varied by the instructor or therapist. In general, practice influences such things as the type and quality of decisions made by the performer, the dynamics of the emerging coordination pattern, and how well the performer is able to exploit the performance environment.

THEORIES OF MOTOR LEARNING

A fundamental assumption associated with traditional motor learning theories is that learning is characterized by the development of an appropriate memory representation of the acquired skill. These representations are then used to guide performance, the specific movement parameters being prescribed according to the goal of the movement. Two theories that foster this assumption are the **closed-loop theory** of motor learning developed by Adams (1971) and Schmidt's (1975) **schema theory.** Indeed, a considerable amount of research conducted in the area of motor learning during the last two decades has been devoted to testing the predictions set forth in each of these theoretical frameworks.

The assumption that the development of some sort of representation is the end product of learning runs counter, however, to a relatively new approach currently emerging in the literature. This alternative view of motor learning, known as the **ecological theory of perception and action** (Gibson, 1966, 1979; Turvey, 1974, 1977; Fowler & Turvey, 1978), dismisses the need for discrete representations of action and focuses on the changing relationship between the learner and the environment in which the learning takes place. Let's examine the basic tenets of each of these theories as they are related to the acquisition of skills within a motor domain. Their respective contributions to our present level of understanding of motor skill learning will also be discussed.

Adams's Closed Loop Theory

Perhaps the first contemporary theory developed to describe how motor skills are learned was advanced by Adams (1971). In an attempt to overcome what he perceived to be the shortcomings of earlier, open-loop accounts of motor behavior, Adams set about developing a theory of motor learning that relied heavily on the availability of feedback to guide the learning of a motor skill. Contrary to the assumptions of open-loop theories, Adams argued that feedback was necessary to guide each performance attempt during the early stages of learning and that it

> Adams's closed-loop theory relied heavily on the availability of feedback to guide learning.

also served as an important source for the detection and correction of errors in performance. Adams's closed-loop theory was predicated on the complementary operations of two distinct memory states. The first of these, called the **memory trace,** was responsible for selecting and initiating a given plan of action. The **perceptual trace** then served as a comparator mechanism, comparing the movement in progress with a correct memory of the movement. Adams considered the strengthening of these two distinct memory states to be central to the learning of a given motor skill.

Adams's theory stimulated a number of research investigations designed to test his two-state memory system (Adams & Goetz, 1973; Newell, 1974; Schmidt & White, 1972). Although a number of these studies provided support for the theory, its value as a comprehensive theory of learning was considered to be limited. This perceived shortcoming was based on the overuse of slow, linear-positioning movements to test the various predictions associated with the theory. These slower movements were not considered sufficiently representative of the full range of movements possible.

The results of a number of deafferentation studies (Lashley, 1917; Taub & Berman, 1968) also proved difficult to reconcile by using Adams's theory. As you will recall from our earlier discussions of the various motor control theories in Chapter 1, animals and humans deprived of all sensory feedback are still able to accomplish a variety of movements. Given the central role played by feedback in Adams's closed-loop theory, that theory cannot account for this ability to perform movements in its absence.

Schema Theory

In addition to the troublesome empirical findings outlined in the preceding discussion, Schmidt (1975) identified two further theoretical problems associated with Adams's closed-loop theory of motor learning. The first of these problems was related to storage. That is, how is it possible to store a mental representation for every movement ever performed? Surely we would exceed the capacity of human memory at some point. The second problem was related to an individual's ability to perform quite accurately what appear to be novel skills: movements not previously observed or physically attempted. Adams's theory provides no mechanism to explain how skills not previously experienced could be initially performed. These apparent shortcomings of Adams's theory inspired Schmidt to develop an alternative theory of learning. This new theory of motor learning came to be known as schema theory.

Although schema theory retained the need for two independent memory states, the *recall* and *response recognition* schemas proposed by Schmidt were less rigidly conceived and therefore better able to account for a learner's ability to acquire a broad range of movement skills. Like Adams's memory trace, Schmidt's **recall schema** was involved in producing a movement by being responsible for selection of the parameter values that specified that particular movement. Examples of these movements are throwing a ball using an overarm as opposed to underarm pattern or climbing a flight of stairs with different stair riser heights. Once these values were selected and the movement executed, it became the responsibility of the **response recognition schema** to evaluate the correctness of the completed movement in terms of both the amount and the direction of errors. Schmidt further hypothesized that as the learner continued to practice and receive feedback from his or her own sensory mechanisms and other external sources, the strength of both schemas would be enhanced.

> The GMP is thought to contain the spatial and temporal patterns of muscle activity needed to perform a given movement.

In addition to the two schemata, a core feature of Schmidt's theory was the **generalized motor program (GMP)**, an abstract memory structure that could be prepared in advance of a movement. This mechanism provided the means by which a specific movement was executed. It was thought to contain the temporal and spatial patterns of muscle activity needed to accomplish a given movement. Thus, the GMP played a particularly important role in the execution of ballistic movements, where the opportunity to use feedback to guide the movement was limited or nonexistent. Although Adams argued that his memory trace was, in essence, a form of motor program, it operated only long enough to initiate the movement (e.g., a few milliseconds). In contrast, Schmidt's generalized motor program was capable of operating much longer (e.g., one or more seconds) and therefore was not dependent on feedback or on the response recognition schema to complete certain movements.

How were the recall and response recognition schemata thought to be developed? According to schema theory, their development was contingent on the learner's ability to extract four important pieces of information from every performance. These were the initial conditions associated with the movement (e.g., body position, characteristics of the object being thrown or held), the specific movement parameters or response specifications chosen (e.g., force, velocity), the sensory consequences emerging from the actual performance of the movement (e.g., how the movement felt), and the movement's outcome.

Once each individual piece of the movement puzzle was extracted from the performance, the learner would begin to put the pieces together, relating certain individual pieces to others. For example, the relationship between the initial conditions and the particular movement parameters selected was thought to contribute to the development of the recall schema, whereas the response recognition schema's development was assumed to be based more on the relationships among the initial conditions, the movement's outcome, and the sensory consequences generated (Schmidt, 1982, 1988). Once these relationships were abstracted, certain rules or principles of operation could be formulated and used to guide selection of the appropriate motor program for action.

Although interest in schema theory as an all-encompassing account of motor skill acquisition has largely waned, certain theoretical constructs emerging from the theory have endured. These constructs continue to be extensively studied by a number of motor learning researchers. Two of the more often investigated aspects of schema theory are the generalized motor program (Magill & Hall, 1990) and the variability-of-practice hypothesis (Bird & Rikli, 1983; Gabriele, Hall, & Buckholz, 1987). Schmidt argued that learning was not only dependent on how much a skill was practiced but also how the skill being practiced was varied. The variability of practice hypothesis has received a considerable amount of research attention in the past 20 years. At this time, however, the predictions associated with the hypothesis have yet to be unequivocally supported. See Van Rossum (1990) for a comprehensive review of research on the variability of practice.

Ecological Theories of Perception and Action

The beginnings of an ecological approach to perception and action emerged with an influential set of papers written by Turvey and colleagues (Turvey, 1974; Turvey & Carello, 1988; Turvey & Fowler, 1978). In these studies, the authors outlined a new theory of motor learning that not only incorporated the major concepts described in Gibson's ecological theory of direct perception (Gibson, 1979) but also extended Bernstein's work (1967) in the area of movement coordination to the learning of motor skills. You may recall that Gibson and Bernstein provided the impetus for development of the dynamic systems framework of motor control that we described in Chapter 1. These two theories share a common theme: interaction between the performer and the dynamics of the environment in which she or he is moving. The ecological approach has therefore extended the ideas embodied within the dynamic systems approach to a perceptual level of analysis.

In contrast to the more traditional motor learning theories developed by Adams and Schmidt, which describe the products of learning in terms of schemas or memory traces, the ecological theory of perception and action dismisses such memory-based explanations of learning. Central to the ecological approach to perception and action is the idea that the learner seeks to discover the lawful properties or invariant relationships between, among things, the physical features of objects in the environment that make it possible to learn certain motor skills. Having discovered these properties, the learner becomes better able to generate a solution for any given movement problem that is encountered. Just as the dynamic systems approach focused on the interaction between performer and environment in the control of movement, the ecological approach emphasizes the changing relationship between the perceptions of the performer and the action environment in which the learning takes place.

> Ecological theories emphasize the changing relationship between a performer's perceptions and the action environment.

In a recent review article contrasting the various theories of motor learning, Newell (1991) identifies two major weaknesses associated with the more traditional theories of motor learning. The first is their inability to explain how new patterns of coordination are learned. At best, schema-based accounts can only describe how modifications to existing patterns of movement are accomplished. The second weakness identified by Newell is the inability of traditional theories to account for the spontaneous compensations made in response to perturbations, or changes, that occur in the environment while a movement is in progress. Ecological approaches to motor learning appear better able to address this ability without resorting to elaborate cognitive processing or the need for a pre-existing reference of movement correctness (such as a memory trace or motor program).

Traditional motor learning theorists have, of course, countered the claims made by ecological theorists by pointing out certain perceived weaknesses of their own. Schmidt (1988), the originator of schema theory and of the generalized motor program concept, argues that the role of the GMP has been misinterpreted by advocates of the ecological approach and that it is considerably more flexible and nonspecific in its function than ecological theorists imply. A second criticism of the ecological approach is that it places relatively little importance on the role of cognition during learning. In a recent review article addressing the controversy, Colley (1989) describes a number of movement scenarios in which some form of cognitive processing or mental representation is needed to guide the action. Certainly, it is difficult to imagine how we are capable of performing the appropriate actions in a variety of rule-based sports settings without resorting to a mental representation of some kind. For example, how does one know how to interact with an approaching soccer ball unless the conditional rules are already stored in memory? As we noted in Chapter 5, simply seeing the approaching soccer ball is insufficient to define the nature of the interaction.

Even though the basic tenets of the ecological approach have only just begun to be systematically applied to the acquisition of movement skills, a growing base of support for this new theoretical approach is building among the scientific community. At the very least, the emergence of this alternative approach to studying skill acquisition has renewed interest among researchers in better understanding how novel motor skills are learned. As was the case in our earlier discussion of the various theories advanced to explain how movements are controlled, it is unlikely that a single, all-encompassing theory of motor learning will emerge.

STAGES OF MOTOR LEARNING

Despite the fact that considerable controversy exists about which theory of motor learning best describes how motor skills are acquired, existing theories offer practitioners much help in understanding the nature of the learning process. One aspect of applying what we know about motor learning that is of great practical significance is being able to describe the nature of the behavioral changes we can expect to see during various stages of the learning process. Fortunately, a number of useful models have been developed that eloquently describe the behavioral changes that accompany learning. We will consider three such models.

Fitts's Three Stages of Learning

As early as 1964, a prominent researcher by the name of Paul Fitts identified three major stages of motor skill acquisition. The first, which Fitts called the **cognitive stage,** is thought to be characterized by a learner's attempt to understand the nature of a particular motor skill using information from a variety of different sources. This information may be derived from watching a peer or instructor perform the skill, receiving verbal feedback from a coach who observes the learner practice the skill or, from attending to the learner's own sensory feedback generated through physical practice. Numerous errors that are quite gross in nature typically accompany performance during this stage, and learners can often be seen talking to themselves as they attempt to produce an appropriate movement pattern. Through a trial-and-error process, novice performers are beginning to discover both the kinematic (form) and the kinetic (force) properties that define the skill being learned.

> The learner attempts to understand the nature of the movement skill during the cognitive stage.

As they enter the second stage of the learning process learners begin to find it easier not only to detect errors in performance but also to prescribe the appropriate solutions. Although the movement pattern is still not flawlessly reproduced, the learner who has entered the **intermediate** or **associative stage** is beginning to understand how the various components of the skill are interrelated. The learner also begins to modify and/or adapt the movement pattern as the movement situation demands. These abilities may be observed in the young tennis player who is able to direct her forehand stroke to different areas of the court because she better understands how the position of her body and the movement of her feet prior to ball contact can be altered to produce a different outcome. Similarly, a patient entering this phase of relearning during rehabilitation is capable of detecting errors and solving problems, independent of the therapist. Thus the use of facilitation techniques and/or manual guidance is counterproductive after the patient enters this second stage of learning.

> The learner begins to modify and/or adapt the movement pattern as needed during the intermediate stage.

Once the learner has reached the **autonomous stage** of learning, the focus is on automatizing the movement pattern so that attention can be directed to other aspects of the performance. These aspects might include the position of other players on the court or the development of movement strategies that can be used to guide subsequent movements. Learners in this stage are now able to perform the necessary set of movements consistently in a variety of different movement situations. Errors become much less frequent during performance, and learning begins to slow during this stage, as the subtle changes necessary to improve performance become more difficult to master.

> During the autonomous phase, movement execution becomes more automatic, and attention can be directed elsewhere.

It is also argued that the cognitive aspects of the performance are no longer accessible to the learner, who has largely given over control of the movement to other subsystems at lower levels within the central nervous system. The clinician should now be able to introduce distracters during the patient's treatment session. Ongoing conversations should be possible while the patient is performing a well-practiced task. The introduction of multiple tasks should also be possible if the patient has reached this level of learning. As O'Sullivan (1994) warns, however, many patients who have experienced traumatic head injuries affecting motor control will never reach this level of performance. They may perform consistently in very structured or stable environments, but any change that renders the environment more unstable or unpredictable often results in a dramatic deterioration in performance.

Although it remains difficult to know exactly when a learner is entering each of these learning stages, Fitts's description nicely illustrates how motor behavior changes as a function of instruction and/or practice. Thus it provides the teacher of motor skills with valuable observational clues from which to develop appropriate instructional strategies. This description of learning continues to appear in various instructional textbooks and literature read by instructors and therapists alike (Magill, 1993; Christina & Corcos, 1988; O'Sullivan & Schmitz, 1994).

A Neo-Bernsteinian Perspective

A different view of the learning process has recently emerged in the writings of ecological theorists (Vereijken, van Emmerik, Whiting, & Newell, 1992). For want of a better label, we will call it the Neo-Bernsteinian perspective. This perspective can be traced back to the writings of Bernstein (1967) in which he described the learning process in terms of "mastering redundant degrees of freedom" (p. 127). According to Bernstein, the learning of a motor skill can be likened to the solving of a problem, the problem being how best to harness the many degrees of freedom available in the human motor system.

Combining the intuitive logic of Bernstein's early writings and the ideas embodied within an ecological framework, Vereijken (1991) recently proposed a three-stage model of learning that describes how the learner attempts to manipulate the dynamics of a movement in order to "solve" a given movement problem. During the **novice stage**, the learner simplifies the movement problem by "freezing out" a portion of the degrees of freedom. This reduction in the number of degrees of freedom is thought to be accomplished in two ways. The first involves keeping all joint angles in the body rigidly fixed throughout the movement, and the second involves temporarily constraining, or coupling, multiple joints so that they are forced to move almost in unison. Unfortunately, either solution results in a performance

> During the novice stage, the learner simplifies the movement problem by "freezing out" some of the available degrees of freedom.

that is rigidly executed and unresponsive to changes in the action environment. One has only to observe the rigidly constrained swinging action of a novice batter attempting to hit a pitched ball to see how counterproductive these types of "freezing out" strategies are.

As learners move into the **advanced stage** however, they begin to reinstate degrees of freedom and/or release additional degrees of freedom. These released joints are now incorporated into larger functional units of action or, to use dynamic systems terminology, coordinative structures. During this advanced stage of learning, the dynamics of the action are becoming more apparent to learners as they begin to alter the kinematics associated with the movement. The relationship among the joints and their associated muscle synergies is altered, permitting some joints to continue to move in synchrony while others move independently of each other. The result is a more fluent performance that can be readily adapted to changes occurring in the action environment.

> During the advanced stage, the learner begins to reinstate, and/or to release additional degrees of freedom.

Finally, Vereijken hypothesizes that during the **expert stage** of learning, the learner continues to release additional degrees of freedom and reorganize others until all the degrees of freedom needed to accomplish the goal of the task have been manipulated in the most economical fashion. What differentiates this stage of learning from the previous one is the learner's ability not only to manipulate his or her own degrees of freedom but also to exploit additional passive forces (such as inertia and friction) that are external to the learner but inherent in the movement situation. Thus the relationship between the learner's perception of what is required to solve the movement problem and the emerging dynamics of the resulting action is permanently redefined.

> The performer's ability to exploit additional passive forces that are external to him or her is evident during the expert stage.

Gentile's Two-Stage Model

A third description of the learning process that warrants discussion was developed by Gentile (1972). Her description was originally intended to provide, for teachers of motor skills, a more cohesive account of motor skill acquisition than appeared in many of the motor learning textbooks available at that time. Gentile not only considers how the nature of the movement environment in which the task is to be performed influences the nature of the information a learner must acquire, but also provides a number of instructional strategies that a teacher can implement to facilitate a learner's progress through each stage. Our discussion in this chapter will be largely theoretical, but many of the practical strategies she describes in her working model will be incorporated in our discussions of practice and feedback in later chapters.

According to Gentile's model, the learner's goal during the first of two stages of learning is **getting the idea of the movement**—that is, discovering how the movement must be organized to accomplish a particular goal within the constraints of the movement environment. In order to accomplish this goal, however, the learner must identify and selectively attend to those aspects of the skill and environment that are directly relevant to the performance. Gentile referred to these relevant aspects as the **regulatory conditions** associated with the learning environment. In the case of a child attempting to catch a fly ball, for example, the regulatory conditions include the ball and its trajectory as it moves through space. These two characteristics determine how the performer organizes his or her movement pattern to reach the desired position in space at the appropriate time to interact successfully with the ball. How the performer then spatially orients the catching limb to position the glove hand to intercept the ball constitutes a second set of regulatory conditions to which the learner must selectively attend.

The regulatory conditions associated with catching a ball include the trajectory of the ball and how the child spatially orients the glove hand in order to intercept the ball.

Getting the idea of the movement is often made more difficult for the learner by the fact that nonrelevant aspects of the environment often distract the performer from the task at hand. In order to accomplish the goal of the movement, the learner must ignore these nonrelevant or **nonregulatory conditions.** As we know from the developmental literature, however, this task is not an easy one for young children, who tend to be overexclusive in their attentional reference frame (Thomas, 1984).

> During the first stage, the learner must learn to identify and selectively attend to the regulatory conditions related to the movement.

As the learner reaches the second stage of learning, described by Gentile (1972) as the **fixation/diversification stage,** the objective becomes matching the newly acquired movement pattern to the environment in which it is to be performed. If the environment is generally stable, the emphasis falls on making the movement pattern as consistent as possible on each successive attempt. For example, a performer

Crowd noise and movement are examples of the nonregulatory conditions associated with this movement scene.

> During the second stage, the learner attempts to match the newly acquired movement pattern to the performance environment.

attempting to learn a new dive from the tower and a gymnast learning a new floor routine are both operating in a stable environment and are therefore more concerned with developing a movement pattern that can be performed consistently on every attempt.

On the other hand, if the skill being learned is to be performed in a variable and often unpredictable environment, the primary goal for the learner is to learn to diversify the movement pattern so that it permits flexibility of action. This is certainly the goal for a soccer player, who must be able to pass the ball to other team members from stationary and moving positions and at a variety of different angles. Developing a flexible locomotor pattern is also the goal for a patient who is learning to walk again. After completing the initial stage of gait training using parallel bars and/or assistive devices, patients must learn to alter their gait pattern to accommodate changes in terrain, surface, and a number of obstacles or people moving along a crowded corridor or street. Although Gentile's working model was originally developed and applied to the teaching of motor skills in physical education settings, she has recently extended many of the ideas embodied in this early model to the physical therapy domain (Gentile, 1987).

The three descriptions of learning that we have just discussed enhance our knowledge of the learning process in a number of different ways. Whereas Fitts helps us better understand the nature of the cognitive and behavioral processes that characterize a learner's progression through the various stages of learning, Vereijken explores the changing relationship between the learner's perception and the dynamics of the action environment that contribute to the learning process. In so doing, she links the learner to the environment in which the learning is taking place. Gentile adopts a similar approach in her working model of skill acquisition by also considering how the nature of the environment in which the skill is ultimately to be performed influences the goals to be achieved by the learner. This is particularly evident in her description of the second stage of learning. Gentile's application of the model's theoretical constructs to the development of instructional strategies for use in applied settings also distinguishes her model from those developed by Fitts and Vereijken.

In addition to offering insights into the learning process from a theoretical standpoint, these three different descriptions provide the practitioner with a multilevel perspective on the learning process. They illuminate the changing nature of the cognitive processes used by the learner and also address the dynamics of action we can expect to see at various points in the learning process. Vereijken and Gentile, in particular, stress the important role played by the environment in which the skill is to be learned. Only by considering the individual in the context of the learning environment can we truly understand *all* the variables that contribute to learning. Armed with this knowledge, the practitioner can begin to manipulate the learning environment in a way that fosters optimal learning.

THE GENERALIZABILITY OF LEARNING

One final issue that is integral to any discussion of learning is the generalizability, or **transfer,** of that learning. Indeed, Schmidt and Young (1987) argue that "transfer and learning are indistinguishable and that care should be taken when searching for the principles of transfer as if they were distinct from those of learning" (p. 49). The interrelatedness of the two concepts is perhaps most evident when we consider a definition of the term *transfer.* Quite simply, transfer is the degree to which the learning of one skill influences the learning of a subsequent skill. This influence may be in a positive, negative, or neutral direction. For example, learning the overhand throwing pattern should positively influence our subsequent learning of more complex actions, such as the spiking action in volleyball or the overhead serve in tennis.

In contrast, learners often go through a period of frustration when they begin to learn a forehand stroke in badminton just after having learned how to hit a forehand stroke in tennis. This period of negative transfer may be triggered by the subtle alterations in the pattern of coordination, or by the altered force, necessary to hit a forehand in badminton relative to the forehand tennis stroke. The equipment being used and the characteristics of the object being struck have also changed markedly between skill settings. In simulating this very type of situation in a laboratory setting, however, Ross (1974) found only minimal levels of negative transfer. Playing a new position on a softball or football field often creates negative transfer, because the way in which a player responds to the same set of visual information must now change as a function of the new set of responsibilities associated with the second position. As Ross also discovered, however, negative transfer effects are temporary and can be quickly ameliorated with additional practice of the transfer skill.

> Transfer of learning may occur in a positive, negative, or neutral direction.

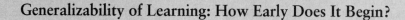

HIGHLIGHT

Generalizability of Learning: How Early Does It Begin?

In the motor development laboratory at Indiana University, infants as young as 12 months of age have demonstrated the ability to generalize their learning in one movement context to vastly different movement contexts (Titzer, Smith & Thelen, 1995). This rather surprising finding emerged when young infants who had participated in an earlier study designed to investigate whether infants could learn the perceptual properties associated with opaque and transparent surfaces were subsequently able to perform a very different movement task not usually observed at such a young age.

In the first of the two studies, 8-month-old infants were provided with an assortment of either transparent or opaque containers with which they played for 10 minutes per day over a 2-month training period. The researchers were primarily interested in knowing whether increasing an infant's exploratory experience with the different types of containers would enhance her or his ability to retrieve objects placed within the different types of containers.

Not only did the 2 months of playing experience with the containers lead to greatly improved performance on an object retrieval task performed by the trained infants, but it also facilitated their performance on a second, very different developmental task: crawling across the well-known "visual cliff." After watching four of the infants who had partici-

Playing with transparent containers helped the infants derive important haptic, visual, and auditory information that could be used to develop a perceptual category for transparency.

pated in the earlier container study cross the transparent cliff surface with little hesitation in a later study, the researchers decided to test whether playing with transparent containers, in particular, contributed to the infants' ability to cross the visual cliff. The now 12-month-old infants who had played with transparent containers between 8 and 10 months of age were brought back into the laboratory, and their performance on the visual cliff task was compared to that of the infants who had played with opaque containers.

The results indicated that 71.4% of the infants in the transparent container group crossed the visual cliff, whereas only 30% of the infants in the opaque container group could perform the task. A second observation of special note was that all the infants in the transparent container group patted the cliff's transparent Plexiglas surface before crossing. None of the infants who crossed the cliff in the opaque container group patted the surface prior to crossing.

The researchers concluded that the activity of playing with transparent containers, in particular, assisted the infants in deriving haptic, visual, and auditory information that could be used to develop a perceptual category for transparency. They further reasoned that touching the visual cliff's surface prior to crossing reinforced the infant's decision that the surface was navigable.

Results such as these clearly illustrate the importance of enriching young infants' environments as a means of developing their knowledge of different perceptual properties that can then be applied to performance in future movement contexts. The study also illustrates just how early we can begin to generalize global perceptual knowledge acquired in one movement context to other, quite different settings.

Understanding the Relationship between Learning and Transfer

Why is it important for the practitioner to understand the relationship between transfer and learning? Schmidt and Young (1987) identify three important reasons. First, the practitioner who is familiar with the principles that govern transfer can develop a better understanding of how certain skills contribute to or interact with other skills being practiced in a particular training situation. Second, the use of simulators to train space shuttle personnel, commercial pilots, and military personnel to operate expensive and often very complex equipment rests on the assumption that the skills and/or knowledge acquired in training will positively transfer to the actual performance situation. The use of dry-land training to introduce complex swimming and/or diving maneuvers also incorporates important transfer principles. Third, the use of various instructional strategies (such as lead-up activities) is based on knowledge about

The use of simulators rests on the assumption that the skills and/or knowledge acquired in training will transfer to the actual performance situation.

transfer. A practitioner who understands this important relationship will be more likely to structure an optimal learning environment.

THEORETICAL VIEWS OF TRANSFER

Identical-Elements Theory

One of the earliest theories of transfer was developed by Thorndike and Woodworth (Thorndike & Woodworth, 1901; Thorndike, 1914). The essence of their **identical-elements theory** was that in order for the transfer of learning between skills and/or movement contexts to occur, the elements underlying the two skills or situations must be identical. Thus a major assumption of this theory was that transfer of learning was not based on any general extraction of knowledge, but rather, was very specific in nature.

Osgood (1949) and Holding (1976) extended and modified the ideas proposed by Thorndike by exploring the relationship between the stimulus prompting an action and the action itself. Holding predicted that in situations where much similarity existed between the stimulus and the response of the first task learned and those of the task currently being practiced, high

> According to identical-elements theory, transfer of learning will occur only if the elements underlying two skills or situations are identical.

levels of positive transfer would occur. Conversely, as the degree of similarity between the stimuli and response associated with the two tasks declined, any transfer would grow less likely. For example, because of the dissimilarity between the two sports, learning to play tennis after being taught to play golf is not likely to foster any positive transfer.

Transfer-Appropriate Processing

A more recently developed view of transfer was first proposed by Bransford and colleagues (Bransford, Franks, Morris, & Stein, 1979; Morris, Bransford, & Franks, 1977), who were largely interested in studying how people learn verbal skills. This view has become known as **transfer-appropriate processing (TAP)**. The major assumption underlying the TAP framework is that the learning of any movement skill is enhanced if the nature of the processing activities engaged in during the practicing of that skill is similar to the type of processing that underlies the performance of the same skill in a different performance context or in a different movement pattern from the one practiced. In contrast to the earlier identical-elements theory, which considered the similarity of task elements to constitute the major factor governing transfer, advocates of this view suggest that it is the similarity of the *cognitive processing* that determines whether transfer occurs.

> According to TAP, transfer of learning will occur if similar processing activities are required for the two movement skills or contexts.

Lee (1988) has recently explored the relevance of TAP to the learning and subsequent transfer of movement-related skills. Although much research remains to be done to validate the basic assumptions of the theory as it is applied to the domain of movement skills, the TAP framework provides an alternative and potentially interesting method of promoting transfer. According to the framework, practicing a variety of structurally *dissimilar* skills that nevertheless require the same types of cognitive processing needed to perform other related movement skills should promote positive transfer.

From a practical viewpoint, then, practitioners who wanted to structure a learning environment based on the TAP concept would try to match the type of processing activities in which the learner engaged during practice to those that would be required in a future transfer situation (such as different movement context or the performance of a new but similar movement pattern). Positive transfer is thought to be optimized by making the *processing activities* similar between the practice and the transfer situation. For example, a coach who structures a practice situation wherein a gymnast is learning a new and more difficult somersault while suspended in a harness above a trampoline expects that, although the practice situation is unlike the context in which the skill will ultimately be performed, the type of cognitive processing in which the gymnast engages during practice will be highly similar to that required when the skill is later performed on a floor exercise mat.

Similarly, if the rehabilitation setting can be structured so that the patient, while performing various rehabilitation exercises, engages in processing activities similar to those required to perform various activities of daily life, then positive transfer should be expected. Support for the idea that such an approach fosters positive transfer was provided in a recent study involving a group of older adults who were experiencing balance problems (Rose & Clark, 1995). These adults participated in a three-month training program and performed a wide variety of dynamic balance activities on specialized balance training equipment. In order to investigate whether the adults could transfer what they had

According to the TAP framework, if a rehabilitation setting is structured so that the patient engages in processing activities similar to those required to perform various activities of daily life, then positive transfer should be expected.

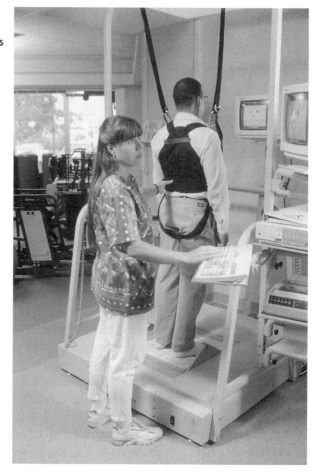

learned during training to gait, the adults were filmed walking over a firm and over a compliant surface before and after training. Large improvements were observed both in the level of intra- and interlimb coordination exhibited by the adults and in the overall control of the locomotor pattern.

APPLICATION OF THEORY

Make Practice Difficult

In light of the importance placed on the transfer of learning, what practice or training methods might a practitioner use to promote better transfer capabilities? Three promising methods are outlined by Christina and Bjork (1991) in a discussion devoted to the issue of long-term retention and transfer of movement skills. The first method involves making the practice situation more difficult by having learners practice several skills during each training session. This practice method, known as **contextual interference**, has been shown to promote significantly better retention and transfer of certain movement skills. Christina and Bjork suggest that introducing high levels of contextual interference to the practice situation promotes the development of cognitive strategies that are less dependent on context or skill and therefore are well suited to guiding the performance of other skills in different movement contexts. We will discuss both the theoretical and the practical aspects of this practice technique in Chapter 10.

> Practice can be made more difficult by having learners practice several skills interchangeably.

Vary the Type of Practice

The second method creates a less complex practice situation by simply providing learners or patients with the opportunity to practice many variations of one movement skill in a variety of different contexts. For example, having learners practice striking objects of different weights and shapes with a number of different implements not only improves their learning of the general skill of striking, but also enhances their ability to transfer the knowledge they have acquired during practice to the performance of other striking skills not previously encountered. Structuring a practice situation that requires CVA patients to reach and grasp objects of different weights and shapes, placed at different heights relative to their starting position, should also foster high levels of

> Having learners practice many variations of one movement skill in a variety of different contexts promotes positive transfer.

positive transfer to other daily living settings (such as selecting items from supermarket shelves or from cupboards in the home). Variable practice has been shown to be a particularly useful instructional method for teaching a variety of different movement skills to children (Pigott & Shapiro, 1984), who may not yet be prepared for the more difficult practice situation created when contextual interference is used (Wrisberg & Mead, 1983).

Reduce the Frequency of Feedback

The final method that Christina and Bjork describe involves reducing the frequency with which external feedback is provided to a learner. As counterintuitive as this may initially appear, particularly for the physical therapist who typically gives a patient a great deal of verbal feedback during a therapy session, there is a growing body of convincing research literature that argues against the presentation of too much feedback. This argument is based largely on the results of no-feedback retention or transfer tests wherein subjects who were provided with a high frequency of feedback performed much more poorly than subjects provided with considerably less feedback during the learning phase (Sherwood, 1988; Winstein & Schmidt, 1990).

Essentially, the authors agree that providing too much feedback creates dependence in the learner on the external feedback. This leads to negative consequences when learners are required to perform the same skill in a situation where no feedback is provided or to transfer what they have learned about one skill to a second skill not previously experienced. Conversely, those learners who receive less frequent feedback rely more on the information available from their own internal sensory sources of feedback (e.g., proprioception and vision), while also engaging in problem-solving behaviors that can be applied in subsequent learning environments. The role of feedback in the learning and transfer of movement skills will be explored in greater detail in Chapter 11.

> Learners who receive feedback less frequently learn to rely more on information available from their own internal sensory sources.

Although continued systematic research is still needed to elucidate the reasons why transfer occurs, it is clear that the major goal for the practitioner is to structure a skill-learning or rehabilitation environment that facilitates the same type of *cognitive processing* that will be necessary to perform the skill in a subsequent learning or daily life situation. In some situations, this may best be achieved by practicing activities that are very similar to those that will be performed in a subsequent performance setting (e.g., specific gait-training activities for certain patient populations). In other situations, providing activities that promote the same type of cognitive processing (e.g., machine-based dynamic balance training) may yield very similar results. Therefore, identifying situations in which one type of training (e.g., specific vs. nonspecific) should be used in preference to another will much enhance our understanding of transfer.

The manipulation of certain practice variables may also provide the practitioner with useful strategies for promoting positive transfer. The use of practice strategies that are designed to introduce high levels of contextual interference or variability into a practice setting requires the learner to engage in more effortful and thoughtful processing activities that will foster high levels of positive transfer in subsequent performance situations. Finally, reducing the amount of external feedback provided during learning appears to simulate the eventual performance situation better. The endorsement of each of these practice methods reflects a growing belief among learning theorists that the goal of learning is not just to learn a set of inputs for later retrieval, as Bransford and colleagues put it in the quotation that opens this chapter. Rather, the goal is to develop the knowledge necessary to generate the most appropriate solution for any given movement problem.

SUMMARY

Motor learning involves internal processes that lead to a relatively permanent change in an individual's capability for skilled performance. Given the covert nature of the learning process, we cannot observe it directly but must infer that it has occurred on the basis of repeated observations of performance.

Unlike motor performance, learning occurs as a function of practice and experience on a given motor skill. It is therefore not influenced by motivational, maturational, or training factors.

Both the structure and the function of the CNS are altered in numerous ways as learning proceeds. The level of communication is enhanced as a result of increased dendritic branching, synaptic connections, and the rerouting of pathways throughout the nervous system.

Several theories have been advanced to explain how the learning of motor skills is accomplished. Whereas closed-loop and schema theories of motor learning emphasize the development of memory-based representations of action, the ecological theory of perception and action emphasizes the changing relationship between the performer and the movement environment. According to the ecological perspective, rather than broadening their repertoire of memory-based representations, learners discover and exploit the lawful properties of the environment that define the type of action most appropriate for solving a given movement problem.

We discussed three models that describe the performer-related changes evident during various stages of the learning process. Fitts's (1964) three-stage model describes the cognitive and behavioral changes that occur at each stage, whereas Vereijken's (1991) three-stage description of learning is focused at the level of the action itself. According to this second model, the learning process is characterized by the "freezing" and subsequent "releasing" of the degrees of freedom available within the motor system. The antecedents of this model are evident in the writings of Bernstein (1967).

A third model of motor skill acquisition, developed by Gentile (1972), considers how the regulatory and nonregulatory conditions associated with a given motor skill influence the movement goals to be accomplished by a learner at each stage of the learning process.

Integral to any discussion of motor learning is the generalizability, or transfer, of that learning. Factors that have been considered to influence the transfer in a positive, negative, or neutral direction include the degree to which the elements of the respective skills are similar and the similarity of the processing activities that are required for the respective skills.

Introducing high levels of contextual interference into the practice setting, introducing variability and reducing the amount of external feedback provided to the learner are three promising instructional methods designed to foster positive transfer across different types of performance settings and between different movement skills.

IMPORTANT TERMINOLOGY

After completing this chapter, readers should be familiar with the following terms and concepts.

advanced stage
autonomous stage
closed-loop theory
cognitive stage
contextual interference

ecological theory of perception
    and action
expert stage
fixation/diversification stage
generalized motor program

getting the idea of the
   movement
identical-elements theory
intermediate or associative
   stage
memory trace
morphological
motor learning
nonregulatory conditions

novice stage
perceptual trace
recall schema
regulatory conditions
response recognition schema
schema theory
transfer
transfer appropriate processing

SUGGESTED FURTHER READING

Gentile, A.M. 1987. Skill acquisition: Action, movement, and neuro-motor processes. In *Movement science foundations for physical therapy,* eds. J. Carr, R. Shephard, J. Gordon, A.M. Gentile, & J. Held, pp. 93–130. Rockville, MD: Aspen.

Schmidt, R.A. 1992. Motor learning principles for physical therapy. In *Contemporary management of motor problems* (Proceedings of the II STEP Conference), pp. 65–76. Alexandria, VA: Foundation for Physical Therapy, Inc.

TEST YOUR UNDERSTANDING

1. Define the term *motor learning*. Identify the various factors that influence learning.

2. Cite the kinds of neurological changes that occur as the individual learns a new motor skill or movement pattern.

3. List the fundamental assumptions of the closed-loop and schema theories of motor learning. How do the fundamental assumptions associated with these two theories differ from those that characterize ecological theories of perception and action?

4. Briefly identify the major empirical and theoretical weaknesses associated with the theory of motor learning developed by Adams (1972).

5. Identify the major theoretical weaknesses associated with traditional theories of motor learning.

6. Compare and contrast the various models that describe the performer-related changes occurring during each stage of learning.

7. According to Gentile (1972), how do the regulatory and nonregulatory conditions associated with the learning of different types of motor skills influence the nature of the movement goals to be accomplished by the learner?

8. Define the term *transfer*. Provide one example of a movement situation in which the direction of the transfer is likely to be positive, one in which it is likely to be negative, and one in which it is likely to be neutral.

9. Briefly describe two theoretical views that have been advanced to explain why transfer occurs between different movement skills and/or performance settings.

10. Identify practice variables that can be manipulated for the purpose of promoting high levels of positive transfer. Provide examples of how each one of these variables could be manipulated in a specific skill situation.

About the Quote

What is it that we actually derive from learning motor skills? Bransford et al. (1979) suggest that we acquire knowledge about the skill, rather than an image or representation of the skill itself. This knowledge can then be applied to the learning of a variety of different skills and thus promote transfer of learning. Unfortunately, as plausible as their assertion might seem, it has been a difficult one to test experimentally. This difficulty may soon be remedied through the transfer-appropriate processing (TAP) view, which provides researchers with a theoretical framework and a testable set of assumptions. This relatively new approach to the study of transfer, first developed by Bransford and colleagues, was described in this chapter.

CHAPTER 7

SCIENTIFIC MEASUREMENT AND MOTOR LEARNING

CHAPTER OBJECTIVES

■ Become familiar with the various measurement techniques used to distinguish temporary changes in performance from the relatively permanent changes that accompany learning.

■ Understand and be able to distinguish between tests designed to measure how well a learner can recall a newly acquired movement skill and tests designed to demonstrate how well a learner can transfer what has been learned to a new performance or skill situation.

■ Become familiar with the various measurement techniques used not only to discover the types of abilities that distinguish experts from novice performers but also to quantify the learning-related changes in perception and cognition.

■ Become familiar with the types of measurement techniques used to quantify the learning-related changes in how the pattern of coordination is controlled.

"For both the experimental effects of learning in the laboratory and the practical effects of learning in the gymnasium or on the playing field, measuring learning and evaluating progress are critical."

—Schmidt (1991)

How do teachers of movement skills and clinicians determine whether the instructional or treatment methods they are using are producing the desired changes in behavior? Certain practitioners tend to rely on the accuracy of their qualitative observations of repeated performances over time, but others try to find measurement tools and/or testing procedures with which to quantify the behavioral changes that are occurring as a result of their instruction. The growing interest among practitioners in identifying valid and reliable measurement techniques is being catalyzed, in part, by the demand for more objective evaluations of what has actually been learned during the course of a physical education curriculum or a therapeutic intervention. Fortunately, just as there are a number of measurement techniques that enable researchers and practitioners to quantify certain aspects of the control of movements, are there also a number of ways in which both the amount and the type of learning can be measured. This chapter focuses on the techniques and methodologies most commonly used in motor learning research.

MEASUREMENT AND MOTOR LEARNING

Performance Curves

The repeated observation of practice performances is still the most commonly used method of evaluating performer or patient progress in applied settings. The changes that occur in one or more appropriate measures of performance (e.g., peak torque output, movement speed, or number of errors) are systematically documented over the course of many practice trials to produce what many practitioners erroneously call a learning curve. These indices of change, more appropriately called **performance curves,** give practitioners some insight into the short-term changes in behavior occurring as a function of practice and/or instruction. However, they are considered to be inadequate indicators of the relatively permanent behavioral changes associated with learning as we defined it in Chapter 6.

Performance curves were once used more extensively in experimental settings than they are today as a means of studying how a particular instructional or practice strategy influenced the amount and/or rate of learning (Bilodeau, Bilodeau, & Schumsky, 1959). Invariably, a particular performance measure was plotted against a number of practice trials, producing a curve that was thought to represent the nature of the learning taking place. Many different types of performance curves are possible, but the typical performance curve is characterized by a steep rise or fall during the early practice trials followed by a more gradual sloping as the trials progress (Figure 7.1). This type of negatively accelerated curve, as it is often called, indicates that the learning of a skill occurs quickly at first but then becomes progressively slower. This typical performance curve has long been thought to represent a fundamental principle of practice known as the **power law of practice** (Snoddy, 1926).

The use of performance curves as an index of learning has received a considerable amount of criticism in recent years. Schmidt (1991) has identified two major disadvantages associated with the use of performance curves in this way. The first problem is the method's inability to establish the relative permanence of the changes observed in repeated observations of performance. How does one know, for example, whether the

> Performance curves are inadequate indicators of the relatively permanent behavioral changes associated with learning.

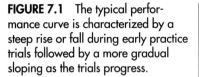

FIGURE 7.1 The typical performance curve is characterized by a steep rise or fall during early practice trials followed by a more gradual sloping as the trials progress.

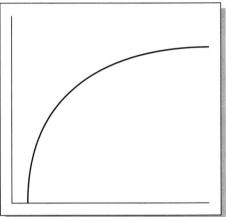

skill has actually been learned unless the performer is also tested after the intervention has been withdrawn and, preferably, after a period of time has elapsed following the last practice trial? Invariably, these performance curves are developed during a single experimental session in which a given number of trials are completed on a criterion task.

A second problem Schmidt pointed out in the use of performance curves to infer learning is the apparent insensitivity of these curves to both the individual differences between performers and the amount of variability evident in the trial-to-trial performances of each performer. This insensitivity to between-subject individual differences is illustrated in Figure 7.2, which shows the performance curves of two individual performers and a third, averaged performance curve. The two performers' performance curves are considerably different, but these differences are no longer discernible when the information obtained from both performers is averaged. The result is a third curve that masks these individual differences, leading us to infer wrongly that learning progressed in a smooth and continuous fashion.

In addition to these two criticisms, Newell (1991) has argued that a similar averaging procedure also eliminates the natural fluctuations between practice trials that individual performers exhibit. Too often, groups of trials are organized into blocks represented by a single mean. Although this averaging method produces a smoother performance curve, it minimizes the amount of information available about the learning process. In fact, Newell contends that if one really wants to know how a learner solves any given motor problem, then "the change in performance with practice needs to be examined on an individual-subject basis over individual practice trials" (p. 223).

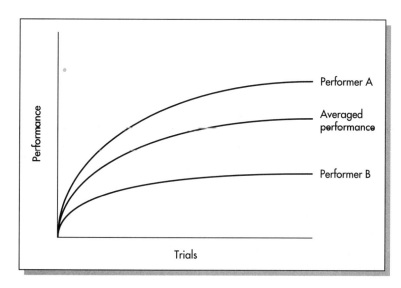

FIGURE 7.2 Performance curves averaged across a group of learners mask the individual differences and trial-to-trial variations, leading to the erroneous conclusion that learning was smooth and continuous.

Retention Tests

An alternative method used to infer that learning has occurred is to administer a **retention test** one or more times during the acquisition of a particular movement pattern and/or skill. A practitioner often uses this type of test to evaluate how well a particular skill or set of strategies has been learned over the course of an instructional unit. This same retention test also provides practitioners with an opportunity to evaluate their own teaching effectiveness.

> In contrast to the acquisition phase, performers receive no feedback during a retention test.

Absolute Retention Scores. In experimental settings, retention tests have traditionally been administered at the completion of a set of acquisition trials in which one or more experimental groups attempt to learn a given motor skill. After some interval of time has elapsed during which the skill is not performed, the groups are again tested on their ability to perform the same skill. Unlike the acquisition phase, however, the groups no longer receive any feedback related to the outcome of the performance or the performance itself. The **absolute retention score** derived from this retention test is thought "to reflect the amount retained of what was originally learned in acquisition" (Christina & Shea, 1993, p. 218). As we will discover in later chapters, this type of retention test measure has been used to evaluate the relative effectiveness of different types of instructional strategies, of different practice schedules, and of different methods of administering feedback during the learning of a variety of motor skills.

Relative Retention Scores.   In two review articles devoted to a discussion of how best to measure what a performer has learned, Christina and Shea (1988; 1993) have advocated the calculation of two additional types of retention scores. The first of these, a **relative retention score,** is obtained by calculating the difference between the performance score achieved on the last trial or block of trials of the acquisition phase with that obtained on the first trial or block of trials during the retention test. In contrast to the absolute retention score, this measure reflects how much task-related information was gained or lost during the retention interval.

Savings Scores.   The second type of retention score Christina and Shea consider important is a **savings score.** This score, thought to measure how quickly an individual is able to relearn a skill following a no-practice retention interval, is obtained by summing the number of trials required for individuals to regain the level of performance demonstrated at the completion of the acquisition phase.

Christina and Shea recommend that researchers consider calculating all three of these types of retention scores because "the various kinds of performance information added by using the different types of retention scores can complement each other to provide a more inclusive understanding of the memory constructs underlying the retention of motor learning" (p. 221). Of course, the authors also acknowledge that the nature of the research question being asked should ultimately determine whether one or all of these different types of retention scores are calculated.

Transfer Tests

As important as it is to know that a recently learned skill can be recalled at a later time in the absence of any feedback, a larger issue—and one of particular interest to the practitioner—is the transferability of learning. Practitioners are concerned not only with a learners' ability to recall a skill at the completion of an instructional unit but also with whether they can transfer what they have learned to a new performance situation or a related skills unit. Let us consider two examples to illustrate the different types of **transfer tests** traditionally used in motor learning research.

In the first type of transfer test, a researcher is interested in knowing whether learning a particular movement skill in one set of practice conditions is transferable to a second set of performance conditions. For example, a therapist may want to know whether a patient who has learned to walk again after several months of gait training in a clinic can demonstrate the ability to perform that same skill in a second set of performance conditions that more closely resemble a real-world setting (such as a crowded corridor). Similarly, a gymnastics coach may be interested in finding out whether having a gymnast practice a particular somersault in a harness suspended above a trampoline will facilitate his or her performance of the same skill on a floor exercise mat. In this first type of transfer situation, the learner will be asked to perform the same skill in a very different set of performance conditions. This type of transfer test is often referred to as a test of **intra-task** transfer, because only the conditions in which the skill is to be performed are altered.

> Transfer tests are used to measure the degree to which the learning of a motor skill generalizes to other performance contexts and/or skills.

In a second type of transfer test, known as an **intertask** transfer test, the learner is required to perform a movement skill quite different from the first skill learned or a variation of a movement skill just learned. This type of transfer may be observed when a learner is introduced to the skill of swinging a golf club after having previously learned to hit a baseball. Although these two skills are quite different in some respects, they have some elements in common (e.g., transfer of weight onto the front foot, the follow-through component, and so on). In the second type of intertask transfer situation, a learner who has just learned to juggle using the cascade pattern of juggling may be confronted with learning a column juggling pattern. In order to successfully perform this new variation of the juggling skill, the learner attempts to apply the knowledge and certain strategies used to learn the cascade pattern to the new set of conditions.

As we will see in later chapters, these two different types of transfer tests are often administered shortly after a retention test or as the only test of learning. How and when they are used during an experiment are generally determined by the nature of the research question being explored.

MEASURING LEARNING-RELATED CHANGES IN PERCEPTION AND COGNITION

In addition to the information provided by the use of retention and/or transfer tests, the practitioner and researcher alike are also interested in discovering the types of abilities that distinguish expert from novice performers and the nature of the perceptual and cognitive changes that can be attributed to learning. Fortunately, several measurement techniques and methods of analyzing experimental data have been developed to assist us in this endeavor. We will begin with a discussion of the most common techniques and methods used to make comparisons between expert and novice performers and also to measure the learning-related changes in perception and cognition.

Expert–Novice Comparisons

Perhaps the most popular experimental approach currently being used to describe the characteristics of motor performance at various points along the learning continuum involves the comparison of expert and novice performance across a broad range of cognitive and motor skills. The **expert–novice approach** has been used primarily to compare the perceptual–cognitive characteristics that appear to differentiate elite from sub-elite and/or novice performers. This approach has been successfully applied to a number of cognitive and motor skills, including chess playing (Chase & Simon, 1973), physics problems (Chi, Feltovich, & Glaser, 1981), dinosaur knowledge (Chi & Koeske, 1983), basketball (French & Thomas, 1987), tennis (McPherson & Thomas, 1989), and baseball (McPherson, 1993).

In general, such studies have identified significant perceptual differences between expert and novice performers. These differences have specifically involved how a given visual display is searched, the speed at which it is searched (Bard & Fleury, 1981), what elements of the display are selectively attended to (Allard & Starkes, 1980), and how quickly

> The expert–novice approach has been used to determine what perceptual–cognitive characteristics differentiate elite from novice performers.

the important information is extracted from the visual display prior to movement (Abernethy & Russell, 1984; 1987). Expert performers search a visual display more quickly than novice performers but they are also able to locate quickly and extract only those elements of the display that are relevant to the forthcoming response (see Highlight on whether experts see things differently in a field of play). In addition to these perceptual inequalities, cognitive differences are also readily apparent. For example, expert performers are better able to interpret and organize skill-related information in memory so as to facilitate superior recall of that knowledge (Allard, Graham & Paarsalu, 1980; Borgeaud & Abernethy, 1987).

The research tools used to identify the perceptual and cognitive differences that differentiate expert from novice performers typically include visual occlusion techniques, eye movement recordings, and memory recall tests. A discussion of each technique and how it has been used in various experimental settings follows.

Visual Occlusion Techniques

Visual occlusion has been used in a series of studies designed to investigate whether expert and novice performers attend to and extract the same types of visual cues from a visual display (Abernethy & Russell, 1987; Starkes & Deakin, 1984). Vision of the movements of a videotaped or filmed performer is blocked at certain points during the action sequence, and the observer is asked to make certain predictions about the outcome of the movement. This same technique has been used to occlude certain body parts of a performer during execution of a movement. By doing this, researchers can begin to identify what aspects of the performer's movement appear to provide the most meaningful information for the forthcoming response.

Abernethy and Russell (1987, Experiment 1) used the visual occlusion technique to demonstrate that expert badminton players were significantly better than novice performers at predicting the landing location of an approaching badminton shot when the film was stopped at the exact moment of racquet-shuttlecock contact or as early as 83 milliseconds before contact. The researchers demonstrated that the expert performers were extracting meaningful information from the display much more quickly than the novice performer. In a second experiment conducted by the same authors, certain body parts of the filmed performer were occluded during the performance. During one sequence, the racquet and arm of the performer was eliminated; the lower body, face and head, or racquet only was occluded during other sequences. The results indicated that novice performers attended primarily to the movements of the racquet in order to anticipate where the shuttlecock would travel. In contrast, the expert performers made their predictions by watching the movements of the arm and the racquet held by the performer. Monitoring the location of the arm controlling the racquet was clearly providing the expert performer with information about the direction of the shot much earlier than watching the racquet alone.

> Visual occlusion techniques are used to investigate whether expert and novice performers attend to and extract the same types of visual cues from a display.

Although such visual occlusion techniques have advanced our knowledge concerning the aspects of visual information that appear to be important to skilled performance, the limitations of the methodology have prohibited its use as a perceptual training and assessment tool in actual play situations. As a result of recent advancements in technology, however, visual occlusion techniques may become an extremely useful perceptual training tool in the years to come. Starkes and colleagues (Starkes, Edwards, Dissanayake & Dunn, 1995) recently completed the first field test using a new technology known as liquid crystal visual occlusion spectacles (Milgram, 1987). The lenses of these spectacles can be manipulated to provide full or occluded vision by means of an electrical pulse manually delivered to the glasses.

Using the visual occlusion spectacles, Starkes and colleagues were able to manipulate the visual fields of a group of volleyball players during various stages of a live serve. Following the serve, each player was required to place a marker on the court where she thought the ball had landed and then rate how confident she felt about her decision. The results of this study were similar to those of previous studies using more traditional visual occlusion approaches, which suggests that the new technology may eventually assist researchers in conducting studies in more realistic sports situations than has ever been possible.

Eye Movement Recordings

An alternative method of determining exactly what aspects of a visual display performers are attending to while they are watching a movement or play situation unfold involves the use of more sophisticated devices to record eye movement. This computer-based technique is designed to track the movements of the observer's eyes while also providing information about gaze fixation time (i.e., the length of time the eyes are fixed on a given area of the display). Bard and Fleury (1981) have successfully used this technique to demonstrate that expert ice hockey goal tenders fixate for a longer period of time on the stick of the shooter, whereas novice goal tenders fixate more on the puck. As was the case in the badminton study conducted by Abernethy and Russell (1987, Experiment 2), watching the arm and implement being controlled, instead of the object being contacted, gives expert performers more time to anticipate what type of shot will be performed and therefore enables them to initiate a response more quickly. Eye movement recordings have also been used to identify differences among expert and novice performers in tennis (Goulet, Bard, & Fleury, 1989), soccer (Helsen & Pauwels, 1990), and gymnastics (Vickers, 1988).

> Eye movement recordings track the movements of the fovea and also provide information about gaze fixation time.

Certain problems with the use of eye movement recordings to compare the perceptual abilities of expert and novice performers have been identified. First, the device itself has not yet been refined to the point where it can be worn in the actual movement setting. In order for the recordings to yield accurate eye movement data, the observer must be stationary and must generally be seated in a chair. The ecological validity associated with the use of this technique remains questionable as a result. Second, Adams (1966) correctly points out that the recording of eye movements identifies only what the observer is looking at, not what she or he is actually seeing. Thus eye movement recordings do not necessarily indicate what cues are being extracted for the purposes of making a response. One final criticism involves the device's inability to monitor peripheral vision as well as focal vision. We already know, from our discussions on the role of vision in motor control, that peripheral vision can provide the performer with important information on which to formulate a response.

Memory Recall Tests

The method most often used to investigate the cognitive processes that appear to form the basis of expertise has been the **pattern recognition** or **memory recall test**. This test has been used to demonstrate that expert performers not only take in very large quantities of information from a visual display in a very short period of time but also organize it in a form that facilitates superior recall of that information. This organization of the information is thought to involve the **"chunking"** of individual pieces into larger units in memory. We will discuss this memory process in more detail in the next chapter.

> Pattern recognition or memory recall tests have shown that experts are able to extract large amounts of information quickly from a visual display and that they organize it in a form that promotes superior recall.

DeGroot (1966) and Chase and Simon (1973) were among the first researchers to use this type of test successfully to study cognitively based skills such as playing chess, writing computer programs, and solving mathematical problems. In using the test to compare expert and novice chess players, Chase and Simon (1973) found that expert players were able to recall the exact location of a significantly higher number of chess pieces immediately following a 5-second look at a game board. Less skilled players were able to recall the locations of significantly fewer chess pieces. What is most interesting about their findings, however, is that experts demonstrated superior recall only when the locations of the chess pieces conformed to an actual game setup. On those trials where the pieces were randomly located, there were no differences found in recall ability among the various skill levels. This suggests that the expert performer's ability to chunk information is dependent on his or her familiarity and experience within the specific skill environment rather than on a pre-existing ability to store more information in memory.

Pattern recognition and memory recall tests have since been used to study open sport skills that are primarily performed in variable environments. Unlike closed skills, open skills test a performer's ability to extract large amounts of information from a continuously changing

Do Experts See Things Differently in a Field of Play?

Williams and colleagues (Williams, Davids, Burwitz, & Williams, 1994) have recently demonstrated that in contrast to an inexperienced group of soccer players who tend to watch the ball and the player who is passing it, expert players focus on the more peripheral aspects of a game scene, such as the positions and movements of players "off the ball." These systematic differences in visual search strategies are evident in the accompanying graph, which shows how long experienced and inexperienced players fixated on certain areas of the playing scene.

To demonstrate these contrasting visual search strategy patterns, Williams et al. used an eye movement recording system capable of monitoring the eye movements of a group of inexperienced and experienced soccer players as they watched a series of soccer action sequences on a large projection screen. In order to determine how the different visual search strategies might influence the decisions made by players, the researchers also measured how quickly and accurately each player decided where on the field the ball would be passed. They did this by asking the player to announce aloud the grid number corresponding to the selected pass destination on the field. Not surprisingly, the experienced players demonstrated significantly faster response times than their inexperienced counterparts. The experienced players were clearly anticipating the ball's destination even

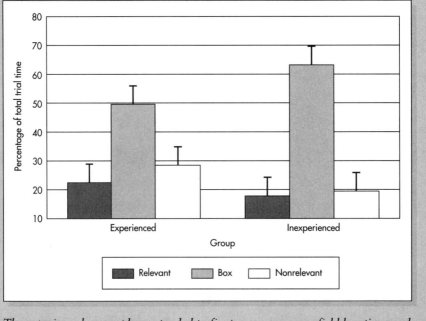

The experienced soccer players tended to fixate on many more field locations and to alternate their fixations more frequently than inexperienced players.

before the ball was kicked, an outcome that underscores their ability to make better use of advance information.

Perhaps one of the most interesting findings of this study was that the experienced players tended to fixate on many more field locations and to alternate their fixation locations more frequently during each trial. The faster scan rates observed by Williams et al. were in contrast, however, to those recorded in previous studies (Helsen & Pauwels, 1992). The authors attributed these differences to the fact that they had created a more complex open-play situation by representing more players in each of the filmed sequences.

According to the authors, research findings such as these emphasize the need for coaches to help inexperienced players develop more appropriate visual search strategies that not only encompass the passing player and the ball being passed but also acknowledge the importance of the positions and movements of players in the immediate vicinity of the unfolding play. The authors conclude their discussion by suggesting a number of soccer-related training activities that coaches might use to help players develop more effective visual search strategies. These include using activities such as "one touch" and "silent" play lead-up games.

visual display. (See the Highlight on the classification of motor skills.) In one such study, Allard, Graham, and Paarsalu (1980) presented several slides of basketball play situations to varsity and intramural level basketball players. Half of the slides depicted players in structured game positions; the remaining half showed random game positions such as scrambling for a loose ball. Following a 4-second viewing of the slide, players were asked to recall the position of as many players as possible by placing a magnet on a game board provided. As was the case in Chase and Simon's study, the varsity players exhibited superior recall when compared to intramural players, but only for those slides that depicted structured play situations. These findings have since been replicated using other sports, such as field hockey (Starkes & Deakin, 1984) and volleyball (Borgeaud & Abernethy, 1987).

Limitations of the test.   As effective as the use of this recall test appears to be in differentiating between expert and novice performers in their perceptual abilities, it is not without its limitations. These limitations were highlighted in a recent article by Abernethy and colleagues (Abernethy, Burgess-Limerick, & Parks, 1994), who share the concerns expressed by advocates of direct theories of perception (see Chapter 5).

The Classification of Motor Skills

It has been a common practice in research on motor skill learning to categorize motor skills according to different criteria. One classification system that has been referred to extensively in the motor learning literature categorizes skills into two general classes according to the type of environment in which they are performed. The two classes of skills are closed and open. Let us briefly contrast the defining characteristics of these different types of motor skills.

Open skills have customarily been described as those skills that are performed in variable environments and therefore must be repeatedly adapted to the changing demands of the environment. Given that a changing environment rarely permits the use of the same movement response on two successive attempts, it is important that the performer be able to execute many subtle variations of the skill. Examples of open skills can be found in soccer, basketball, football, and ice and field hockey.

Closed skills are performed in stable, unchanging environments. The goal for the learner in these types of movement situations is the development of a consistent movement pattern that can be performed in exactly the same way from trial to trial. Examples of these types of skills include springboard and platform diving, figure skating and, gymnastics.

Unfortunately, this method of classifying skills has created as much confusion as clarity for the reader of motor skills research. This is

They also suggest that the use of static "snapshots" of action may not adequately capture the dynamic nature of perception in a real sports environment. It is clear that this method of exploring perceptual differences between expert and novice performers is based on an indirect/computational view of perception. Recall that researchers aligned with this more traditional view of perception assume that the visual image received at the level of the retina is both static and impoverished and therefore in need of considerable elaboration before the observer can perceive it as meaningful. A second concern raised by Abernethy et al. involves the erroneous conclusion that the superior perceptual abilities demonstrated by experts are the sole cause of differences in the quality of performance observed. They argue that improved perceptual abilities may simply be by-products of other factors, such as

Platform diving has traditionally been classified as a closed skill, whereas the skills performed in ice hockey have been classified as open skills.

because many skills are really neither open skills nor closed skills. Consider, for example, golf and pole vault. Although both skills are performed in relatively stable environments, subtle changes are occurring from trial to trial. Wind direction and velocity may change between golf strokes, and the height of the bar to be jumped in the sport of pole vault is raised repeatedly throughout a competition. Couple this problem with the fact that many open skills have components that can be classified as closed skills (e.g., free throw shooting in basketball), and the dichotomous classification of skills becomes still more imperfect.

Contemporary writers such as Magill, 1993 have suggested that much of the confusion can be avoided if we consider these two very different types of skills to represent the two opposite extremes of the motor skill continuum. Thus there is room between the "poles" to place a number of motor skills that are more like one than the other type of skill.

task experience and familiarity, that might contribute more to the differences observed in performance.

Development of a Knowledge Base

Although comparisons between expert and novice performances have provided us with knowledge about the attention and cognitive abilities that appear to differentiate novice from expert performers, this methodology has contributed little insight into *how* a novice performer actually learns to become an expert. This major shortcoming of the expert–novice paradigm was first identified by Thomas, French and Humphries (1985), who called for a more systematic approach to the study of motor skill acquisition—one that better elucidates the processes underlying the acquisition of what the authors referred to as a domain-specific knowledge base. Thomas and colleagues (Thomas & French, 1987; McPherson & Thomas, 1989; McPherson, 1993) have since developed a comprehensive **knowledge-based paradigm** and successfully applied it to a variety of sport-related settings.

The paradigm developed by Thomas et al. involves the administration of appropriate knowledge tests and skill-specific tests to children at different levels of learning: extensive verbal interviews designed to test the children's knowledge of a game's rules (declarative knowledge) and their understanding of when to apply certain game-specific strategies (procedural knowledge). Each of these tests is supplemented with the videotape coding of game performances. These videotape recordings are then used to evaluate the learning-related changes in the level of skill exhibited, in the quality of decision making during match play, and in the performer's ability to execute the decisions successfully.

> The difference in knowledge base lies in the expert's ability to incorporate the DO portion into the IF-THEN-DO productions.

As a consequence of their efforts to explore all these relationships simultaneously, Thomas and colleagues have been able to show that expert performers possess a larger, more complex, and better organized knowledge base than novice performers in certain sports settings. The authors further speculate that this major difference in knowledge base lies in the expert performer's tendency to develop IF-THEN-DO productions with incorporation of the DO portion being the defining element of expertise (see McPherson & Thomas, 1989, for a more detailed review).

MEASURING LEARNING-RELATED CHANGES IN THE DYNAMICS OF ACTION

In addition to the many perceptual–cognitive changes that occur in connection with learning, it is clear that many subtle and not-so-subtle changes are also taking place in the pattern of coordination at various points along the learning continuum. Although the practitioner with acute observational skills is able to observe directly many of the not-so-subtle changes in the dynamics of the action that evolve with practice, more sophisticated technology and methods of analysis are necessary if the more subtle changes in behavior are to be identified.

We will discuss two types of measurement in this section: physiological and mechanical measures of efficiency. Both of these measurement techniques have been successfully used to quantify the more subtle learning-related changes that occur in the dynamics of the action.

Measures of Metabolic and Mechanical Efficiency

If, indeed, one of the defining characteristics of skilled performance is movement efficiency, then research directed at studying how this component changes as a function of practice would seem worthwhile. Sparrow and colleagues (Sparrow, 1983; Sparrow & Irizarry-Lopez, 1987) have shown particular interest in this aspect of performance and have employed physiological and mechanical indices of efficiency to explore the relationships among practice, mechanical work rate, and metabolic energy expenditure.

In one such study, Sparrow and Irizarry-Lopez (1987) examined the changes in the amounts of metabolic energy expended and mechanical work accomplished by the legs and arms of adults who repeatedly practiced a crawling movement on a motor-driven treadmill over the course of ten days. The authors hypothesized that changes in these two aspects of performance would be closely related to any modifications being made to the movement pattern during practice. This initial hypothesis was generally supported when the various physiological and mechanical parameters measured were correlated. The authors found that as subjects "optimized" their pattern of interlimb coordination, the amount of energy expended decreased. And although the improvement was not statistically significant, the level of mechanical efficiency demonstrated by the subjects had also improved as much as 13.7% by the last day of practice.

> The level of metabolic and mechanical efficiency has been shown to increase as a movement skill is learned.

Considerably more research is necessary to examine fully the relationship between movement kinematics and mechanical efficiency, but the results of this study suggest that this will be a fruitful area of research. Research in this area may also yield important practical information for rehabilitation therapists concerned with helping patients learn functional movement patterns. The development of a movement pattern that minimizes the amount of energy expended and the mechanical work involved is an important goal for the patient.

IDENTIFYING THE LEARNING-RELATED CHANGES IN PERFORMANCE

It is clear that the use of the many experimental methods and techniques described in this chapter has contributed much to our understanding of the perceptual, cognitive, and mechanical processes that form the basis of skilled performance. More research is needed to delineate exactly how a performer progresses along the skill-learning continuum, but we can identify a number of performer characteristics that are directly influenced by learning.

- The focus of attention. As learning progresses, performers allocate attention to different types of salient cues and become able to extract meaning from a visual display with greater speed and precision.

- Knowledge base. Both the breadth and the structure of the knowledge base can be expected to change as a function of learning. Expertise appears to be accompanied by knowledge not only of what to do but also of when to do it.

- Dynamics of the action. The learner begins to manipulate more appropriately the degrees of freedom available within the motor system to accomplish the goal of the movement. Changes in the temporal and spatial patterning of musculature are also evident as the learner searches for the optimal solution to the motor problem at hand.

- Metabolic and mechanical efficiency. There is some evidence to suggest that modifications in the kinematics of movement associated with learning are strongly related to reductions in the amount of physiological and mechanical energy expended.

SUMMARY

This chapter described a variety of methods and measurement techniques designed to help those of us interested in learning to document the many changes that occur within the performer in the course of learning a new motor skill or movement pattern.

Various types of retention and/or transfer tests have been successfully used to evaluate the effectiveness of different instructional and/or practice strategies in facilitating the learning of a variety of motor skills and to determine whether what has been learned can be applied to different performance settings (intra-task transfer) or different variations of a skill (intertask transfer).

Differences in perceptual abilities between novice and expert performers have been demonstrated by using two related research methods: visual occlusion techniques and eye-movement recordings. As a consequence of attending to different salient cues in a visual display, expert performers are able to extract more meaningful information more quickly than novice performers. These perceptual differences ensure that the expert performer is able to respond more quickly and appropriately in game situations.

The use of memory recall tests has revealed differences in cognitive abilities between expert and novice performers. In general, expert performers have learned to organize, or "chunk," large amounts of information into larger memory units that can then be retrieved with greater speed and ease of recall.

The relationships among development of a knowledge base, skill performance, and decision-making abilities is currently being systematically explored in a number of different sports contexts. The present research findings suggest that as the learning of a sport proceeds, the learner develops more and more IF-THEN productions, which are then linked to a number of DO productions. The successful linking between these two sets of productions may herald the arrival of expertise in a given sport.

The changing dynamics of action that accompany learning are being quantified using a variety of measurement and analytical techniques, which include measures of physiological and mechanical efficiency. Research conducted using these techniques has provided evidence that as individuals 'optimize' their pattern of interlimb coordination, the amount of energy expended decreases. The mechanical efficiency associated with the optimized movement pattern also shows improvement.

IMPORTANT TERMINOLOGY

After completing this chapter, readers should be familiar with the following terms and concepts.

absolute retention score
chunking
expert–novice approach
intertask transfer test
intra-task transfer test
knowledge-based paradigm
memory recall test
pattern recognition test

performance curves
power law of practice
relative retention score
retention test
savings score
transfer tests
visual occlusion

SUGGESTED FURTHER READING

Snyder, C.W. Jr., & Abernethy, B. In press. *Understanding human action through experimentation*. Champaign, IL: Human Kinetics.
McPherson, S.L. 1994. The development of sport expertise. Mapping the tactical domain. *Quest*, 46, 223–240.

TEST YOUR UNDERSTANDING

1. Describe the major weaknesses associated with the use of performance curves as an index of learning.

2. How are retention tests used to measure learning-related changes in performance? In what fundamental way do they differ from transfer tests?

3. In what way does the information provided by an intra-task transfer test differ from the information provided by an intertask transfer test? Provide two practical examples to illustrate your answer.

4. Describe two experimental methods used to identify the perceptual characteristics that differentiate novice from expert performers. Explain the nature of the perceptual differences revealed by these two methods.

5. How have memory recall tests been used to identify differences between experts and novices in cognitive abilities? Describe the major research findings that have emerged from the use of such tests.

6. Briefly describe a research paradigm that has been used to study how the novice performer learns to become an expert. How does the expert's knowledge base appear to differ from that of a novice performer?

7. Describe two methods that have been used to investigate how the dynamics of action change as a function of learning. Outline the major findings that each method has yielded.

About the Quote

Schmidt reiterates the importance of finding meaningful ways to measure learning. Of course it is important for the experimenter to measure accurately the changes in the performance of a group of subjects who receive a particular intervention. And Schmidt argues that it is equally important for the practitioner to use measurement to evaluate the progress of a group of learners in the gymnasium or on the playing field. This chapter presented a number of different measurement tools, many of which can be used effectively in both experimental and practical settings. Time is of the essence in many practical settings, but so too, is the need to be accountable for one's teaching practices.

CHAPTER 8
MEMORY AND LEARNING

CHAPTER OBJECTIVES

- Become familiar with contemporary models of memory that have guided research in the area of human memory during the past two decades.

- Understand and be able to identify the areas within the central nervous system that appear to play important roles in memory-related functions.

- Understand the different types of memory and how they contribute to the learning of movement skills.

- Understand and be able to describe the factors that influence the long-term retention and recall of movement skills.

- Become familiar with the techniques and strategies a practitioner and/or clinician can employ to enhance the learning and subsequent recall of movement skills.

> *"Since memory is largely reconstructive, we should, wherever applicable, teach concepts, principles and rules to complement or supplement teaching rote knowledge or facts."*
>
> —Farr (1987)

How is it that we are able to remember hundreds of seemingly unrelated events, countless procedures for assembling equipment or operating a computer, and the abstract rules associated with playing a particular game or solving a complex mathematical equation? The answers to these questions appear to lie in a construct known as **memory.** Gordon (1989) states that "the term 'memory' is most often defined as an internal record or representation of some prior event or experience" (p. 9). Thus it is intimately related to learning, which we discussed at length in Chapter 6.

Is memory a structure that can be traced to a particular area of the nervous system? Or is memory best conceptualized as a cognitive process that enables us to act upon a continual flow of externally and internally generated information in a meaningful way? This is just one of the many questions addressed in this chapter. No doubt many more questions will emerge as the discussion unfolds, and some will remain unanswered at its conclusion. Let us begin our discussion by describing two contemporary yet contrasting views of the construct called memory.

CONTEMPORARY MODELS OF MEMORY

Numerous attempts by researchers to describe the intricacies of human memory have yielded a variety of theories and models over the years. One has only to read the literature to encounter descriptions of memory that range from reverberating circuits in the brain (Hebb, 1949), to computer analogies wherein memory is likened to a central processing unit consisting of a set of structures through which all information must pass. Two contemporary models of memory that have contributed to a renewed research interest in human memory over the past three decades are discussed in this section. The first of these two models represents a more structural view of memory. The second proposes an alternative view that emphasizes a more functional approach to the study of memory.

Atkinson and Shiffrin's Multistore Model

One of the most highly developed multistore models of memory was proposed and empirically tested by Atkinson and Shiffrin (1968, 1971). Drawing heavily on the computer analogy, they conceived of human memory as a set of clearly defined structures (i.e., hardware) in which various types of processing occurred (i.e., software). Atkinson and Shiffrin distinguished among these hypothesized memory stores on the basis of their different retention characteristics and the types of processing activities that took place in each. The processing activities included such things as memory coding, rehearsal, organization, and retrieval of information from memory. Each process was also considered to be under the control of a processor that used each of these mnemonic strategies to move information through the system in a highly regulated fashion.

According to the multistore model, environmental information enters the first of three memory structures, called a **sensory register,** where it is stored for no longer than a second. This relatively large-capacity store is responsible for registering the physical features of an environmental display provided by any and all of our sensory systems (e.g., visual, auditory, haptic). These features registered might include the shape of an object, the feel of a surface, and sound coming

> According to the multistore model, human memory consists of clearly defined structures in which various types of processing occur.

from a nearby location. In order to preserve a proportion of the stimuli entering this sensory register, however, an individual must direct his or her attention to certain aspects of the registered stimuli that are selected for further processing in memory. The remaining stimuli, to which we choose not to attend, simply disappear as quickly as they appeared.

Once the selected information is passed to the next structure represented in this multistore model, we become consciously aware of its presence. In this second memory structure, which the authors refer to as the **short-term store (STS)**, much of the active processing necessary to transfer the selected information into the third and more permanent storage area takes place. Unlike the sensory register, the STS is much more limited in its capacity but capable of more sophisticated processing. One control process in particular serves an extremely important function in this compartment of memory. This process, called rehearsal, is important for the maintenance and/or elaboration of information reaching the STS and for its subsequent transfer to the third memory structure.

This final storage area, known as the **long-term store (LTS)**, is viewed as a relatively permanent store with an essentially unlimited capacity for storing information. It is here that the individual is thought to store knowledge of the world in various forms. These various forms include important facts (declarative knowledge), operations (procedural knowledge), and/or concepts (semantic knowledge). Although it is represented only once in the model constructed by Atkinson and Shiffrin, the LTS is actively involved in the flow of information before it actually reaches this final storage area. For example, information entering the sensory register cannot be labeled or categorized until it is compared with information already stored in the LTS. Similarly, the strategies that govern the movement of information through the system must first be represented in the LTS in the form of rules or principles.

> Much of the active processing necessary to transfer information to the LTS occurs in the STS.

The multistore model developed by Atkinson and Shiffrin has guided research in the area of human memory during the past two decades. It has been used to describe how adult memory operates and has also proved to be an effective framework for interpreting age-related changes in various aspects of memory capability (Chi, 1976, 1977; 1975; Ornstein, Naus, & Liberty, 1975).

Levels-of-Processing Framework

Despite the evidence compiled in support of Atkinson and Shiffrin's multistore model of memory, a growing number of researchers began to question the usefulness of this approach. Two particularly avid critics of structural accounts of memory were Craik and Lockhart (1972), who preferred to view the phenomenon of memory very differently. Unlike other cognitive psychologists of that time, they believed that research attention should be directed solely toward better understanding of the processes used to acquire, store, and then recall memories. They further argued that clear distinctions between the various structures of memory were not so distinctive as previously thought and that the projected capacity of each store could be significantly influenced by other variables. These might include the type of information processing necessary or the time available to process the incoming information. Craik and Lockhart were to develop an alternative memory framework that focused on how information was processed at different levels within a unitary memory structure.

> **The levels-of-processing framework focused on the processing of information at different levels within a unitary memory structure.**

Craik and Lockhart believed that two primary factors determined how much information was eventually stored in memory. These were the number of memories an individual was capable of processing at any one time and the depth to which the incoming information was processed. The authors realized that not all the information presented to an individual at any given time could be processed and that, therefore, the learner needed to choose which information would be processed. Craik and Lockhart hypothesized that although the most recently presented information was more likely to be processed, given its importance in changing the nature of the problem being explored or the action being performed, the performer could also choose to continue processing previously presented information. Information processed by the learner constituted primary memory; the remaining, unprocessed information occupied secondary memory. How deeply the incoming information was processed was the second important factor assumed to determine the degree to which it was retained in memory. Again, an individual could choose to process the information at a shallow level or at progressively deeper levels that provided a greater opportunity for elaborating the information or rendering it more distinct in some way.

Like Atkinson and Shiffrin's model, Craik and Lockhart's alternative framework for studying memory has had its critics (Baddeley, 1978; Morris, Bransford, & Franks, 1977). The major criticisms include there being no way to measure the depth to which information was processed, a problem Craik and Tulving (1975) were unable to solve, and the framework's preoccupation with how information is encoded in memory as opposed to how it is retrieved. Each of these drawbacks has limited the robustness of the levels-of-processing perspective.

NEUROBIOLOGY OF MEMORY

A question one might aptly raise at this point is whether there is any neurological evidence in support of Atkinson and Shiffrin's structural claims or any areas within the nervous system capable of serving the type of processing functions described by Craik and Lockhart? Certainly, the interest in human memory has not been confined to a psychological level of analysis. It has fascinated an equal number of neuroscientists, who have attempted to identify regions within the nervous system that might subserve memory. A review of their research efforts and limited findings is the topic of this section.

The search for neuroanatomical sites corresponding to memory dates back to ancient times and the study of phrenology, a pseudoscience whose adherents traced the contours of the skull in an attempt to reveal an individual's character and mental faculties. Today, the experimental paradigms and measurement techniques used to study memory are not only more sophisticated but also more extensive in scope. They range from the ablation and lesion techniques used to study memory in animals (Lashley, 1950; Mishkin, 1982) to a variety of noninvasive brain-scanning techniques used to study the time course of electrical activity in the human brain during the performance of memory tasks. Systematic clinical observations of patients with neurological damage that has caused different types of amnesia have also helped researchers identify areas in the human nervous system that may be involved in several important memory functions.

One early pioneer in memory research was Karl Lashley (1929; 1950), who spent a number of years trying to identify specific brain structures that might be responsible for coding and storing mnemonic information. Using an animal model to study memory, Lashley systematically ablated or introduced lesions to increasingly large areas of an animal's cortex. The results of his work indicated that how well the animal was able to remember a given task was determined primarily by the total amount of cortex destroyed rather than by the specific region affected. Lashley's conclusions were to become the cornerstone of a memory principle called **equipotentiality**: the idea that no one area of the cortex is more likely than any other to be involved in the storage of memories. This same distributed view of memory still exists today.

> Research has shown that no one area of the cortex is more involved than any other in the storage of memories.

Despite the fact that researchers have been unsuccessful in identifying a specific area in the nervous system that might subserve memory, a number of areas and/or structures have been shown to play important roles in memory-related functions. The areas most often implicated as serving memory functions include portions of the limbic system, thalamus, temporal lobe, prefrontal cortex, basal ganglia, cerebellum, and association and motor areas of the cortex (Dudai, 1989). In the paragraphs that follow, we briefly discuss the nature of the research findings and the proposed functions of each of these areas.

The Limbic Connection

The research of Thompson (1980) and O'Keefe and Nadel (1978), in particular, has shown that the hippocampus and amygdala of the larger limbic system play an important role in memory. According to O'Keefe and Nadel, the primary function of the hippocampus involves spatial memory, or the storage of cognitive maps. These maps can then be used for recognizing places, spatially coding scenes, and navigating through space. This hypothesized role has received further support from a number of other researchers interested in the neurobiology of memory. They propose that the hippocampus and its interconnections serve a mediating function in working memory and that another memory system, located elsewhere in the brain, is responsible for long-term memory functions.

> The primary function of the hippocampus is thought to involve spatial memory, or the storage of cognitive maps.

The rhinal cortex, situated immediately below the hippocampus and amygdala, has also been shown to play a crucial role in recognition memory. When all three of these limbic system structures are removed from the brains of monkeys, they are no longer able to distinguish between familiar and unfamiliar objects presented to them (Mishkin, 1978). The removal of these structures creates a condition known as **anterograde amnesia.** This condition results in a loss of memory for the most recently occurring events. This same type of amnesia is often observed in patients who have sustained a moderately severe cerebral concussion and in individuals with Korsakoff's syndrome, which is commonly associated with chronic alcoholism. Additional research has also shown that damage to certain areas in the thalamus or frontal lobe (e.g., the prefrontal cortex) produces the same type of memory loss (Aggleton & Mishkin, 1983). The subsequent discovery of interconnecting neural pathways among these areas further suggests the presence of neural circuitry in the form of feedback loops that are responsible for the learning and storage of recent memories.

In addition to the neural circuitry just described, a second set of neural circuits that link other areas in the central nervous system have also been identified as serving a memory function. These circuits appear to include specific nuclei within the basal ganglia (e.g., the caudate nucleus, putamen, and substantia nigra) and their numerous interconnections with sensory, association, and motor areas at higher cortical levels (Cook & Kesner, 1984; Martone et al., 1984; Mishkin, 1982). Among the many memory functions attributed to this second circuit are the encoding and retrieval of information concerning the spatial and response aspects of a task, the association of incoming sensory information with existing memories, and the storage of cognitive maps.

Dual-Systems Theory of Memory

The theoretical position most widely adopted by neurobiologists now studying human memory is that at least two fundamentally different learning and memory systems exist. According to Petri and Mishkin (1994), these two memory systems "use different circuitry within the brain, store different aspects of experience, and follow different rules of storage" (p. 36). In this **dual-systems model** of learning and memory, the first system is believed to be involved in the storage of neural representations that can be used to form associations between specific memory episodes or events (cognitive memory), whereas the second system is associated with the development of habitual behavior. The information stored in this second memory system (habit memory) is thought to be accessed at subconscious levels for the performance of well-learned skills, be they verbal or motor in orientation. It is interesting to note that this two-system model, developed by neurobiologists, is not unlike other memory frameworks developed by cognitive psychologists such as Baddeley & Hitch (1974).

> The dual-systems model partitions memory in terms of the functions it serves.

TYPES OF MEMORY

Short-term and Long-term Memory

Short-term memory, or working memory (Baddeley, 1981) as it is often called because of its active role in the processing of information, is assumed to contain all the information we are currently thinking about or are conscious of at any particular point in time. How much information is this component of memory capable of storing at any given time? Miller (1956) proposes that we are capable of temporarily storing as few as five separate units of information to as many as nine individual units. Given this limited capacity of working memory, it is fortunate that phone numbers rarely exceed seven digits in length and that social security numbers are limited to nine! The temporary storage of information in working memory also enables us to compare and contrast the items being held there and even to associate current information with information that has previously been stored in a repository of more nearly permanent memory known as **long-term memory (LTM)**.

Unlike short-term memory, LTM is considered to have a limitless capacity for the storage of information. Moreover, once the information to be retained has been transferred to this large-capacity store, it is believed to remain there for an almost indefinite period of time. You will recall that the control process Atkinson and Shiffrin identified as instrumental in the transfer of information from short-term to long-term memory is rehearsal.

> The temporary storage of information in working memory enables us to compare and contrast stored items.

Long-term memory has been described as a relatively permanent storage area for memories, but it is not uncommon for us to be unable to remember an event witnessed many years ago or to find ourselves unable to perform a skill we had learned as a child. Although some researchers attribute the tendency to forget information already stored in long-term memory to the natural decay of the memory trace over time, others argue that forgetting is caused by different types of interference. Still more recently, a number of researchers have begun to turn to alternative explanations for forgetting that focus on the larger issue of retrieval failure. These contemporary theorists acknowledge that interference plays a role in forgetting, but they consider it only one explanation for our inability to retrieve information from memory.

Declarative and Procedural Memory

A second way of categorizing memory has been proposed by a number of researchers (Anderson, 1981; 1987; Tulving, 1985) interested in distinguishing among different types of memory on the basis of the types of knowledge stored there. Although Tulving originally proposed three types of memory (episodic, procedural, and semantic), there has been a tendency in recent years to describe only two types of memory. The first of these is called **declarative memory**, the second is **procedural memory** (Anderson, 1987).

> Declarative memory assists us in knowing "what to do," whereas procedural memory assists in knowing "how to do" a particular skill.

"Knowing what to do" in any movement situation is an important part of the learning process and appears to be subserved by declarative memory. Information stored in this area of memory may include the rules of a game, the components of a skill, or the facts of a particular situation. In contrast, procedural memory assists us in "knowing how to do" a particular skill.

The Relationship between Learning and Memory

Gordon (1989) has characterized the relationship between learning and memory as one where learning acts as the trigger or catalyst for the formation of memories and/or knowledge about a particular action. In light of the importance of this relationship between memory and learning, we will examine it more closely in this section.

> The process of knowledge compilation is used to convert knowledge from a declarative to a procedural form.

In attempting to describe the way the role of memory changes during the acquisition of cognitive skills, Anderson (1982) has developed a theoretical framework that is highly reminiscent of Fitts' (1964) three-stage model of motor skill acquisition (see Chapter 6). According to Anderson, during the first stage of learning a cognitive task, information about the skill is encoded as factual or **declarative knowledge.** This type of knowledge can be interpreted and then used to generate a solution. In this stage, a learner may continually rehearse the information presented in order to hold it in working memory for later interpretation. The overt signs of this rehearsal may include mutterings or visible lip movements.

As the learner enters the second stage of learning, the existing knowledge is gradually converted from a declarative to a procedural form. This process of **knowledge compilation** not only vastly reduces the burden placed on working memory's small capacity but also enables the learner to apply the knowledge directly to the task at hand. There is no longer a need for intermediary interpretation of the factual information, which tends to be slow and prone to error. Recall that Fitts described a similar transition stage at the behavioral level. He characterized the second associative stage of learning as one in which performers begin to blend individual components of a motor skill into a smooth sequence of movements.

During the final stage of learning, which Anderson called the procedural stage, learners continue to fine-tune their **procedural knowledge** to a level where it can be quickly and appropriately applied to a specific problem. The sequence of productions that are performed can be likened to a set of cognitive steps one might use to structure a geometry proof or perhaps to move a chess piece into a "checkmate" position. Anderson's three-stage description has been applied primarily to the acquisition of cognitive skills, but it can be useful in describing the role of memory in the learning of many different types of motor skills.

FACTORS THAT INFLUENCE MEMORY SKILL

Now that we have described the various changes in how knowledge is represented in memory as a learner progresses through the various stages of skill acquisition, let us consider the factors that are most likely to influence how well a particular skill is retained for later recall. It is possible to identify many of these factors by examining three important components of any learning situation: the characteristics of the movement skill to be learned, the environmental context in which the skill is to be learned, and the learner. The interaction among all of these components significantly influences how well a particular skill is learned. For example, we can expect a young child who is introduced to a new skill in an unfamiliar skill setting to operate very differently from an older child who is familiar with both the skill to be learned and the environment in which it is to be learned. Similarly, we will find that some skills are just inherently easier to remember than others.

Characteristics of the Movement Skill

The type of movement skill to be learned has been shown strongly to influence long-term retention. For example, motor skills that require continuous motor control in response to the ongoing presentation of information appear to be remarkably resistant to forgetting. Examples of these skills include riding a bicycle and driving a car. In contrast, skills that are more discrete or consist of a series of procedures are much more difficult to retain if they are not performed on a regular basis. Whereas discrete skills usually involve a specific response to a given signal (e.g., serving a volleyball after the whistle is blown by the referee), procedural skills involve a sequence of operations that must be performed in a specific order. The technique of administering cardiopulmonary resuscitation is an example of a procedural skill (see the accompanying Highlight).

Why is it so much easier to remember one type of motor skill than another? One possible reason involves the organizational complexity of the skill to be learned. Among the criteria for determining organizational complexity are the number of steps the skill involves, whether the order of the sequence can be varied in any way, the extent of planning required to perform the skill, and the degree to which one operation or part of the skill cues the next part (Christina & Bjork, 1991). Prophet (1976) has shown that the procedures involved in piloting a plane are particularly susceptible to forgetting, particularly when pilots are required to fly a plane using the instruments only. The inherent *lack* of

H I G H L I G H T

The Skill of Resuscitation

Have you ever wondered why you are required to renew your cardiopulmonary resuscitation (CPR) certificate every year? The reason lies in the inherent organization and cohesion of the skill itself, which consists of a number of operations that must be carefully timed if the technique is to be administered correctly. Although cardiopulmonary resuscitation has been shown to enhance by as much as 40% a person's chances of surviving a serious accident, skill in CPR is difficult to retain for a long period of time.

In order to determine just how quickly the technique is forgotten, Glendon, McKenna, Blaylock, and Hunt (1985) tested a group of individuals who had successfully mastered the resuscitation skill and received their certificate of mastery some three months earlier. Four aspects of their performance were measured:

1. The *performance* and timing of the heart compression component.

2. The *technique* used to inflate the lungs and depress the chest in the correct area.

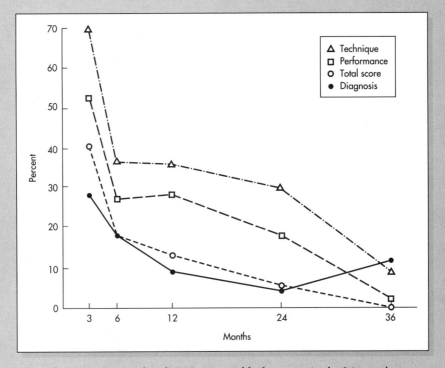

The techniques associated with CPR are quickly forgotten in the 36 months following certification.

3. The quality of the initial *diagnosis* in which the level of consciousness, breathing, and pulse were checked.

4. The outcome of the performance as measured by a *total score* representing the predicted survival rate of the patient.

As the graph on the preceding page indicates, the likelihood that Resusci-Anne, the mannequin used to teach resuscitation skills, will survive drops within a year from a level of 100% immediately following training to a low of 15%. After 36 months, the likelihood of survival is zero. It is clear that regular practice in administering this technique is critical if the skill is to be retained. When was the last time you renewed your own certification?

internal organization associated with piloting skills has been offered as the primary reason for the poor recall. It has also been suggested that continuous skills are much easier to "overlearn" because it is impossible to determine when one trial of the skill ends and the next begins (Schendel, Shields, & Katz, 1978). Considerably larger amounts of practice are therefore possible in any given practice session.

The Initial Learning Environment

A number of authors interested in the long-term retention of motor skills (Annett, 1979; Hurlock & Montague, 1982; Prophet, 1976; Schendel, Shields, & Katz, 1978) strongly argue that how well a particular motor skill is learned following its initial introduction constitutes the most potent variable determining whether a skill is forgotten over time. This conclusion is echoed in the more recent writings of Christina and Bjork (1991), who, in addition to providing a comprehensive review of the related literature, also discuss a number of strategies designed to optimize the level of original learning and thereby positively influence retention.

> The characteristics of the movement skill, learning environment, and learner all influence how well a particular skill is learned.

The initial level of learning is believed to be completed when a predetermined criterion of mastery has been reached. For example, a baseball coach might regard mastery of the skill of bunting as having been achieved when a player is able to bunt successfully on eight of every ten attempts. How automatically a learner is able to perform a particular skill has also been used as an indicator of learning. One very important way of determining the degree to which a skill has become automatic is to introduce a second skill and observe whether the learner has a sufficient reserve of attention to allocate to performance of the second skill while continuing to perform the first. How well the learner performs the two skills concurrently is a measure of the degree to which the primary skill has been learned.

The Learner

An instructor has only to watch a class of students trying to recall a motor skill presented in a previous class to see that certain students are better able to recall the skill than are their classmates. Despite the fact that the instructor gave the same verbal instructions, demonstrated the skill in the same way, and provided the same amount of practice opportunities to everyone, some students are simply better able to recall the information necessary for performing the skill accurately. Why do these individual differences exist? More often than not, the ability level and past experiences of the learner affect how well a particular skill is remembered. Farr (1987) suggests that these characteristics of learners "have equipped them with a larger and more varied repertoire of memory-enhancing strategies" (p. 95).

The existence of a greater repertoire of memory strategies can therefore be expected to not only influence how long information can be retained but also how quickly it can be retrieved from memory at the appropriate time (see the Highlight that describes the skilled memory capabilities of J.C., the waiter). These memory differences were highlighted in a study conducted by Anderson and Reder (1979), who were able to distinguish between individuals who could recall historical facts well and those who could not. Those individuals with the better memory strategies were able to elaborate the information far beyond the content presented to them in a fictitious history passage during a free-recall test.

Although the instructor has little control over the abilities and past experiences an individual brings to a learning situation, it is important that individual differences be considered when designing the curriculum and instructing the class. It is clear that instructor-dominated approaches do little to capitalize on the strengths of the learner. In contrast, programs that emphasize self-paced learning or that place the responsibility for learning squarely in the hands and minds of the learner foster superior learning and long-term retention of skill-related knowledge.

APPLICATION OF THEORY

Practical suggestions for enhancing the learning and subsequent recall of a variety of different movement skills have been made on the basis of several experimental studies. The techniques advocated include (1) setting a higher criterion for "mastery" or otherwise increasing the amount of original learning, (2) using qualitative explanations designed to foster understanding of the task to be learned, (3) presenting mnemonics (memory aids) that enable the learner to create a more elaborate and/or distinctive memory of the skill-related information, (4) increasing the level of contextual interference present during practice, and (5) adequately spacing practice and refresher training. Let us see how each of these suggestions can be put into practice.

Increasing the Amount of Original Learning

What type of strategies can an instructor or clinician use to optimize the original learning of a movement skill? Christina and Bjork (1991) suggest that the criterion for mastery be set at a higher level. Let us return to the bunting example to illustrate their suggestion. Instead of requiring only that the player be able to complete a certain number of successful attempts, the coach might require that the player also be able to direct the ball along the first or third baseline on command before being satisfied that the skill has been adequately learned. In order for the learner to meet this more difficult criterion, additional practice will be required beyond the amount necessary simply to acquire the mechanics of the skill itself.

In addition to raising the criterion for mastery, an instructor can also implement additional practice beyond criterion in an attempt to increase the original level of learning. The term most often used to describe additional practice of a skill beyond mastery is **overlearning.** As theoretically implausible as it might seem to consider any skill to be overlearned, this term appears repeatedly in the motor skills literature. It is operationally defined as the number of practice trials completed beyond a predetermined criterion level of mastery. Although supplementing practice of a skill has been demonstrated to enhance original learning, it has also been noted that beyond a certain level, additional practice begins to yield diminishing returns. That is, increasing the amount of practice time beyond mastery may not yield proportionally greater increases in improvement (see Magill, 1993, for a review of this issue).

> Overlearning involves providing additional practice beyond the criterion level of mastery.

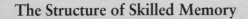

HIGHLIGHT

The Structure of Skilled Memory

How is it that certain people are capable of memorizing entire books, the days of the week associated with dates several thousand years ago, or the entire multiplication table for numbers between 1 and 100? Some researchers have been so fascinated by the abilities of these individuals that they have spent many years attempting to discover the underlying structure of what they refer to as skilled memory. Ericsson and Polson (1984), for example, studied J.C., a waiter who could memorize as many as 20 complete dinner orders. How was he able to accomplish this impressive feat? A review of the detailed observation notes compiled by these authors over a 2-year study period reveals just how J.C. was able to remember such a large amount of information.

Instead of trying to recall each individual order in sequence , J.C. categorized the information into salad dressings that were encoded as a list of first letters corresponding to their names. For example if Blue cheese, Oil and vinegar, Oil and vinegar, and Thousand island dressings were ordered by the first four members of the party, they were remembered as the word BOOT. In order to remember those items that were to accompany the entree, J.C. used a different mnemonic strategy that involved

J.C. had developed a sophisticated set of mnemonics in order to remember large amounts of information and then retrieve it from memory.

encoding the food items into patterns (e.g., baked potato, rice, rice, baked potato = abba). Meat temperatures were encoded by first spatially associating them with a linear increase from rare to well-done and then expressing them with numbers from 1 to 4. J.C. finally associated each of the entrees ordered with the position of the person who was ordering it. What is perhaps most interesting about J.C.'s memory ability is that it was not limited to the recall of dinner orders. When asked to recall a new category of items, such as time intervals ranging from 1 second to a week, J.C. exhibited the same level of recall within two practice sessions. Apparently, the retrieval strategies he had developed for use in one situation were readily transferable to another.

The study of J.C. and many other skilled mnemonists led Chase and Ericsson (1982) to propose a theory of skilled memory that is predicated on three important principles: meaningful encoding, retrieval structure, and speed-up of memorization. They persuasively argue that individuals with skilled memory not only are capable of rapidly storing information in long-term memory (LTM) and then associating it with existing knowledge in a more meaningful way but also can retrieve the information using a special set of retrieval cues that are explicitly associated with the information presented. The speed-up of memorization is a function of practice and can lead to storage rates in LTM that are equal to those of short-term memory (STM). The fact that the average individual can be trained to improve his or her memory skill significantly is an especially promising aspect of the theory.

Perhaps the two most difficult tasks facing an instructor or clinician are choosing a criterion level of mastery that is appropriate for the skill to be learned and then determining the amount of additional practice that is most likely to maximize the original learning. Although Farr (1987) argues that these decisions are often arbitrarily set in laboratory experiments "for convenience and practicality, not for any pedagogically-grounded reasons (p. 48)," Jones (1985) has provided a means by which a less arbitrary decision can be made. Jones suggests plotting an individual's learning curve in order to determine the point at which the curve begins to plateau. This point is then considered the best indicant of "completed" acquisition. Any additional practice beyond this point can be equated with "overlearning" of the skill. As promising as this method appears at first glance, multiple plateaus are often observed in the curve as the learner reaches difficult points in the acquisition of a very complex skill. In these situations it is important not to conclude erroneously, after observing the first plateau, that original learning is complete.

Fostering Understanding of the Task to Be Learned

Augmenting instruction with qualitative explanations can enhance the learner's understanding of the task to be learned (Gentner, 1980; 1982; Kieras, 1981; Smith & Goodman, 1982; Tourangeau & Sternberg, 1982). These explanations may consist simply of telling the learner *what* to do, or they may be more comprehensive. For example, the instructor might also provide information about *how* the skill is to be performed and *why* it should be performed in a particular way. Konoske and Ellis (1985) caution that in order for these ancillary explanations to be useful, they "should include spatial and component-part information as well as goal statements" (p. 13). This type of information can be presented schematically, by illustration, or in the case of motor skills, through demonstration and verbal cueing. Taking the time to foster a better understanding of procedural tasks has also been shown to influence positively the perceived organization or cohesion of a task (Morris, Stein, & Bransford, 1979; Owens, Bower, & Black, 1979). Of course, when the information provided to learners is consistent with what they already know about other learned skills, it is considered even more meaningful.

> Telling learners *what* to do, *how* to do it and *why* it should be performed in a particular way can foster their understanding of the task-to-be learned.

Mnemonics (Memory Aids)

Providing the learner with **mnemonics** (memory aids) can also do much to foster the original learning and long-term retention of a particular motor skill. These mnemonics may be in the form of verbal cues that help the learner remember the critical components of a task or the next step in a set of procedures. Verbal cues that conjure up strong visual images or kinesthetic sensations can be particularly helpful. Cueing a swimmer performing the back crawl to "enter the water at the eleven and one position of a clock" cues the performer to the optimal entry for the arms after the recovery phase of the stroke. Similarly, cues that highlight changes in sensation due to increasing pressure of the water against the arms or a change in temperature as the arm leaves the water can also serve as useful mnemonic aids in the learning of certain swimming strokes. Encouraging the learner to rehearse each of the

> Verbal cues that evoke strong visual images or kinesthetic sensations serve as useful memory aids for learners.

components of a skill verbally or mentally can also be an extremely important way to foster learning and recall.

Contextual Interference during Practice

Battig (1972; 1979) has demonstrated that learners who are required to practice a skill in conditions that promote high interference recall the skill considerably better at a later time. Battig manipulated the level of interference present in the practice environment by changing the requirements of the task from trial to trial. This might involve changing the speed at which a movement is performed or altering the pattern of coordination required. Battig hypothesized that increasing the level of interference made the practice situation more difficult for learners, forcing them to use multiple and variable strategies to encode the skill-related material. He further hypothesized that the type of information processing used would be more elaborate and/or distinctive as a function of the practice situation being more cognitively effortful for the learner.

> Recall is improved by requiring learners to practice different skills or variations of a single skill from trial to trial.

You may recall from our earlier discussion of Craik and Lockhart's levels-of-processing framework that the more distinctively or elaborately we process information, the better able we are to retain and then retrieve those memories for later use. Although Battig studied the role of contextual interference in the learning of verbal skills, the concept was to be applied in the late 1970s to the acquisition of motor skills. Since the publication of the first experiment conducted by Shea and Morgan (1979), a number of researchers have continued to explore the role of contextual interference in the learning and retention of motor skills in both laboratory and gymnasium settings (Lee & Magill, 1983; Goode & Magill, 1987; Shea & Zimny, 1983). We will return to this topic in Chapter 10.

Spacing of Practice

It is generally agreed that the spacing of practices leads to superior learning and later recall of verbal and motor skills alike (Baddeley & Longman, 1978; Bahrick & Phelps, 1987; Lee & Genovese, 1988). Unlike a **massed practice** schedule that calls for significantly longer periods of the practice over fewer days, a **distributed practice** schedule is based on shorter practice sessions separated by longer intervals of rest. Why does a distributed practice schedule produce superior learning and recall? Baddeley (1990) speculates that the spacing of practice may facilitate the physical changes in the brain that are necessary to produce long-term retention by providing more time for certain neurochemical substances associated with these changes to regenerate during the rest interval. During the shorter rest intervals associated with massed practice schedules, there may be insufficient time for these neurochemical substances to regenerate. Baddeley acknowledges that such a hypothesis is difficult to test, but he is confident that the rapid developments occurring in the neurochemical study of memory will make it possible to test this hypothesis in the near future.

Similarity between Practice and Performance

The degree to which the context in which a skill is initially practiced mirrors the eventual performance setting is likely to influence how well a particular skill is retained. Say I learn to serve a tennis ball in a practice environment that is very different from the one in which I will ultimately be required to perform the skill. Is it likely that my memory of that skill will be adversely affected? Tulving and colleagues (e.g., Tulving, 1983; Tulving & Thomson, 1973) suggest that this is indeed the case and have developed what has come to be known as the **encoding-specificity principle** to describe this phenomenon. According to this principle, the ability to retrieve skill-related information successfully depends on the degree to which the setting where the information is to be retrieved is similar to the setting where it was originally encoded.

Similarity between the conditions in which encoding and retrieval occur enhances skill retention because a learner encodes more than just the information related to the skill to be learned. This information is connected with other types of information provided by the environment (e.g., sights, sounds, and smells) that renders the memory more distinctive. For the instructor of motor skills, this principle suggests that the more a practice situation can be made to resemble the final performance conditions, the better the learner's recall of the skill will be. Basketball players might be instructed to practice their offensive and defensive skills in small groups using one half of the basketball court. Volleyball players might practice the skill of spiking against one or more players who are attempting to block the ball as it is hit by the player at the net. For the clinician, this principle suggests having the patient practice each daily activity in the environment in which it will ultimately be performed (e.g., brushing the teeth at a sink in the bathroom rather than at the patient's bed).

It should now be clear that the more an instructor or clinician fosters the active participation of a learner in the learning process, the more successful both the original learning and the subsequent recall of the skill will be. Cooperative learning and/or peer teaching techniques, verbal cueing and/or verbal or mental rehearsal, and large amounts of practice seem to be the most effective means of encouraging learner involvement in the learning process. An active role for the processor is also an important component of both the multistore model and levels-of-processing framework discussed earlier in this chapter. Whether the strategies used to transfer information from one store in memory to another are internally generated or externally provided to the learner, what is crucial is that the learner take an active rather than a passive role in the learning process.

DISORDERS OF MEMORY

Disorders of memory may result from cerebral traumas that are either acute in nature (e.g., head trauma, hypoxia or ischemia, and transient global amnesia) or more gradual in onset (e.g., alcoholic Korsakoff amnestic syndrome, brain tumor, and viral encephalitis). Selective memory loss is also observed: Some patients are unable to recall recent memories (i.e., anterograde amnesia), and others have difficulty retrieving more remote memories (i.e., **retrograde amnesia**). In some cases, these disruptions to memory are temporary; in others, they may be much longer lasting. In either case, the rehabilitation process is negatively affected. For example, recovering stroke patients are often unable to remember a set of instructions given as little as 30 seconds earlier even though they remain able to remember the minute details of events experienced some 30 years before. On some occasions, patients recall only a few bits of information from a series of commands, making it almost impossible for them to perform the activity correctly. The generalization of information is also problematic for these patients. It is most often observed when they are asked to perform an activity learned in one setting in a different setting. For example, a patient may learn to transfer from a hospital bed to a chair but may be unable to perform the same set of movements in the home. This inability to apply what has been learned in a practice situation to similar situations arising in daily life significantly slows the patient's return to independent functioning.

Mills (1988) provides a number of strategies for improving the memory of patients involved in a rehabilitation program (some of these strategies were described in the preceding section). When a skill is first being presented to a recovering patient, for example, it is important to keep to a minimum any verbal descriptions and instructions related to how the task is to be performed. By this means, the therapist minimizes the confusion that can result from the overloading of working memory. One might even dispense with verbal instructions when introducing a skill, particularly when working with patients who have experienced damage to the right hemisphere following a stroke. Because these patients have difficulty remembering language, visual demonstrations may prove much more effective than verbal descriptions in conveying how best to perform a particular skill or exercise.

When verbal instructions *are* used to present a skill, the speed with which they are delivered should be carefully controlled. Speaking slowly and clearly will do much to enhance the amount of information understood. How effective the instructor has been in providing verbal instructions will soon be evident in the patient's or learner's response. The nature of the response should therefore be carefully monitored, and where confusion is evident, subsequent instructions or demonstrations should be modified.

Once the skill to be learned has been introduced, it is important that the patient be provided with an immediate opportunity to practice. Active rehearsal boosts the likelihood that the information will be transferred to long-term memory. Self-paced practice should also be encouraged so that the patient has enough time to process the information presented and then translate it into action. Imposing time constraints on action denies the patient sufficient time to rehearse and organize the information in a manner that is optimal for later retrieval and translation into action. Various part-task training methods are also useful for individuals with memory disorders or as-yet-undeveloped memory functions. These practice methods will be discussed in greater depth in Chapter 10. The "Keep It Simple (KIS)" principle certainly should not be overlooked in these types of learning situations.

> Self-paced practice should be encouraged so that the patient has adequate time to process the presented information and translate it into action.

Mnemonic strategies and devices can enhance the learning process. These are most often provided in the form of verbal cues that the instructor uses to supplement a demonstration of the skill and highlight the important aspects of the task. These cues can then be repeated by the instructor as the learner practices the skill and can even be repeated by the learner as she or he prepares to practice. Encouraging learners to engage in self-talk, or verbal rehearsal, while they practice has been shown to increase how well a particular skill is recalled at a later time (Weiss, 1983, Weiss & Klint, 1987). This instructional technique will be discussed further in Chapter 10. Mnemonic devices in the form of memory boards and logs are also frequently used in clinical facilities to help a patient remember a set of exercises or simply maintain a schedule. Skill-related cues written on sheets posted at activity stations set up in gymnasiums are also valuable for learners engaged in practicing many different types of skills at once.

SUMMARY

The intent of this chapter has been to familiarize the reader with the construct of human memory and the nature of the operations involved in the acquisition, rehearsal, organization, and recall of skill-related information. Memory is generally divided into two components. The terms used to differentiate these two components include short-term and long-term memory, primary and secondary memory, declarative and procedural memory, and cognitive and habit memory. Whatever labels are used, it is the type of memory function that largely differentiates one component from the other.

Several variables have been demonstrated to influence the learning and retention of verbal and motor skills. They include the original level of learning, the characteristics of the skill to be learned, the nature of the learning conditions, and the inherent abilities and past experiences of the learner. Research in this area has yielded several strategies that are recommended for the teacher and clinician whose goal is to optimize the learning and long-term retention of cognitive and motor skills. Integral to all of these strategies is the idea that the learner must be actively involved in the learning process.

IMPORTANT TERMINOLOGY

After completing this chapter, readers should be familiar with the following terms and concepts.

anterograde amnesia	massed practice
declarative knowledge	memory
declarative memory	mnemonics
distributed practice	overlearning
dual-systems model	procedural knowledge
encoding-specificity principle	procedural memory
equipotentiality	retrograde amnesia
knowledge compilation	sensory register
long-term memory	short-term memory
long-term store	short-term store

SUGGESTED FURTHER READING

Baddeley, A.D. 1990. *Human memory. Theory and Practice.* Boston, MA: Allyn and Bacon.

Christina, R.W., & Bjork, R.A. 1991. Optimizing long-term retention and transfer. *In the mind's eye: Enhancing human performance,* eds. D. Druckman & R. Bjork, pp. 23–56. Washington, DC: National Academy Press.

Farr, M. J. 1987. *The long-term retention of knowledge and skills. A cognitive and instructional perspective.* New York: Springer-Verlag.

TEST YOUR UNDERSTANDING

1. Cite the major features of the multistore model of memory. How does this view of memory differ from the levels-of-processing framework proposed by Craik and Lockhart (1972)?

2. What is the memory principle of equipotentiality? What types of measurement were used to provide support for this principle?

3. Identify the areas of the central nervous system that have been shown to play a role in memory.

4. Briefly describe the condition known as anterograde amnesia.

5. According to the dual-systems theory of learning and memory, what are the major functions of the two memory systems?

6. How does declarative memory differ from procedural memory?

7. According to Anderson, how does the role of memory change as a new cognitive skill is acquired?

8. Cite three factors that have been shown to influence how well a skill is retained for later recall.

9. Describe at least five ways in which a practitioner can facilitate the learning and subsequent recall of a movement skill.

10. Describe the various ways in which disorders of memory are most likely to influence an individual's behavior.

11. Mention strategies that are often used to improve the memory of patients involved in a rehabilitation program.

About the Quote

Farr is encouraging practitioners to broaden their teaching beyond the rote learning of motor skills or facts to the inculcation of principles, concepts, and rules. These concepts can prove helpful to the learner who is trying to recall a particular skill or a strategy related to its use in a game situation. Not only does this approach increase the number of mnemonic aids available to the learner, but such teaching is also likely to facilitate the transfer of learning to other types of motor skills. Of course, the practitioner must first undertake a very careful analysis of the skill to be learned in order to foster better reconstruction of the skill by the learner.

CHAPTER 9

SETTING THE STAGE
FOR LEARNING

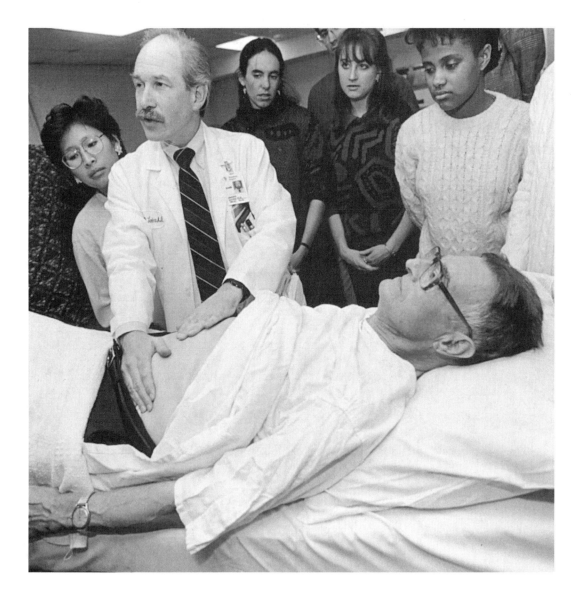

CHAPTER
OBJECTIVES

- Understand and be able to identify the many variables that have been shown to influence the effectiveness of using a model when introducing new movement skills.

- Be able to identify practical strategies and techniques that can be used to enhance the effectiveness of a model in a variety of instructional settings.

- Become familiar with the two primary theoretical explanations of the effectiveness of modeling in the acquisition of movement skills.

- Become familiar with the alternative technique called discovery learning for introducing a new movement skill or pattern of coordination.

- Identify ways in which a practitioner can structure a learning environment to promote discovery learning.

> *"The use of demonstrations at the early stage of skill learning should enable the learner to perceive the important relationships between body parts, namely the relative motions."*
>
> —Scully & Newell (1985)

A recurring issue for teachers and clinicians alike is the construction of an environment in which the learning or relearning of movement-based skills is optimized. Although it is important for the learning environment not to overwhelm the learner with its complexity, it should progressively challenge the individual and eventually mirror the environment in which the skill to be acquired will be performed. For example, during the course of a rehabilitation program in which a patient is learning to regain function following a cerebrovascular accident, the learning environment should resemble the place where the skills will ultimately be performed. To achieve this end, many rehabilitation facilities construct elaborate complexes complete with full-scale kitchens, grocery aisles stocked with items to be selected and carried, and modified motor vehicles designed to train the patient in advanced transfer skills.

In motor skills settings, a similar method is desirable. Once the fundamental skills of a sport have been introduced, further practice should take place in a learning environment that becomes more and more like the game situation. Undesirable complexity can be controlled by reducing the repertoire of skills needed in modified game situations or the number of players participating in any given game situation. In this way, the learning environment is progressively shaped to reproduce that of the game.

Numerous factors must be considered when constructing an environment for learning. We will focus on three very important factors, each of which is considered a critical determinant of effective learning. The first of these factors, setting the stage for learning, is the topic of this chapter. Important issues related to organizing the practice environment and to providing feedback will be discussed in Chapters 10 and 11.

INTRODUCING THE SKILL TO BE LEARNED

Although there are a variety of ways to present skill-related information to a learner, visual presentation is usually chosen. That is, the skill or movement pattern to be learned is modeled or demonstrated a number of times for the observer. In such **observational learning,** learners watch another individual perform the movement before attempting to reproduce the action themselves. Unlike lengthy verbal descriptions during which a learner may stop paying attention or simply fail to remember all that has been said, a visual demonstration of the skill quickly provides the learner with a meaningful image of the act. In choosing a visual model to set the stage for learning, the practitioner must first consider a number of important variables that have been shown to influence the effectiveness of this instructional technique.

Variables That Influence the Effectiveness of Modeling

A number of variables appear to influence how well a modeled skill is initially performed and ultimately retained by the observer. These variables have been identified and incorporated in an eloquent model of observational learning developed by McCullagh, Weiss, and Ross (1989) that is presented in Figure 9.1. It is beyond the scope of this chapter to discuss all the variables identified in this model, but we will look at some of them, particularly those that one should consider before introducing a new movement pattern to a group of observers. These include the developmental characteristics of the observer, elements of

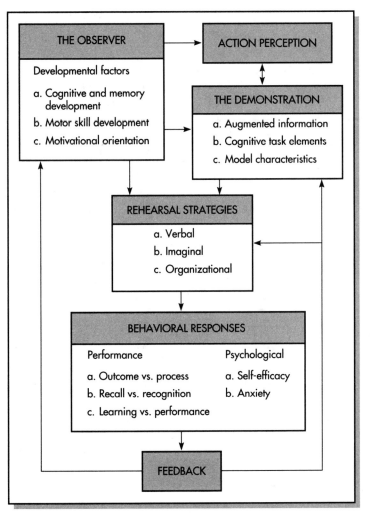

FIGURE 9.1 A number of observer and model characteristics influence the overall effectiveness of demonstrations.

the demonstration (e.g., model characteristics, augmented information, and cognitive task elements), and the type of rehearsal strategies used. We will begin our discussion by considering the characteristics of the observer that appear to affect how the information conveyed by the model is processed.

Characteristics of the Observer. One has only to watch a group of children try to reproduce a movement pattern that has just been demonstrated by a skilled model to realize that few observers processed the modeled information in the same way. Some of the children's first attempts are very accurate, whereas those of other children bear little resemblance to the actual skill modeled. A glance at the model proposed

An observer's level of cognitive and memory development influences both the amount and the type of information extracted from a modeled performance.

by McCullagh et al. provides some clues to why the performances of the observers vary so greatly. First, it may be that not all of the children observing the model are at the same stage of cognitive and memory development. These differences can be expected to influence both the amount of information that is extracted from the modeled performance and the manner in which it is then organized for later recall (Thomas, 1980). In fact, research has shown that younger children (4–7 years) do not effectively organize information derived from a modeled performance, that they fail to label it in a manner that might facilitate later recall, and that they do not spontaneously rehearse the information presented (Thomas & Gallagher, 1986; Winther & Thomas, 1981). Research has also shown that if children of this age are to be successful in reproducing the modeled skill, it is necessary to instruct them to rehearse cognitively before attempting the skill (Weiss & Klint, 1987).

Just as we can expect differences in cognitive ability to influence how effectively an observer extracts and organizes the information derived from a model, differences in children's levels of physical and motor skill development will also influence how well they are able to reproduce the skill physically during practice. The changing size and composition of a child's body affect how well a skill is performed, as does the level of coordination, strength, and balance the child has achieved at the time the skill is introduced. A review of the motor development literature (Clark & Ewing, 1985; Halverson, Roberton, & Langendorfer, 1982; Seefeldt & Haubenstricker, 1982) also suggests that gender differences exist in the quality of motor skill development. Although the differences in motor development observed between males and females are quite small during the preschool and early elementary school years, they become larger with increasing age. It is therefore important to consider these differences when modeling new skills in mixed-gender settings. It has also been shown that the level of exposure children have had to organized sports settings plays a major role in their performance of certain sport-specific skills.

An observer's level of physical and motor skill development influences the observer's ability to reproduce the modeled action physically.

An individual's level of motivation to learn the skill being modeled is another factor that must be considered when introducing a skill. As Brooks (1986) aptly points out, "Neither a balky child nor a disinterested adult learns easily or improves motor skill" (p. 24). Whereas some individuals need little or no encouragement to learn a new skill or movement pattern because they are already intrinsically motivated, others need repeated words of encouragement or incentives to learn. Thus a therapist often rewards a patient who has worked very hard during a rehabilitation session with the opportunity to choose an activity he or she enjoys at the end of the session, and a physical educator may reward a class of children who have been attentive during a skills practice with a few minutes of game play. Yet another effective way of boosting a learner's motivation to learn a particular skill is to explain how the acquisition of that skill will contribute to his or her overall game-playing versatility or (in the case of a patient) ability to perform certain daily activities.

The use of peer models in classroom (Schunk & Hanson, 1985; Schunk, Hanson, & Cox, 1987) and motor skill settings (McAuley, 1985; Lirgg & Feltz, 1991) has been shown to enhance the observer's confidence in his or her own ability to perform the modeled skill. The skilled adult model's ability to perform the skill far exceeds that of younger observers, but the peer model who is perceived as similar to the learner in ability can positively influence the observers' perception of their own ability to perform the skill. The end result is usually enhanced motivation to learn the skill. Although its role in the learning of movement skills has often been overlooked in the motor learning literature, motivation is a fundamental prerequisite to both the learning of movement skills and continued participation in activity settings.

> Peer models can be used to enhance an observer's confidence in his or her ability to perform the modeled skill.

Elements of the Demonstration.   There are several characteristics of the model and of the demonstration itself that one should consider in planning to introduce a new movement pattern via modeling.

Skill Level of the Model. Many writers of contemporary textbooks on motor learning (Christina & Corcos, 1988; Magill, 1993; Schmidt, 1988; 1991) have persuasively argued that the single most important characteristic of a model is his or her ability to perform correctly the skill being observed. These and other authors contend that watching a skilled model ensures that observers correctly imitate the most efficient movement pattern when they begin to practice the skill. This ability to reproduce the modeled action correctly is being guided by a perceptual "blueprint" of the modeled skill that is developed and stored in the observer's memory (Sheffield, 1961). Unfortunately, the claims of these writers and theoreticians have not always been supported by research.

Although a number of research studies have demonstrated superior performance among observers who first watch a skilled model before practicing (Landers & Landers, 1973), Scully and Newell (1985) point out in a recent review of the modeling literature that an equally large number of studies have demonstrated no such effect (Martens, Burwitz,

---

The use of a model appears to be more effective when an observer is required to learn a new pattern of coordination.

& Zuckerman, 1976). Theorists aligned with an information-processing paradigm attribute these equivocal findings to differences in information load among the tasks modeled (Gould, 1980), but Scully and Newell argue that examining the dynamics of the task being modeled provides a more reasonable account of the contrary findings. They suggest that the use of a skilled model is more effective when the observer is required to learn a new pattern of coordination rather than to rescale an already familiar movement pattern. If this line of reasoning is accurate, a learner who is being introduced to the Fosbury flop high-jump technique for the first time will benefit more from watching a skilled model than will another performer who is already familiar with this particular style of jumping and is attempting to clear greater bar heights using the technique.

As common as it is for practitioners to use skilled models when introducing new movement skills, the theoretical assumptions underlying the use of a correct model have only recently been scrutinized by a number of researchers (Lee & White, 1990; McCullagh & Caird, 1990; Pollock & Lee, 1992). In fact, Lee and White have hypothe-

---

Watching an unskilled model more actively involves the observer in the problem-solving activities of the model.

---

sized that the use of correct models may not be the most effective means of conveying movement skill information during the early stages of skill acquisition. An alternative approach is to have them watch an unskilled model repeatedly practice the skill to be learned. The observer who watches an unskilled model is thought to be more actively involved in the problem-solving activities of the model as the model tries to discover how to perform the skill more effectively. It is further argued that the use of skilled models may undermine the problem-solving process because skilled models offer observers very little error information they can use to develop their own error-detection mechanisms (Pollock & Lee, 1992).

Pollock and Lee had observers watch either a skilled or an initially unskilled model practice a computer tracking game. In addition to watching the model, the observer recorded the model's performance score after each trial. When they compared the performances of both groups of observers to those of the skilled and **learning models** who demonstrated the skill, the authors found that both groups of observers performed consistently better during practice than any of the learning models who were paired with observers. On the basis of their findings, the authors concluded that observing a model was equally beneficial for the observers no matter what that model's skill level, particularly during the initial performance of a skill.

McCullagh & Caird (1990) have also demonstrated the effectiveness of learning models. In addition, they showed that the use of a learning model can positively influence how well the skill is later recalled and generalized to the acquisition of a new movement skill. Specifically, the authors demonstrated that observers who watched a model learn a timing task and received information about the correctness of the model's movement pattern performed as well as a group of subjects who physically practiced the skill and received information about their own performance. This same group of observers also performed much better than a group of observers who watched a skilled model perform the skill before they practiced. It is important to note, however, that simply watching a learning model perform a skill did not provide observers with enough information on which to base their subsequent practice. Subjects who watched a learning model but were not privy to the feedback provided to the model about the performance demonstrated little improvement during any of the testing phases. Giving a learner feedback about the model's performance is important, particularly when using learning models.

> Providing performance-related feedback to a learning model as the observer watches results in better retention and transfer of the skill.

Status, Similarity, and Age of the Model. The effects of three additional factors associated with model characteristics have also been investigated. These factors are the perceived status or competence of the model demonstrating the skill (Baron, 1970; McCullagh, 1986), the similarity of the model to the observer (McCullagh, 1987; Gould & Weiss, 1981), and the age of the model relative to that of the observer (Landers & Landers, 1973; Lirgg & Feltz, 1991). In general, although these characteristics of the model appear to influence performance positively by raising the level of attention directed to the model or the motivation exhibited by observers, there is little evidence that any of these model characteristics affect how well a movement pattern or skill is ultimately learned.

Augmented Information. In certain learning situations, the effectiveness of a visual model can be enhanced by augmenting, or supplementing, the demonstration with verbal cues that convey salient information. Verbal cues that highlight important components of the skill can be very useful additions to a modeled performance (Roach & Burwitz, 1986; Weiss, 1983). Such "show and tell" models are thought to focus observers' attention on the most important features of the skill being modeled. The use of verbal cueing has been shown to be particularly helpful to young children attempting to acquire a new movement pattern or sequence of movement, especially when the verbal cueing is

> The status, similarity, and age of the model appear to have little effect on how well an observer learns a movement skill.

The age, status, and skill level of the model relative to the observer are variables that have been shown to influence the effectiveness of a demonstration.

coupled with cognitive rehearsal (Weiss & Klint, 1987; McCullagh, Stiehl, & Weiss, 1988).

Although the addition of verbal cues has been shown to facilitate reproduction of a modeled action, it is important to consider the form in which these cues are provided, their meaningfulness for the observer, and the frequency with which they are provided. Training the observer to use verbal cues that describe the modeled action prior to its presentation also enhances observational learning (Bandura, Jeffrey, & Bachica, 1974). Gerst (1971) has shown that personally generated cues that are imaged by the observer can be more effective than concrete descriptions of the movement pattern. The issue of meaningfulness also looms large in situations where adults are introducing skills to young children. Often, many of the verbal cues the adult instructor chooses to describe an action are too complex for the children

Verbal cueing, coupled with cognitive rehearsal, is particularly helpful to young children attempting to learn a new skill.

to comprehend. Providing opportunities for children to develop their own verbal descriptors of an action may be very useful in the early stages of skill learning.

The Type of Skill Being Demonstrated. A question that has intrigued one group of researchers interested in modeling issues is whether a visual demonstration constitutes the best method for conveying skill-related information when the skill to be learned is one that has a strong temporal component. In these situations, the use of an auditory demonstration may provide the observer with more salient information about the skill to be learned. To address this question, Doody, Bird, & Ross (1985) examined the performance of subjects on a timing task that was introduced with a visual, an auditory, or a visual and auditory demonstration. A fourth group of subjects simply practiced the skill and received knowledge about their performance after each practice attempt.

The results of an immediate retention test indicated that all the groups that received a demonstration performed better than the physical practice group. Comparing the performance scores of the three demonstration groups, however, revealed that the group that received an auditory demonstration of the timing task performed as well as the group that received a visual and auditory demonstration and both groups performed significantly better than the visual demonstration group. These results suggest that auditory demonstrations can be an effective means of conveying information to observers when timing is important in the task being demonstrated. In a more recent study, Rose and Tyry (1994) manipulated the type of demonstration used to introduce the skill of rapid-fire pistol shooting to a group of experienced single-target shooters. Given that shooters must sequentially fire at each of five targets in a prescribed period of time, this task may be considered to have a strong timing component.

> Auditory demonstrations may convey more information than visual demonstrations when the skill to be learned involves a high temporal component.

Unfortunately, Rose and Tyry's results were contradictory to those of Doody et al. Subjects who received an auditory demonstration exhibited the least effective performance when compared to the groups that received a visual demonstration only or a combined visual and auditory demonstration. Why did the visual demonstration group, who received no auditory information during the demonstrations, perform so well at this task? The answer lies in the fact that timing information was available and could be extracted visually from the demonstration. Each time the model fired the pistol, an opaque puff of air could be observed escaping from the pistol's air ports. Apparently, this recurring visual cue was sufficient to provide the timing information that observers needed to perform the skill successfully. The results of this study suggest that timing information does not always have to come from auditory sources alone. In the case of many skills, timing information can be acquired through other means. This finding has important implications for instructors of people who are deaf, because these instructors cannot exploit auditory sources as a means of teaching the timing components of a skill.

Rehearsal Strategies. The type of rehearsal strategies used by the observer prior to practicing the demonstrated movement pattern are also considered an important determinant of effective modeling. McCullagh et al. describe different types of rehearsal, two of which will be discussed here. These are verbal and mental, or imaginal, rehearsal strategies. Verbalizing the components of the skill prior to practice has been shown to be particularly helpful to novice performers, but mental rehearsal can also be used to strengthen the observer's perception of the skill to be performed.

Verbal Rehearsal. **Verbal rehearsal** has proved to be a particularly effective strategy for increasing the selective attention and recall skills of children with various disabilities who are attempting to learn new skills in classroom settings (Meichenbaum & Goodman, 1971; Tarver, Hallahan, Kauffman, & Ball, 1976). In the area of motor skill learning, Kowalski and Sherrill (1992) also found the use of verbal rehearsal particularly effective for a group of young students with learning disabilities who were asked to perform a seven-part sequence of locomotor movements. The children who were trained to rehearse verbally the information presented by a skilled model reached a criterion level of performance on the task in considerably fewer attempts than those children who simply watched the model perform the task prior to practice. Collectively, these research findings suggest that training novice performers, particularly young children with a learning disability, to use verbal rehearsal strategies in motor skills settings is warranted.

> Verbal rehearsal is an effective strategy for increasing the selective attention and recall skills of children with various learning disabilities.

Mental Rehearsal. Imaginal, or mental, rehearsal can also be employed to strengthen the observer's perception of what is required without the need for overt verbalization or, in some cases, physical practice. The effectiveness of this form of rehearsal appears to be influenced by the type of task being rehearsed—that is, whether or not it demands a large amount of cognitive processing. Tasks characterized by a high cognitive component, as opposed to a high motor component, appear to be especially conducive to **imaginal rehearsal** (Feltz & Landers, 1983). Moreover, individual differences in imaging abilities may influence the degree to which imaginal rehearsal leads to improved performance. Research has demonstrated that the recall of certain movement characteristics (such as distance and location) is affected by an individual's visual imaging abilities (Housner & Hoffman, 1981). Unfortunately, researchers interested in the theoretical underpinnings of observational learning have paid little attention to mental rehearsal.

> Skills that demand large amounts of cognitive processing are well suited to imaginal rehearsal strategies.

Evaluating the Effectiveness of a Model

Form vs. Outcome.   One challenge for the instructor or clinician who must often evaluate the effectiveness of a model is determining whether poor skill reproduction is due to inadequate processing of the salient information or to a lack of motor skill development. Indeed, Scully and Newell (1985) warn that evaluating a model's effectiveness solely on the basis of whether the goal of the movement is achieved can provide misleading information, because "observers can pick up information from a demonstration that cannot be immediately realized in producing or mimicking the appropriate action" (p. 183).

Scully and Newell suggest that evaluating the level of control and coordination used to reproduce the skill is a better method of assessing the model's effectiveness than simply recording the score achieved by the performer. This may be why some investigators interested in modeling effects have had different results depending on whether they evaluated movement form or outcome (Feltz, 1982; McCullagh, 1987; McCullagh, Stiehl, & Weiss, 1990). Assessing the form of movement as well as its outcome is an important aspect of several recently published modeling studies (Carroll & Bandura, 1990; Meany, 1994; Weiss, Ebbeck & Rose, 1992).

> Measuring the level of control and coordination used to reproduce the skill is a better method of evaluating a model's effectiveness than considering outcome alone.

The type of performance measurement used should also be an important consideration for practitioners who work with a variety of individuals with disabling conditions. A better way to assess the progress of a patient during rehabilitation may be to evaluate form and obtain standard outcome-based measures.

Performance vs. Learning.   A model's effectiveness may also hinge on whether the observer is asked simply to recognize the correct performance or to recall it from memory without any cues being provided. Similarly, certain characteristics of the modeled performance, such as

FIGURE 9.2 The use of a visual model combined with verbal rehearsal proved to be the most effective means of teaching younger children (5–7 years) a sequence of fundamental motor skills.

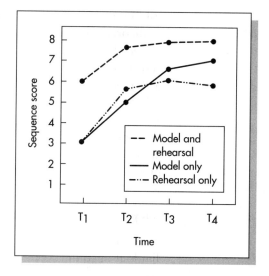

the model's status and his or her similarity to the observer, appear to influence only the quality of the immediate *performance,* not the overall *learning* of the skill (McCullagh, 1986; 1987). You will recall from our discussion of these two terms in Chapter 6 that it is inappropriate to use them interchangeably. Learning, unlike performance, leads to a relatively permanent change in a performer's motor behavior.

In evaluating the influence of verbal cueing and rehearsal on performance and learning, Weiss et al. (1992) recently found that developmental differences exist when the type of model and verbal rehearsal strategies used are evaluated on the basis of immediate performance and later recall. A group of older children (8–10 years) who were provided with a "show and tell" model and verbal rehearsal achieved better performance during early performance trials, whereas those children who watched a visual model only, or such a model combined with rehearsal, performed equally as well in later performance and learning trials. Conversely, the use of a visual model combined with verbal rehearsal proved to be the most effective means of teaching younger children (5–7 years) how to perform a sequence of fundamental motor skills. The results of this study are illustrated in Figure 9.2.

THEORETICAL EXPLANATIONS OF THE MODELING EFFECT

How is it that we are able to learn so much simply by watching someone else physically perform a skill? This question has generated considerable controversy in the past decade and has prompted a number of studies exploring the role of observation in the acquisition of specific behaviors. Two very different theoretical frameworks have guided these research efforts: Bandura's social learning theory (1977; 1986) and, more recently, a direct perception approach (Newell, Morris, & Scully, 1985; Scully & Newell, 1985; Scully, 1986). Social learning theory attempts to explain how an observer processes the information provided by a model, whereas direct perception theory has been used to identify what type of information is being extracted by an observer. Let's look at the major theoretical assumptions underlying each theory and at their contributions to our present understanding of observational learning.

Social Learning Theory

Although Bandura originally developed a theory that was intended to describe how individuals acquire social skills and behavior through observation, it has since been applied to the motor skills domain (Carroll & Bandura, 1982; 1985; 1990). Central to social learning theory is the idea that both the performance and the acquisition of modeled skills are mediated by cognition. Specifically, four subprocesses are believed to govern skill acquisition. These are attention, retention, motor reproduction, and motivation. The observer extracts the dynamic pattern of the modeled action by selectively attending to certain spatial and temporal features of the skill being modeled. This information is then transformed by the observer into a cognitive representation.

> Central to social learning theory is the idea that the performance and learning of modeled skills are mediated by cognition.

According to social learning theory, the observer uses this cognitive representation to guide his or her first attempts at reproducing the movement skill. It also serves as a perceptual reference against which to judge the correctness of the ongoing performance so that errors can be corrected. Finally, motivational mechanisms facilitate the initial processing of the modeled information by raising both the level of attention directed to the modeled performance and the desire to retain the information presented. For the past two decades, the majority of research findings related to observational learning have been interpreted in terms of this theoretical framework.

Direct Perception Approach

An alternative approach to the study of observational learning has been proposed on the basis of research conducted in the area of visual perception of motion (Cutting & Proffitt, 1982; Johansson, von Hofsten,

& Jansson, 1980). The goal of this research was to discover what type of information was being detected by the observers during a modeled action. Using a point-light technique, whereby only an individual's joints were visible to the observer, investigators found that observers were able to identify not only the type of movement pattern represented, such as walking or cycling (Johansson, 1971), but also whether they were viewing a human or a wooden puppet (Johansson, 1976), a male or a female (Barclay, Cutting, & Kozlowski, 1978; Cutting, 1978) or an acquaintance or themselves (Cutting & Kozlowski, 1977) performing the task.

The general conclusion reached on the strength of these varied research findings was that an observer is able to perceive different types of biological motion on the basis of the changing relationships between body parts as a movement is being performed. This **relative motion** of body parts constitutes the "what" being observed during the modeling of an action. These early research findings have since been cited by advocates of direct perception (Newell, Morris, & Scully, 1985; Scully & Newell, 1985; Scully, 1986) in support of their claim that modeled actions can be perceived directly from the visual display, without the need for the elaborate cognitive processing described by Bandura. The central tenets of this approach echo those of the ecological approach to perception and action that we outlined in our discussion of the visual system in Chapter 5.

> The relative motion of body parts constitutes the "what" being observed during the modeling of an action.

DISCOVERY LEARNING

So far in this chapter, we have focused on the use of dynamic models, whether skilled or initially unskilled, as the primary means of setting the stage for learning. As effective as modeling appears to be during the early stages of learning, a number of researchers have demonstrated that alternative ways of meaningfully constructing the learning environment can result in equally effective motor skill learning (Pikler, 1968; van Emmerik, den Brinker, Vereijken, & Whiting, 1989; Vereijken & Whiting, 1988). One such alternative method is discovery learning, wherein the learner is required to discover independently the optimal solution to a given movement problem. Rather than prescribing the appropriate solution for the learner through the use of a dynamic model or a detailed set of verbal instructions, the instructor constructs the learning environment in such a way that the

> In discovery learning methods, the learner attempts to discover independently the optimal solution to a movement problem.

learner is encouraged to employ a variety of different strategies, some more appropriate than others, until he or she finally discovers the best coordination pattern.

Despite the limited number of research studies investigating the merits of discovery learning, a group of researchers at the Free University in the Netherlands have provided some empirical evidence in support of this instructional method (van Emmerik, den Brinker, Vereijken, & Whiting, 1989; Vereijken & Whiting, 1988). A ski-simulation task was used in each of the studies conducted (Figure 9.3). The goal for each performer was to make large-amplitude, high-frequency, and fluent skiing movements. These were performed on a ski apparatus consisting of a platform on wheels that could be moved to the extremities of two bowed, parallel metal rails. When the performance of subjects provided with augmented feedback about critical parameters of the task (e.g., amplitude, frequency, and fluency) was compared to that of a group of discovery learning subjects following four days of training on the task, no differences were found between the groups. Indeed, the performance of the discovery learning group was superior to that of two of the feedback groups.

FIGURE 9.3 An illustration of the ski simulation task used to investigate the merits of discovery learning.

In a second study (Whiting, Bijlard, & den Brinker, 1987), the performance of subjects provided with an expert video model either during each training session or between training sessions was compared to that of subjects who were required to learn the ski-like action through discovery. Prior to training, the discovery group was informed only what movement goal was to be achieved. Following a 4-day training period, the discovery learning group performed significantly better than either of the two groups who were provided with a dynamic model.

How is it that a group of learners given very little information about a skill were able to achieve higher levels of performance than groups provided with repeated and correct demonstrations of the skill to be learned? The authors reasoned that the learners who observed the expert model naturally tried to imitate the model's movement form while also attempting to harness the external forces necessary to move the ski platform. Thus their attention was divided between two aspects of performance during training. In contrast, subjects in the discovery learning group had no preconceived idea about the most appropriate movement form to use and could devote all their attention to producing the forces needed to keep the platform moving. As a result, they were more likely to discover the inherent dynamics of the task and exploit them appropriately.

Applying the Principles of Discovery Learning

From a practical perspective, the use of discovery learning techniques in motor skills settings offers two important advantages. First, it forces the learner to explore the perceptual–motor workspace independently in search of an optimal solution to a movement problem. Second, it shifts the role of the practitioner from that of teacher to that of facilitator, as was once the case when movement education was commonly used in physical education settings. Given that infants learn many phylogenetic skills by means of discovery, it is not unreasonable to think that many ontogenetic skills can be acquired in a similar way. Just how might a practitioner structure a learning environment to promote discovery learning?

> Discovery learning can be promoted by presenting a movement problem and allowing the learner to solve it and by simplifying the learning environment.

Present a Movement Problem.   One way for an instructor to stimulate a learner's desire to discover how best to perform a movement is to pose the movement problem verbally and give a brief verbal explanation of the movement goal to be achieved. In introducing the skill of dribbling with a soccer ball, for example, the instructor might simply state that the problem is to move the ball with the foot from one end of the field to the other in such a way that a defender would find it very difficult to steal the ball away. Having outlined the movement problem to be solved, the instructor then leaves the learner to discover the most efficient method of moving the ball with the foot to achieve the goal. No set of verbal instructions and no dynamic model are provided. Following a sufficient amount of practice, the different dribbling techniques can be compared (if several learners are involved) and/or tested by introducing a defender who tries to steal the ball away. A similar approach to the teaching of motor skills is evident in the writings of George Graham and colleagues (Graham, Holt/Hale, & Parker, 1993) whose nontraditional approach to the teaching of physical education emphasizes the use of inquiry (convergent and divergent) and child-designed instructional approaches.

Simplify the Learning Environment. A second way in which an instructor can facilitate discovery learning, particularly when introducing more complex motor skills, is to simplify the learning environment. This can be accomplished by reducing the number of degrees of

Discovery learning techniques are well suited to learning to ride a bicycle.

freedom the learner must control, making it easier for the learner progressively to discover how best to perform the new movement pattern.
To illustrate how this might be possible, Vereijken (1991) describes the
skill of learning to ride a bicycle. Rather than "teaching" a child how to
ride a bicycle, which Vereijken suggests may not be possible anyway, the
instructor helps the child keep the bicycle balanced while she or he
attempts to discover first how to produce a forward movement and then
how to keep the body balanced on the bicycle at the same time. In this
way, the level of motor control required in the early stages of learning
the skill is significantly reduced while the child discovers the physical
laws governing this particular skill's execution.

SUMMARY

It is common practice to set the stage for learning by first presenting the
learner with a visual demonstration of the skill to be learned. Before
doing so, however, the practitioner should consider a number of factors.
These include the characteristics of the observer that are most likely to
influence what the observer extracts from the modeled performance and
how the observer uses that information to guide subsequent practice
attempts. The level of cognitive development influences both the
amount and the type of information extracted from the modeled performance, and the observer's level of physical and motor skill development
influences how well she or he is able to reproduce the skill physically.

Certain characteristics of the model also seem to influence how well
the skill is first performed and ultimately recalled. The need for a skilled
model does not appear to be as important as previously thought, but
the model's ability to convey adequately the strategy underlying the skill
to be learned is crucial. Augmenting the information provided by the
visual model can be extremely useful, particularly when introducing
young children to new skills. Supplementing a visual demonstration
with verbal cues that can be readily understood by the learner is particularly helpful in conveying the critical components of the skill, especially when they are readily understood by the learner. Providing the
observer who is watching a learning model with information about the
model's performance also appears to increase the effectiveness of this
type of model.

Rehearsal strategies are another way in which a learner's perception
of a modeled skill can be strengthened. This rehearsal may take the form
of verbal "self-talk" or that of imaginal (mental) rehearsal. Encouraging

young learners to rehearse modeled information verbally before practicing has proved to enhance both immediate performance and later recall of a movement skill.

When evaluating the effectiveness of a model, the practitioner must not take into account only a movement's outcome. Given that the information extracted from a modeled performance does not immediately lead to a successful movement outcome, it is important to find additional ways to measure how much the observer has benefited. Measurements designed to assess the changing levels of control and coordination demonstrated by a learner are therefore necessary when evaluating the overall effectiveness of a model.

Two very different theoretical explanations have been advanced to account for the effectiveness of modeling. The first of these (social learning theory) focuses on how the observer encodes and organizes the visually presented information. The second attempts to identify what the observer extracts from the modeled performance. Proponents of the latter theory contend that the observer directly perceives the relationships among the limbs performing the movement (e.g., relative motions) and subsequently uses this perception to guide subsequent physical attempts. Both theoretical accounts will continue to contribute to our understanding of observational learning.

An alternative technique for setting the stage for learning is the discovery learning approach. Instead of providing the learner with a visual model and thereby shaping the image of the movement to be reproduced, advocates of discovery learning construct the learning environment in such a way that the learner is encouraged to discover independently the optimal solution to a given movement problem. This technique not only shifts the responsibility for learning to the learner but also transforms the role of the instructor from prescription to facilitation.

IMPORTANT TERMINOLOGY

After completing this chapter, readers should be familiar with the following terms and concepts.

imaginal rehearsal
learning model
observational learning
relative motion
verbal rehearsal

SUGGESTED FURTHER READING

McCullagh, P. 1993. Modeling: Learning, developmental, and social psychological considerations. In *Handbook on research on sport psychology*, ed. R.N. Singer, M. Murphey, & L. Keith Tennant, pp. 106–125. New York, NY: Macmillian Publishing Co.

TEST YOUR UNDERSTANDING

1. Briefly describe the observer characteristics that have been shown to influence the effectiveness of modeling.

2. Describe three ways in which an individual's motivation to learn a new skill can be enhanced.

3. Briefly discuss the advantages and disadvantages associated with the use of (a) skilled models and (b) learning models.

4. Briefly describe the various ways in which the information provided by a model can be augmented.

5. How does the type of skill being demonstrated appear to influence a model's effectiveness?

6. Describe two types of rehearsal strategies that can be used to strengthen an observer's perception of the skill to be learned. What factors appear to influence the effectiveness of each of these two types of rehearsal strategy?

7. What variables associated with modeled performances affect the observer's performance? What variables affect the observer's learning?

8. Why is it important to measure both movement form and the outcome of movement when attempting to evaluate the effectiveness of a model?

9. Discuss the two theoretical explanations advanced to account for the modeling effect. In what fundamental way do these two explanations differ?

10. Describe an alternative teaching method that seems to promote effective learning of movement skills. Discuss the various ways in which this technique can be integrated into a learning environment.

About the Quote

Drawing on the results of point-light studies conducted in the 1970s and 1980s, Scully and Newell suggest that what observers see when they first view a model are the relative motions of the limbs involved in the movement. What are the implications of such a notion for the practitioner? One might argue that the movement being modeled should be performed in its entirety rather than in parts, thus making the relationships between the moving limbs apparent. The importance of modeling the skill at the speed at which it will be ultimately performed should also not be overlooked. In addition to advocating the use of demonstrations in the early stages of learning, Scully and Newell stress the importance of physical practice. It is through physical practice that the learner becomes able to scale the skill appropriately and acquires the control needed to achieve a satisfactory outcome. How much effort is being used to perform the skill accurately is not readily discernible by an observer. Hence practice is indispensable.

CHAPTER 10
ORGANIZING THE PRACTICE ENVIRONMENT

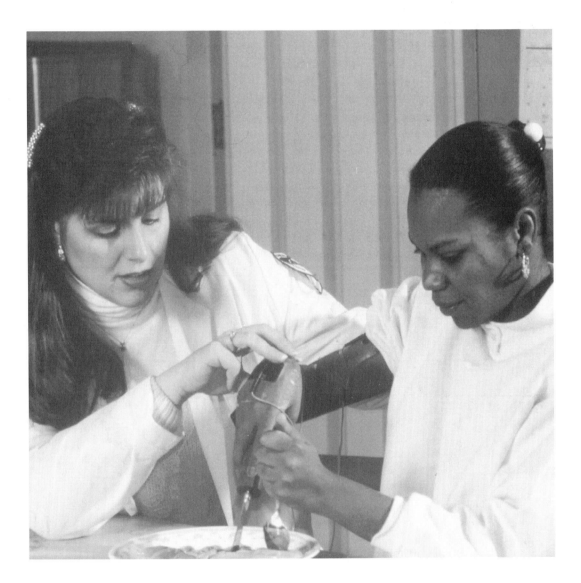

C H A P T E R
O B J E C T I V E S

- Understand and be able to describe how the environment in which a movement skill will ultimately be performed influences the way the skill should be practiced.

- Understand and be able to describe the factors that determine the type of practice schedule selected.

- Become familiar with the major theoretical explanations that have been used to explain why practice schedules that introduce high levels of cognitive effort lead to better retention and/or transfer of movement skills.

- Understand and be able to describe how the spacing of practice within and between practice sessions influences both the immediate performance and the eventual learning of different types of movement skills.

- Be able to identify a number of instructional techniques that can be used to increase the effectiveness of a practice session and help the learner reach a criterion level of mastery in a shorter time.

- Become familiar with the various methods of practicing movement skills in parts and with the variables that are likely to influence the use of these part-practice techniques.

> *"...practice, when properly undertaken, does not consist in repeating the means of solution of a motor problem time after time, but in the process of solving this problem again and again by techniques which we changed and perfected from repetition to repetition."*
>
> —Bernstein (1967)

Having set the stage for learning by introducing the movement skill to be learned, practitioners must now direct their attention to organizing a set of meaningful practice sessions for the learner. Several important decisions about the overall organization of these sessions must first be made. These issues include the length and number of practice sessions per week, the types of activities to be practiced during each session, the order in which they are to be practiced, and the time allotted to each activity. The meaningfulness of any given practice session is further enhanced by the provision of feedback that assists the learner in both identifying and correcting errors in performance. How often and in what form this feedback should be provided will be the subject of Chapter 11.

It is clear that large amounts of practice are necessary for any skill to be mastered. One has only to consider the amount of time that professional athletes continue to spend practicing during a competitive season to realize the importance of regular practice, even after a skill has been initially mastered. Although the amount of time spent practicing a skill or sequence of movements is important, the quality of that practice must not be overlooked. Practice sessions that are relatively short but of high quality generally foster more effective learning than practice sessions that are long and unstructured. What are the necessary ingredients for a high-quality practice session?

> Learning is facilitated by a practice environment that requires the learner to apply different movement parameters to a skill during practice.

STRUCTURING THE PRACTICE SESSION

One of the more important factors to consider in structuring each practice session is the nature of the environment in which the skill is ultimately to be performed. Knowing what environmental demands and/or constraints a learner can expect to encounter during the performance situation makes the task of structuring a meaningful practice environment considerably easier. At one end of the continuum lies a performance environment characterized by stability, whereas the performance environment at the other end is unpredictable and therefore highly variable. In Chapter 1, we discussed stable and variable environments as they influence the demands placed on motor control. We will now consider the role of the performance environment in shaping the structure of practice sessions.

Variability of Practice

One major prediction emerging from schema theory (Chapter 6) is related to the importance of **practice variability.** Schmidt (1975) predicted that practicing a variety of different ways to perform a skill during a practice session would provide the learner with a broader range of movement experiences on which to base the development of a set of rules for action (i.e., movement schemas). For example, structuring a practice environment that gives the learner an opportunity to apply different parameters of a movement skill is considered an effective means of facilitating learning. Thus a learner may practice throwing a ball at targets of different sizes placed at increasingly longer distances from a throwing line, or may practice hitting objects of different sizes that are pitched at different speeds, over the course of a number of practice trials.

Constructing a practice environment that introduces a large amount of variability has been shown to be particularly effective for young children attempting to learn skills that will ultimately be performed in variable performance environments (Shapiro & Schmidt, 1982). In these types of performance situations, it is unlikely that a movement will be performed in exactly the same way twice in succession. The benefits of practice variability are thought to be even greater when learners are required to perform a skill they have not previously practiced, because this type of practice environment promotes **generalizability.** You will recall from Chapter 6 that the ability to generalize, or transfer, the knowledge acquired in learning one skill or practice situation to a second skill or practice context is perhaps the single most important outcome of learning.

Promoting variability of practice in a clinical setting is also likely to benefit the patient in light of our discussion related to generalizability. Unlike the carefully structured environment in which the task of walking is practiced during rehabilitation (which includes parallel bars, stable surfaces, and quiet corridors), the real-world context in which the task will ultimately be performed is very different. Introducing opportunities for patients to practice walking over a variety of different surfaces, in crowded corridors, and while conversing with a second person will better prepare them to return to their former living environments. Also unlike the clinical setting, where a patient is able to perform a task at a self-determined speed, in daily contexts certain external constraints will be imposed on performance of the task (crossing the road in traffic is a good example). Practice that requires patients to manipulate all the various movement patterns of the same task (such as velocity, force, and direction) should also improve their ability to generalize across settings.

Although the findings of a number of research studies provide support for the use of variable practice techniques in the learning of a variety of different movement skills, the practitioner must decide *when* it is appropriate to begin introducing variability into the practice setting. Should practice variability be introduced at the outset of learning or should some initial practice precede its introduction? A review of Gentile's (1972) model of motor learning, which we looked at in Chapter 6, provides a partial answer to this question. Recall that during the first stage of learning, the goal for the learner is to understand better how to perform a particular skill. During the second stage of learning, the goal changes to one of either fixating or diversifying the movement pattern, depending on the type of movement environment in which it will be performed.

Two guiding principles for the practitioner emerge from Gentile's model. The first is that variability of practice should not be introduced until the learner understands the dynamics of the task. Consistent practice of the desired movement pattern may better foster this early understanding of the skill. Second, according to Gentile, the type of variability that should be introduced will differ with the type of skill being learned and the environment in which it will ultimately be performed. For example, the pattern of coordination being learned for hitting a ball will eventually be performed within the context of a tennis or racquetball game. Varying that pattern should be an integral component of any practice session once the learner has acquired a global understanding of the skill's dynamics. Recall that Gentile refers to those factors that directly influence the way a skill is executed as the regulatory conditions. This type of practice variability can be introduced by manipulating variables such as distance, angle, and direction of the stroke during the practice of these skills. By doing this, the instructor can increase the repertoire of possible actions available to the performer in a game situation.

> Practice variability should not be introduced until the learner understands the dynamics of the skill to be learned.

On the other hand, skills that must be performed with a high level of movement consistency in stable environments (e.g., platform diving and gymnastics vaulting) are less well suited to being practiced in a variety of different ways. What *should* be varied during the practice of many of these movement skills is the context in which the skill is practiced, or the nonregulatory conditions. For example, a gymnast must learn to perform a skill or routine in a competition while other performers are simultaneously performing their own routines. The situation is rendered even more potentially distracting by music being played nearby for another gymnast who is performing a floor routine. Opportunities to practice while these nonregulatory conditions are manipulated will better prepare the athlete for the final performance situation. In performance situations similar to this one, then, it is the factors *not* related to movement (e.g., presence of other performers and crowd noise) that should be varied during practice.

> Regulatory conditions are factors that directly influence the way in which a skill is executed.

ORGANIZING THE PRACTICE SCHEDULE

The previous discussion clearly indicates the importance of organizing a practice environment that engages the learner or patient in practicing variations of a movement task, particularly for those skills that will ultimately be performed in variable performance environments. The next step for the practitioner is to decide exactly *how* this variability should be organized. Fortunately, the issue of how best to schedule practice variability in movement skill settings has been systematically investigated by Magill and colleagues, in particular, over the past decade (Lee & Magill, 1983; Magill & Hall, 1990; Lee, Magill, & Weeks, 1985). In the next section, we will review their work and consider its implications for constructing practice sessions.

> **Nonregulatory conditions are external factors that are not directly related to the performance of the skill.**

Introducing Interference

Contextual interference (CI) is functional interference introduced into a practice situation as a result of several movement skills being practiced at once. As we noted in Chapter 8, introducing high levels of interference into a practice setting is believed to enhance the learner's ability to remember skill-related information. Certainly Battig (1972, 1977) found this to be the case when the concept was applied to the learning of verbal skills. The level of contextual interference present in a movement skill setting has been effectively manipulated by altering the type of practice schedule adopted (e.g., blocked vs. random). In the case of a **blocked practice** schedule, the learner practices multiple variations of a skill, but each variation is practiced for a given period of time before the next variation is introduced. For example, during the course of a volleyball unit, a group of learners may practice setting a volleyball for 10 minutes, then work on bumping techniques for the same period of time, and practice spiking in the final 10 minutes of a 30-minute practice session.

> **Contextual interference is functional interference introduced into a practice situation as a result of practicing multiple movement skills.**

Conversely, practicing according to a **random practice** schedule requires that the performer practice each of the skill variations in random order. Let us consider the same three volleyball skills to illustrate how this type of practice schedule differs from a blocked practice schedule. When the same 30-minute practice session is organized according to a random practice schedule, a learner may practice the setting technique followed by the volleyball spike and the bumping technique on three consecutive practice attempts, and the order in which the skills are practiced constantly changes throughout the practice session. In this latter practice situation, the learner does not practice the same skill for any length of time, as was the case in a blocked practice schedule. This random presentation of skills ensures that the level of CI introduced is

> **The level of contextual interference is highest when a random practice schedule is used.**

considerably higher than that introduced when skills are practiced according to a blocked practice schedule.

Influencing Factors

What factors should a practitioner consider when deciding how much CI is appropriate for a given practice situation? In a recent review of CI research findings, Magill and Hall (1990) identified three important factors that affect the degree to which the practice schedule chosen influences how well a skill is retained and then later recalled. These include task-related characteristics, learner characteristics, and whether we measure performance or measure learning and/or transfer. We will first consider how the characteristics of the task to be learned influence whether the positive recall effects associated with random practice schedules are observed.

Task-Related Characteristics.   The beneficial learning effects of practice schedules that promote high levels of contextual interference have been repeatedly observed when multiple tasks that require *different* patterns of coordination are practiced (Lee & Magill, 1983; Poto, French, & Magill, 1987; Shea & Zimny, 1988). Conversely, when only the parameters (such as movement, speed and amplitude) of a movement task that involves the *same* pattern of coordination are manipulated, the learning-related benefits of these same practice schedules are less evident (Poto et al., 1988; experiment 2). In laboratory settings, different coordination patterns have been created using multisegment barrier tasks that require subjects to practice knocking barriers down according to different spatial patterns displayed. In one of the few non-laboratory settings in which the positive recall effects of a random practice schedule have been observed, three different types of badminton serves were practiced (short, long, and drive serves). Each of these different serving techniques involves subtle variations in the pattern of coordination required (Goode & Magill, 1986).

> The beneficial learning effects of random practice schedules are observed more often when multiple skills that require different patterns of coordination are practiced.

The fact that random practice does not yield learning benefits in situations where only the parameters of a particular set of skills were manipulated during the acquisition phase has been primarily interpreted within the framework of the generalized motor program (GMP) concept first developed and subsequently modified by Schmidt (1975; 1982; 1988). According to Magill and Hall, only those skill variations that are controlled by *different motor programs,* as opposed to the same underlying motor program, will benefit from a random practice schedule. The authors concluded that the same motor program was being used to guide the execution of each skill practiced if "the relative timing, sequence of events, and/or spatial configurations remained constant across the skill variations that were practiced" (p. 254).

Learner Characteristics. Several characteristics of the learner also appear to influence whether practicing skill variations in situations of high contextual interference positively influences the retention and subsequent transfer of skill-related information to other movement skill settings. These learner-related characteristics include age, level of experience, intellectual capacity, and learning style.

Age. It is difficult to assess fully the influence of age as it relates to the contextual interference issue, because so few studies have been conducted in which the age of the subject has been manipulated. Of the few studies reported in which age was manipulated, the findings are somewhat mixed. Edwards, Elliott, and Lee (1986) demonstrated superior learning among young children (e.g., 5–8 years) who practiced variations of an anticipation timing task according to a random practice schedule, but some other authors either found no differences in learning to exist as a function of the practice schedule used or found that blocked practice schedules led to superior learning effects (Del Rey, Whitehurst, Wughalter,& Barnwell, 1983; Pigott & Shapiro, 1984).

Level of Experience. Del Rey and colleagues (Del Rey, 1989; Del Rey, Wughalter, & Whitehurst, 1982; Del Rey, Whitehurst, & Wood, 1983) have conducted a series of experiments designed to investigate the relationship between previous movement skill experience and practice schedules that incorporate high contextual interference. The authors reasoned that novice performers who have had little exposure to the types of skills being learned or to the kind of perceptual processing involved would not benefit from random practice schedules as much as a group of more advanced performers. This is not an unreasonable claim in view of our discussion in Chapter 6 of the stages of learning. Recall that learners in the first stage of learning are, among other things, struggling simply to understand the idea of the movement to be learned (Gentile, 1972). As a result, they engage in arduous cognitive processing of the task's demands at one level (Fitts, 1964), while at a second level attempting to "freeze" the many degrees of freedom available to them by constraining multiple joints to act together (Bernstein, 1967). Given that this account was intended to describe what learners attempt to do during the first stage of learning a *single*

> Learners who are limited in their experience with related skills, or with movement settings in general, may not benefit from random practice schedules.

movement pattern, one can only imagine how much more difficult these various operations would be if multiple skill variations were being practiced concurrently!

The predictions of Del Rey and colleagues have been partially supported by their own work and that of other authors who also argue that random practice schedules may be inappropriate for learners until they better understand the demands of a particular skill (Goode, 1986; Goode & Wei, 1988). In one particularly interesting study, Goode and Wei introduced a third type of practice condition that combined blocked and random practice schedules. A group of inexperienced females, unfamiliar with sport skills performed in variable environments, began practicing an anticipation timing skill according to a blocked practice schedule before switching to a random schedule of practice. The results of a transfer test indicated that this mixed practice schedule promoted the best performance. From a practical perspective, these findings suggest the need for practitioners to consider a learner's past experience with related movement skills, or with movement settings in general, when deciding how best to organize practice sessions for optimal learning and transfer.

Intellectual Capacity. Although very little research has been directed to exploring the effectiveness of random practice for individuals who have impaired intellectual capacity, Edwards and colleagues (Edwards, Elliott, & Lee, 1986) compared the effectiveness of blocked and random practice schedules for a group of adolescents with Down syndrome who were learning three variations of an anticipation timing task. Although age-matched control subjects who did not have Down syndrome and who practiced according to a random practice schedule benefited more than a second group of control subjects who practiced according to a blocked schedule, random and blocked practice schedules produced similar levels of learning among the adolescents with Down syndrome. Thus the superiority of a random practice environment was not established for these learners.

In order for individuals with reduced intellectual capacity to benefit from practice schedules that introduce high levels of contextual interference, it may be necessary to provide mixed practice schedules similar to those used in earlier studies (Goode & Wei, 1988). Additional research is clearly needed before definitive recommendations can be made with respect to the most effective practice schedules to use when teaching variations of a skill to individuals with reduced intellectual capacity.

Learning Style. The degree to which a learner exhibits either a reflective or an impulsive cognitive style, particularly in the performance of skills that require both speed and accuracy, has recently been explored as it relates to the contextual interference effect (Jelsma & Pieters, 1989; Jelsma & Van Merrienboer, 1989). These authors predicted that a learner exhibiting an impulsive cognitive style who is asked to perform a task as quickly and accurately as possible will tend to ignore the accuracy component in favor of speed. Conversely, the more reflective learner is more likely to place the importance of being accurate above that of being fast. The authors further reasoned that reflective learners would benefit more from practice schedules incorporating high levels of contextual interference than would more impulsive learners. Whereas random practice schedules require high levels of problem solving and therefore greater reflection, blocked schedules require no such reflection. The results of both a retention test and a transfer test provided support for the authors' predictions. The reflective learners benefited more from random practice schedules than learners characterized as impulsive. Although more research is needed in this area, the cognitive style of a learner would appear to be yet another variable that is likely to influence the effectiveness of certain practice schedules.

> Random practice schedules require higher levels of problem solving and greater reflection than blocked schedules.

Measurement of Performance or of Learning and/or Transfer.   If the effectiveness of random practice schedules had to be evaluated on the basis of testing the performance of a group of learners at the conclusion of a single practice session, instructors would probably abandon this type of practice immediately. Their decision would be based on seeing a set of performance results similar to those illustrated in Figure 10.1. These results clearly demonstrate significantly better performance for a group of learners who practiced according to a blocked practice schedule (e.g., low contextual interference) than for a second group of learners who practiced according to a random practice schedule (e.g., high contextual interference).

However, when the same two groups of learners are compared again at a later time, perhaps at the start of the next practice session, their respective performances are quite different. In contrast to the earlier performance results, the results of a retention test (illustrated on the righthand side of the same graph) indicate that the performance of the random practice group on the same movement skill is now superior to that demonstrated by the blocked practice group. How can we account for this rather dramatic reversal in performance? The answer appears to lie in whether it is performance or learning that is being

> Practicing according to a blocked schedule has been shown to produce superior performance but inferior learning and/or transfer.

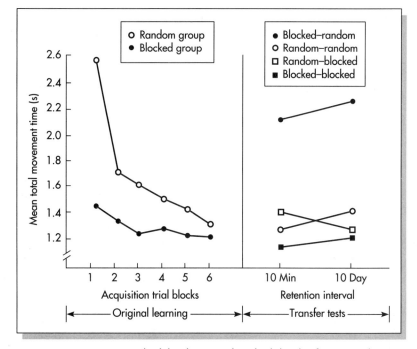

FIGURE 10.1 Practice schedules that introduce high levels of contextual interference appear to affect performance adversely but lead to superior retention of the skill.

measured. You will recall from our discussion in Chapter 7 that retention tests, performed in the absence of feedback and administered some time after completion of practice, are assumed to measure the more permanent learning effects. Performers practicing under the more difficult random practice conditions do not exhibit the same quality of performance, even though they are developing a better understanding of the skill itself. But when they are asked to perform the skill again after a period of rest, and in the absence of any feedback about their performance, the greater benefits of the more difficult practice schedule become evident.

The same is not true for the blocked practice group, who in some retention situations actually perform more poorly than they did right after the first practice session. The superior performance of the random practice group is also evident when the results of transfer tests are considered. In these tests, the learner is required to perform a new variation of the skill not previously practiced.

Two theoretical explanations for this CI effect have been described in the literature and will be the topic of the next section in this chapter.

THEORETICAL ACCOUNTS OF THE CONTEXTUAL INTERFERENCE EFFECT

Practice schedules that introduce high levels of contextual interference into the practice setting have been repeatedly shown to enhance the learning of a skill among adults, even though the benefits are not readily apparent during the practice session itself. Two very different explanations have been developed to identify the type of cognitive processing that produces the contextual interference effect. The first of these, the **elaboration view,** draws on many of the concepts described in the levels-of-processing framework that was originally developed by Craik and Lockhart (1972) and that we discussed in Chapter 8. The early ideas of Battig (1972; 1979) related to intertask transfer in verbal learning situations are also encompassed within this theoretical viewpoint. The second explanation, which has been called the **action-plan reconstruction view,** is strongly influenced by motor program theory. We will begin by outlining the major assumptions of the elaboration view.

Elaboration View

According to the elaboration view, individuals who practice according to a random practice schedule engage in a variety of cognitive processing activities that have the net effect of making the task-related information more distinctive. These multiple processing strategies ensure that the memory representation is also more elaborate, because the information is more "deeply" processed in memory. The learner who practices in conditions of high contextual interference is thought to store all of the variations of the task simultaneously in working memory. This makes the processing more difficult for the learner, but it also provides the opportunity to compare and contrast the different versions during practice. The resulting memory representation for each variation is therefore more distinctive and more likely to be recalled at a later time. In contrast, the learner who practices according to a blocked practice schedule has no opportunity to engage in such complex processing, because only one variation of the skill is stored in working memory.

> The multiple processing strategies engaged in during random practice ensure that the memory representation is elaborately processed in memory.

The intuitive logic encompassed in this viewpoint has had great appeal for researchers seeking a theoretical explanation for the contextual interference effect. As a result, a number of research findings have been interpreted according to this view (Shea & Morgan, 1979; Shea & Zimny, 1983, 1988; Wright, 1988).

Action-Plan Reconstruction View

An alternative explanation for the contextual interference effect has been advanced by Lee and Magill (1983; 1985). These authors argue that learners involved in random practice are required to regenerate the plan of action each time that particular variation is presented. It is thought to be necessary to regenerate, or reconstruct, the plan because the previous plan is temporarily forgotten between practice attempts. For example, plan A is formulated for task variation A but is needed for only one practice trial. Plan B must then be formulated for task variation B, which is being practiced on the very next trial. Plan C must then be formulated for practicing the third variation of the task. As a result of forgetting plan A in the interim, the learner is forced to regenerate the plan when task A is practiced again. A similar type of regeneration process has been proposed by Cuddy and Jacoby (1982), who compared the recall abilities of two groups of children who practiced solving mathematical problems according to a random or a blocked practice format. They also found that children who practiced in conditions of high contextual interference demonstrated superior recall at a later time.

> Because of forgetting, the plan of action must be continually reconstructed each time the skill variation is presented.

SPACING/DISTRIBUTION OF PRACTICE

Another issue that arises for the practitioner designing an instructional unit in physical education or a rehabilitation program for a patient is how to space or distribute practice for optimal learning. The practitioner not only must decide how many practice sessions to schedule each week but also must determine how practice will be temporally distributed in any given practice session. This second type of scheduling has attracted considerable interest among experimental psychologists and motor learning researchers. The effects of two very different types of practice schedules have been investigated over the years. In **distributed practice,** the amount of time that the learner is resting between practice attempts during any given practice session is equal to or greater than the amount of time that the learner is engaged in the practice of the movement skill. In **massed practice,** the amount of time that the learner is engaged in practicing a movement skill during any given practice session is considerably greater than the amount of time devoted to rest.

Although a number of research studies have been conducted to determine which practice schedule leads to better performance and learning, little consensus has been reached among researchers. Whereas some authors conclude that the massing of practice negatively affects both performance and learning (Oxendine, 1984; Schmidt, 1988), others argue that the negative effects of massed practice schedules are confined to performance (Adams, 1987; Magill, 1993; Singer, 1980).

Why do motor learning researchers appear to be so divided on this issue? In a recent review article devoted to the topic, Lee and Genovese (1988) suggest that the lack of consensus is largely due to the different measures that researchers have chosen to assess learning. These have included the use of an absolute retention score that reflects performance on a retention and/or transfer test and relative retention measures that consider performance on a retention test relative to performance at the end of the acquisition phase. (We discussed both types of retention scores in Chapter 7.) Unfortunately, a relative retention score is not considered a pure measure of learning, because it is calculated by using a performance-related value as well as a retention test score. This procedure is therefore considered to produce "contaminated" data (Salmoni, Schmidt, & Walter, 1984).

> The lack of consensus about which practice distribution schedule is best for learning is largely due to the different retention scores used by researchers.

As a result of the review they conducted, Lee and Genovese (1988) concluded that "distributed practice is beneficial to both the performance and learning of motor skills, although the effect on performance is greater than the effect on learning" (p. 282). In their final discussion, the authors raise one point of potential interest to the practitioner that no doubt partly accounts for the conclusion. It involves the type of task that has been commonly used to investigate the spacing-of-practice effects observed. Lee and Genovese point out that in almost all the research studies devoted to this issue, the type of task used has been exclusively continuous—that is, one that has no definite beginning and end (e.g., pursuit tracking). Given that these tasks are, by their very nature, more likely to result in increasing fatigue if continuously practiced without rest, it is perhaps not surprising that the superior beneficial effects of distributed practice compared with massed practice are more evident in immediate performance than after a rest interval.

As Figure 10.2 shows, once the effects of fatigue associated with practicing a continuous task according to the more demanding massed practice schedule have dissipated, the two different practice groups exhibit very little difference in quality of performance. The fact that two studies (Carron, 1969; Lee & Genovese, 1988) using a discrete skill produced quite different performance and learning effects from those observed when a continuous task was employed suggest that the effects of a massed or a distributed practice schedule on performance and learning vary as a function of the skill to be learned.

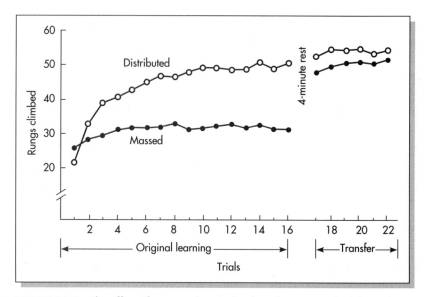

FIGURE 10.2　The effect of a massed vs. a distributed practice schedule on the performance and learning of a continuous ladder-climbing skill.

Practical Implications

The collective results of the studies just described are thought-provoking. They suggest a need to consider the characteristics of the learner, the type of skill that is to be learned, and the goal of the practice session when deciding how best to organize the practice schedule temporally. For example, massed and distributed practice may be equally effective for the learning of discrete skills such as free-throw shooting, batting, and a variety of daily activities that involve discrete movements. The goal of the practice session will also strongly influence the type of practice schedule chosen. If the goal for the session is to provide the learner with as much practice as possible and the quality of the performance is not an issue, then a massed practice schedule is preferable. Conversely, if a quality practice session is the goal, then a more distributed type of practice should be chosen. This may be a very appropriate strategy for the last practice before an important game or tournament as a means of creating a positive mental attitude in the players.

> When choosing a practice distribution schedule, it is important to consider the learner, the type of skill to be learned, and the goal of the practice session.

Although the research evidence suggests that both practice schedules may prove equally effective in promoting learning, particularly when the skill being learned is discrete, the decision may not be quite so simple for practitioners. They generally teach much more complex skills than those used in laboratory research, and they teach these skills to more diverse groups of learners (e.g., young children, recovering patients, and persons with disabilities) and under conditions that often impose many more constraints (e.g., a fixed number and/or length of practice sessions). The practitioner must consider each of these factors when deciding how best to organize each practice session temporally. Let us consider some practical examples to illustrate the importance of these additional factors.

When first analyzing the movement skill that will be introduced to a particular group of learners, the practitioner must consider, among other things, both the complexity and the energy demands associated with the skill being introduced. This analysis is particularly important for skills that are more dangerous to perform and will render the performer vulnerable to injury if practiced in conditions that promote high levels of fatigue (e.g., massed practice). For example, certain gymnastics and diving skills, although discrete by classification, are extremely complex and often require high levels of energy to perform. To minimize the chance of injury to the athlete, a coach is likely to choose a more distributed practice schedule, even though a massed practice schedule has been shown to be equally effective in promoting learning.

A similar decision to use a more distributed practice schedule may be wise when a complex motor skill is first being introduced to a group of novice performers. During the early practice sessions, novices are initially preoccupied with learning how to perform the skill. In these situations, a massed practice schedule may be counterproductive because it allows very little time for the learner to process the skill-related information. A massed practice schedule may be implemented once the performer achieves a certain level of proficiency or with more skilled performers who will benefit from more continuous practice. The decision to use a distributed rather than a massed practice schedule, regardless of the type of movement skill being practiced, may also be warranted in a clinical setting when the practitioner is working with recovering patients who are already highly susceptible to fatigue.

The fact that the relearning of certain activities requires considerable cognitive effort on the part of the patient may also lead the therapist to choose a distributed practice schedule. Such a schedule gives patients more time between practice attempts to process the sensory feedback they derived from performing the skill and any additional feedback provided by the therapist. A massed practice schedule, which limits the amount of rest between practice attempts, would offer little time for this type of reflection. The need to maintain the motivation of the patient during the rehabilitation process may also dictate the type of practice schedule. Although a massed practice schedule provides a greater amount of practice time, the fact that the quality of an individual's performance is likely to decline as the session progresses may result in increasing levels of frustration for the patient during the practice session.

TECHNIQUES FOR ENHANCING THE EFFECTIVENESS OF PRACTICE

Although a large amount of practice is necessary for successful learning, practice in and of itself is not sufficient for the majority of individuals trying to learn or relearn a particular pattern of movement. Fortunately, a number of instructional techniques can be used to increase the effectiveness of any practice session and help the learner reach a criterion level of mastery in a shorter period of time. These techniques may take many forms: verbal instruction, videotape replays of performance, physical guidance, and/or instrumentation designed to amplify a performer's own level of sensory feedback. The next section of this chapter is devoted to a discussion of the utility of each of these techniques in a variety of learning environments.

Guidance Techniques

A number of different practice techniques are available that are designed to help learners acquire a certain movement pattern with a minimum of error. These **guidance techniques** range in strength from intermittent verbal cues provided to a learner to assist him in recalling the steps of a new dance routine to mechanical performance aids such as harnesses designed to prevent a gymnast from injuring herself as she practices a difficult somersault or a patient from falling during the early stages of a balance retraining program. In the absence of these often expensive mechanical devices, an instructor or therapist may physically guide the limbs of a learner through an entire movement pattern or a portion of it. When teaching a child how to perform a forehand tennis stroke, for example, the instructor may stand behind the performer and guide the hitting limb through the desired movement trajectory. During the warm-up before a gymnastics meet, a coach may act as a spotter in the corner of the floor exercise mat and briefly make physical contact with the gymnast's back during the first rotation of a double somersault. This brief moment of physical contact may help the gymnast impart just a little more vertical lift during the rotation, or it may simply provide psy-

Physical guidance may be used during the early stages of learning to convey the general idea of a movement pattern.

chological support during certain maneuvers that the gymnast has previously found difficult to complete successfully.

In clinical settings, physical guidance is regularly used to assist a patient in a variety of different ways. In Bobath's (1965; 1978) neurodevelopmental treatment approach, particular handling techniques are used to guide the patient toward a more nearly normal movement pattern in the early stages of rehabilitation. Physical guidance techniques can also be useful for patients who lack confidence in their ability to perform certain activities or suffer from impaired vision and/or hearing. In these situations, a therapist's supportive touch can reduce the patient's anxiety or provide an important means of communication. In general, the use of physical guidance techniques in clinical settings is predicated on the assumption that compensatory or abnormal movement patterns must be eliminated as soon as possible during the relearning of movement patterns. Therefore, therapists often use physical guidance during the cognitive phase of learning (see Chapter 6).

Although the use of physical guidance clearly has many positive effects on the early performance of a new and often complex movement pattern, the general view among motor learning researchers (Annett, 1959) is that such techniques do little to promote movement skill learning and often result in undesirable dependence on the individual providing the guidance. Schmidt (1991) attributes the ineffectiveness of physical guidance as a learning tool to the fact that it does not enable the learner to experience errors during practice. As a result, the learner fails to develop the necessary error detection and correction skills that will be needed for success in later performance situations where guidance is no longer available. In a discussion of treatment strategies designed to improve a patient's motor control, O'Sullivan (1988) further concludes that the "key to success in manually guided movements is knowing when to remove support and to let the patient move independently" (p. 270). In order for learning to occur, individuals must engage in active movement so as to benefit from the rich sources of intrinsic sensory feedback available to them (such as somatosensation and audition). Passively driven movements tend to eliminate and/or distort the quality of these intrinsic sensations.

> Physical guidance techniques, though useful for learners who lack confidence, do little to promote movement skill in learning.

If physical guidance does little to promote learning, then why is it used at all? Used intermittently, physical guidance can successfully convey the general idea of a movement pattern not previously experienced. Although the use of modeling techniques can often provide the same information, individuals with visual impairments are much less likely to benefit from a modeled performance. Other learners may simply be unable to derive enough clues from a visual model or set of verbal instructions on which to base their first few practice attempts. Recall that one of the important variables influencing model effectiveness is the degree to which the underlying strategy of the to-be-learned movement pattern is evident to the learner. In these situations, physical guidance can serve such a function.

A second value of physical guidance that has already been mentioned is psychological in nature. Manual guidance, if progressively withdrawn, can be extremely effective in helping a learner overcome any initial fears related to an activity. Feltz (1982) demonstrated the effectiveness of physical guidance in helping a child overcome his fear of diving into a pool head first. No doubt many of us can remember a time when this same activity caused us much nervousness. In fact, physical guidance techniques are still commonly used during the early stages of learning this complex skill. Finally, physical guidance in some form is recommended during the early stages of learning skills that may lead to injury if performed incorrectly. A number of gymnastics maneuvers and diving techniques could not be safely taught if mechanical aids were not at first available as a means of constraining the movement pattern and thereby simplifying the learning environment.

Whole-Task vs. Part-Task Practice Strategies

A question that has often proved difficult for the researcher and practitioner to answer is whether it is better for the learner to practice the entire movement pattern from the outset or to practice it in parts until each one has been thoroughly learned. Although part-task practice simplifies the practice environment for the learner, there is some concern that this type of practice will prevent the learner from acquiring a fluent pattern of coordination. To further complicate the issue, a number of research studies have produced equivocal results. The different findings have once again been largely attributed to the type of task used to investigate the issue (Naylor & Briggs, 1963; Stammers, 1982; Wightman & Lintern, 1985).

Nature of the Skill.   What is it about certain movement skills that makes part-task training effective or ineffective? Naylor and Briggs (1963) suggest that the inherent complexity (e.g., the number of components involved) and organization (e.g., the extent to which the components are interrelated) of a given

> The inherent complexity and organization of a skill determine whether part-task practice is appropriate.

movement skill largely determines whether part-task practice is appropriate. For example, movements such as a dance or a gymnastics floor routine, which comprise many individual skills that are simply combined to form a new movement sequence, are considered high in complexity but low in organization. Accordingly, the authors consider these movement skills well suited to part-task practice.

Conversely, movement skills that are much less complex but are highly organized in terms of their component parts are better suited to whole-task practice methods. Two examples of such skills are hitting a baseball and locomotion. Both skills comprise components that are temporally linked, in particular (e.g., the backward-swing and forward-swing components in hitting). As simple as it would seem to be to recommend part-task or whole-task practice on the basis of this simple formula, a closer look at the relationship between these two characteristics of a skill complicates the decision. For example, what type of practice is best in the case of skills that are both high in complexity and high in organization? Serving a tennis ball and serving a volleyball by using an overhead motion might be good examples of such skills.

Capabilities of the Learner.   In deciding whether to implement part-task or whole-task practice methods, a practitioner must also consider the capabilities of the learner. It is likely that a novice performer who has little or no experience of the skill being introduced—or of motor skill settings in general—will not benefit from practicing the entire skill. In these practice situations, the higher demands placed on the learner from a processing and control standpoint may actually hinder the learning of the skill. Partitioning a skill into meaningful parts that are practiced first alone and then in combination may be a more suitable practice method to employ in the case of inexperienced performers.

> The extent to which a skill is partitioned can be significantly reduced if the learner has already mastered any prerequisite skills or abilities.

Of course, the extent to which a skill must be partitioned during the early stages of learning a new movement skill can be significantly reduced if the learner has already mastered any of the prerequisite skills that invariably precede more complex skills. For example, a learner who has not yet mastered the skills of dribbling and shooting in basketball will find it extremely difficult to perform the more complex lay-up skill, which requires both of these skills to be reasonably well developed. In many situations, the breadth of the learner's repertoire of known fundamental motor skills (e.g., throwing, catching, running, and hopping) will also determine whether whole-task practices are possible. Finally, the intellectual and physical capacity of the performer will influence the type of practice method chosen. Patients with cognitive deficits and individuals with certain types of physical disabilities may find it extremely difficult to practice skills as a whole during early practice sessions.

Part-Task Practice Methods

Segmentation. Wightman and Lintern (1985) have identified three methods of part-task practice that may be appropriate for use in certain movement skill learning situations. They are segmentation, simplification, and fractionization. **Segmentation** involves partitioning the skill according to certain spatial and/or temporal criteria. Once partitioned, the components are practiced separately until a certain level of success has been achieved. These learned components are then combined to form the whole skill. A variation of this method involves practicing the first part of a skill, then the second, and then the combination of the two before proceeding to the third component. This approach is often used in the teaching of dance and gymnastics floor routines. In a clinical setting, this type of part-task practice can be useful when teaching bed-to-chair transfer skills. This method has been called progressive-part practice elsewhere in the literature (Magill, 1989; Schmidt, 1988).

> Segmentation involves partitioning a movement skill according to certain spatial and/or temporal criteria.

Simplification.   A second method of part-task practice is called **simplification.** In this method, various aspects of the skill and or environment are simplified. This might involve the removal of accessory parts that are normally used when the whole skill is performed or the use of equipment that reduces the level of control required to perform the skill. For example, a ski instructor often has the novice performer practice without ski poles, thereby simplifying the level of coordination needed to perform the skill. The use of scarves instead of balls when first teaching juggling to beginners also serves to simplify the practice environment and give the learner more time to catch the slower-moving scarves. When first teaching a CVA patient to walk again, the therapist often provides the patient with a walking frame or wide-based cane. The use of such assistive devices reduces the level of dynamic balance and lower-extremity strength required to walk.

> The complexity of various aspects of the skill and/or environment are reduced in the part-task practice method known as simplification.

Scarves are often used to teach the fundamental skill of juggling. This is an example of the simplification method of part-task practice.

Fractionization. The third method of part-task practice involves **fractionization** of the skill, whereby two or more components of the skill that are normally performed simultaneously are practiced in isolation. An example is to practice the diagonal-stride leg action independently of the arm action when first learning classical cross-country skiing techniques. Unfortunately, this method of part-task practice has proved to be the least successful means of fostering learning of the whole skill. This is not surprising, given that two components performed simultaneously in an entire skill would be highly interdependent and therefore largely invariant from a timing perspective.

> Fractionization of a skill involves practicing, in isolation, skill components that are normally performed together.

Attentional Cueing and Whole Practice

Perhaps a compromise approach is one that allows performers to practice the skill in its entirety while their attention is directed to one or two important aspects of the skill. For example, an instructor might direct the learner's attention to particular aspects of the skill, such as the transfer of weight from the rear to the front foot as the ball is contacted during performance of the forehand tennis stroke. Similarly, a therapist may ask the patient to focus on moving the trunk forward over the base of support before attempting to stand from a chair or bed. Although the performers' attention is focused on one or (at most) two parts of the skill while they practice, the whole skill is continually being performed.

One possible advantage of this **attentional cueing** technique over other part-task practice methods is that both the spatial and the temporal patterns of coordination are maintained when the skill is performed as a whole. One has only to observe a number of recreational players who were taught the tennis serve using part-task practice methods such as fractionization to see how much the temporal fluency of the serving motion has been compromised.

> Both the spatial and the temporal patterns of a skill are maintained when it is performed as a whole while attention is directed to one or two parts of the skill.

Whatever method of part-task practice is used, it is important that learners understand how the part or parts they are currently practicing are related to the whole skill. Newell and colleagues (Newell, Carlton, Fisher, & Rutter, 1989) found this to be an important component of part-task practice in a study that compared two groups of novice performers attempting to learn a rather sophisticated video game. Both groups practiced the skill in parts, but one group was also privy to the overall strategy needed to be successful when performing the whole skill. Needless to say, those who had this additional information learned the task considerably better than those who were not aware of how the various parts of the skill being practiced related to the performance of the whole game. In teaching the group of learners about the game's strategy, the authors had fostered the learner's understanding understanding of the skill to be learned. You will recall from our discussion of memory in Chapter 8 that using such a teaching technique also fosters the long-term retention and transfer of the skill-related knowledge that is acquired.

SUMMARY

The influence of both the amount and the type of practice on the learning or relearning of any given movement skill has been the subject of a considerable amount of research in the area of movement skill learning. The primary goal of this research has been to identify various theoretical principles that can be used to facilitate the learning of movement skills by improving the quality of each practice session. The collective results of these research endeavors can be used to guide practitioners in structuring meaningful and efficient practices.

For example, the practitioner now knows that it is important not only to introduce practice variability, whatever the type of skill to be learned, but also to consider organizing that variability according to the principles of contextual interference. Although practicing a skill under conditions of high contextual interference (random practice) does not always promote good initial performance of that skill, it often leads to superior movement skill learning and transfer. In determining what level of contextual interference is most appropriate for any group of learners however, the practitioner should first consider the past experiences of the learner with respect to open skills in particular and movement skills in general. The intellectual capabilities of the learners and their predominant learning style (reflective or impulsive) must also be considered. The type of movement skill to be learned has also been shown to influence the extent to which high levels of contextual interference promote learning.

The elaboration view and the action-plan reconstruction view have been advanced to explain why high levels of contextual interference often promote superior learning. The two accounts differ with respect to exactly *how* the interference produced by the practice situation influences the nature of the processing operations performed by the learner. But the proponents of both views agree that making the practice more difficult requires the learner to adopt a more active and independent role in the processing of skill-related information.

Finally, the spacing, or distribution, of practice between and within sessions must be considered when structuring an efficient practice environment. Whether a practitioner should use massed or distributed practice schedules depends on a number of factors. These include the characteristics of the skill, the individual characteristics of the learner, and the external constraints that are imposed in a practical setting.

Attempts by practitioners to help learners or patients achieve a level of skill mastery in a shorter period of time have also prompted the use of a number of different practice techniques. Two of the more commonly used are guidance techniques and part-task practice strategies. Manual guidance techniques are effective in minimizing the amount of error produced by learners and the tendency for patients to enlist abnormal or compensatory movements early in rehabilitation. When overused, however, they are likely to hinder the learner's development of error detection and correction skills that will be needed when the guidance is removed. The importance of engaging in active movements in order to benefit from the rich sources of intrinsic feedback they offer is another reason for quickly reducing the amount of guidance provided to a patient or young learner.

Part-task strategies are also used to boost the speed with which a particular skill is mastered by reducing its overall complexity. Various part-task methods can be implemented, depending on the characteristics of the skill to be learned and the capabilities of the learner. Three part-task practice methods are fractionization, segmentation, and simplification. An alternative practice strategy—attentional cueing—provides for practice of the whole skill while the learner's attention is directed to specific aspects of the skill. The primary advantage of this technique may be preservation of the spatial and temporal coordination of the skill during practice.

IMPORTANT TERMINOLOGY

After completing this chapter, readers should be familiar with the following terms and concepts.

action-plan reconstruction view	generizability
attentional cueing	guidance techniques
blocked practice	massed practice
contextual interference	practice variability
distributed practice	random practice
elaboration view	segmentation
fractionization	simplification

SUGGESTED FURTHER READING

Chamberlin, C., & T. Lee. 1993. Arranging practice conditions and designing instruction. In *Handbook of research on sport psychology,* ed. R.N. Singer, M. Murphey, & L.K. Tennant, pp. 213–241. New York, NY: Macmillian Publishing Co.

Lee, T.D., S.P. Swinnen,, & D.J. Serrien. 1994. Cognitive effort and motor learning. *Quest,* 46, 328–344.

TEST YOUR UNDERSTANDING

1. Briefly explain why the introduction of large amounts of practice variability is believed to enhance the learning of movement skills.

2. According to Gentile's two-stage model of motor learning, at what stage in the learning of a movement skill is the introduction of practice variability considered most appropriate? Explain your answer.

3. Identify ways in which variability of practice can be introduced in the learning of different types of skills (i.e., closed skills vs. open skills) in a physical education or clinical setting. In what way does the type of variability introduced differ in different learning situations?

4. Briefly describe how the principle of contextual interference is related to the concept of practice variability.

5. Describe how a practitioner might structure a practice session that introduces a high level of contextual interference. Choose a particular sport skill or activity of daily living to illustrate your answer to this question.

6. Identify the various factors that a practitioner must consider when deciding how much contextual interference is appropriate for a given practice situation.

7. How does the type of measurement used to evaluate the benefits of contextual interference influence the conclusions that are reached?

8. Compare and contrast the assumptions underlying the two theoretical accounts advanced to explain the contextual interference effect.

9. Briefly describe the controversy that exists with respect to the spacing, or distribution, of practice within a particular practice session. Identify various factors that might influence a practitioner's decision to choose one type of practice distribution schedule over another.

10. Briefly describe the advantages and disadvantages associated with the use of guidance techniques in physical education and clinical settings.

11. Outline certain guidelines that you, as a practitioner, would follow when considering the use of guidance techniques in any movement skill learning environment.

12. When are part-task practice strategies most likely to be used in the teaching of movement skills? Describe three common part-task practice methods that are used to help learners reach a level of skill mastery in a shorter period of time. Provide examples of skills that are most suited to each type of part-task practice method.

13. Describe an alternative practice method that appears to combine the advantages of part-task practice with those associated with the whole-task practice of movement skills.

About the Quote

According to Bernstein, the essence of practice and learning is being able to solve a motor problem repeatedly and not simply reproduce the solution. Bernstein believes that the learner, by actively engaging in the processes necessary to solve the problem time and time again, becomes better able to refine the solution process until it is honed to perfection. That the practice environment should be organized in a way that requires the learner to be actively engaged in the learning process is the primary conclusion that has emerged from a number of experiments discussed in this chapter. As cognitively effortful as these practices appear to be for the learner, they are more likely to provide the learner with the techniques necessary to solve a variety of different motor problems in a variety of different movement contexts.

CHAPTER 11
AUGMENTED FEEDBACK AND LEARNING

CHAPTER
OBJECTIVES

■ Understand and be able to describe the various types of augmented feedback used to facilitate the learning of movement skills.

■ Become familiar with the various forms of augmented feedback that focus on the kinematic aspects of a performance and with those forms that emphasize the unobservable kinetic parameters of movement.

■ Become familiar with the type of augmented sensory feedback that is used to promote better control and learning of movement by providing the learner with information about internal physiological events.

■ Understand and be able to describe the various factors that must be considered when deciding how precise the augmented feedback that is provided to a learner should be.

■ Understand how the frequency with which augmented feedback is provided to the learner influences the performance and/or learning of movement skills.

■ Understand and be able to explain how the timing of augmented feedback following a practice attempt influences the learning of movement skills.

> *"Motor learning is best viewed as a problem to be solved, where S tries a movement, is given KR, tries again on the next trial, and so on, and the KR is the information used to solve the problem."*
>
> —Adams (1971)

Now that we have considered the many issues involved in organizing the practice environment, let us turn to a discussion of how the practitioner can further shape the quality of each practice session by providing information to the learner about the nature of his or her practice performance. We read in Chapters 4 and 5 that learners possess a sophisticated repertoire of internal sensory feedback mechanisms (such as vision, audition, and somatosensation) that acquaint them with many aspects of a movement. We will now consider a second source of movement-related information that can be provided to the individual. This second and external source of feedback can be used to supplement the

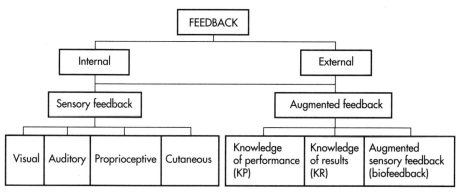

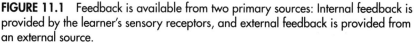

FIGURE 11.1 Feedback is available from two primary sources: Internal feedback is provided by the learner's sensory receptors, and external feedback is provided from an external source.

feedback already available from internal sensory sources. (Figure 11.1 illustrates the relationship between these two categories of feedback.)

This supplementary type of information, called **augmented feedback,** consists of information provided to the learner from an external source. Three characteristics of this type of feedback are notable. First, it may be provided in a verbal or nonverbal form. Second, augmented feedback may be provided during, immediately following, or some time after a movement has been completed. Third, the augmented feedback may describe the outcome of the movement and/or the movement pattern itself.

Augmented feedback that is provided after the completion of a movement and describes the *outcome* is called **knowledge of results (KR),** whereas information specific to the *quality* of the movement pattern produced is known as **knowledge of performance (KP).** These two components of augmented feedback have inspired a number of research endeavors during the past several decades. The purpose of this chapter is to discuss the general findings of these numerous studies and their practical relevance.

> Augmented feedback is information provided to a learner from an external source that describes the outcome of a performance and/or the quality of the performance itself.

Providing meaningful augmented feedback to a learner during practice is one of the most important responsibilities of an instructor or clinician. Not only can augmented feedback help the performer identify and correct errors in performance, but it can also serve as an important mediator for motivating learners during practice. Three important issues related to feedback will be discussed in the remaining sections of this chapter. These are the form of the feedback provided to the learner, the precision of the feedback, and the frequency with which it is presented during practice.

FORM OF THE FEEDBACK

There are many ways to provide learners with information about their performance during a practice session. The forms most commonly used are verbal instructions, videotape playbacks of performance, and **augmented sensory feedback**. Verbal feedback provided by a teacher or clinician still tends to be the form most commonly used in sport and clinical settings. A variety of alternative feedback techniques have also been shown to facilitate the learning and/or relearning of movement skills. The discussion that follows focuses on a variety of alternative forms of augmented feedback that can be conveniently divided into those methods that emphasize the kinematic aspects of a performance and those that focus on the unobservable kinetic parameters. As we will see, kinematic feedback can be provided by using videotape replays of actual performance or graphic displays of limb displacement, velocity, and/or acceleration. Kinetic aspects of a performance can be revealed by using similar types of graphic visual displays or auditory signals associated with EMG activity, torque output, and/or ground reaction forces. One or both of these forms of augmented feedback may be presented to the performer for any given performance. And either form may be provided while the performance is occurring or following its completion.

Kinematic and Kinetic Visual Displays

Newell and colleagues (Newell & McGinnis, 1985; Newell, Quinn, Sparrow, & Walter, 1983) have demonstrated the effectiveness of using both **kinetic** and **kinematic** forms of feedback in the learning of a variety of movement skills that involve rapid limb movements or the generation of criterion levels of force. Newell and Walter (1981) argue that the use of traditional forms of KR (such as movement time and peak force) can specify only what *not to do* on a subsequent trial following an incorrect attempt, whereas the use of kinetic and/or kinematic representations of movement can provide useful information about what *to do* on the next trial (p. 246).

> Traditional forms of KR can specify only what *not* to do on a subsequent trial following an incorrect performance.

Unfortunately, the value of these types of displays is often limited to describing only one, or at most two, parameters of performance. This may be viewed as a drawback when the movement skill to be acquired is considerably more complex because of the number of degrees of freedom involved. In these situations it may be necessary to represent the dynamics of the movement by using a display that combines multiple segments. Alternatively, one or more parameters of performance might be identified that, if specifically practiced, will benefit the overall performance of the task. Of course, identifying these critical parameters requires a thorough understanding of exactly what parameters are being manipulated to produce a particular coordination pattern. Given that a primary focus of the dynamic systems approach is to identify the equations of motion that govern both the stability and the instability of a particular pattern of coordination, it will become easier to identify the critical parameters that can be represented either kinematically and/or kinetically.

Although kinematic representations of a movement's dynamics have been shown to benefit learners performing single-degree-of-freedom movements, Swinnen and his co-investigators (Swinnen, Walter, Lee, & Serrien, 1993) have recently provided empirical support for the use of feedback based on movement outcome (i.e., KR) rather than detailed kinematic information in more complex skill situations. In a series of three experiments, the authors demonstrated that subjects provided with general information on outcome were better able to learn a bimanual coordination task that required them to perform different limb movements than were subjects provided detailed kinematic feedback (Figure 11.2).

The authors reasoned that because the movement goal was made clearly apparent to the performers, "they were largely capable of comparing what was done with what should be done, using the limited amount of extra KR feedback" (p. 1341). These more recent findings of Swinnen et al. are also in agreement with those described earlier by Young and Schmidt (1990), who suggested that global information about a movement's outcome may be more effective when the skill to be learned involves a greater number of degrees of freedom.

> Global information about a movement's outcome may be more effective when the skill to be learned involves a high number of degrees of freedom.

Videotape Feedback

The effectiveness of videotape replays focusing on the kinematic aspects of performance appears to be influenced by a number of factors. These include the skill level of the learner, the period of time over which the videotape feedback is used, and whether it is supplemented with additional verbal feedback. In reviewing a number of studies in which videotape feedback was used, Rothstein and Arnold (1976) found that skilled performers tended to benefit more from the use of unguided videotape feedback than did novice performers. It has been argued that the large amount of information available from videotape feedback has a tendency to overwhelm the novice performer who has not yet learned how

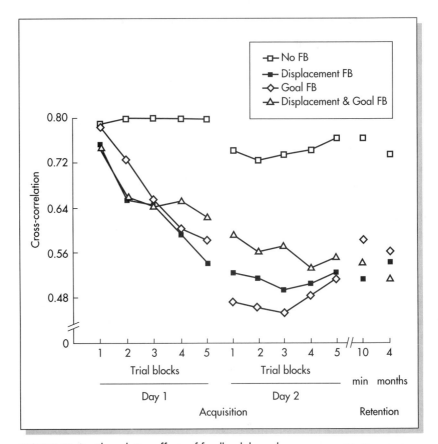

FIGURE 11.2 The relative effects of feedback based on movement outcome vs. performance-based kinematic feedback in the learning of a bimanual coordination task (FB means feedback.)

to attend selectively to the important aspects of the performance (Newell & Walter, 1981). Rothstein and Arnold did find, however, that in those studies in which the videotape feedback provided to novice learners was supplemented with specific skill-related verbal cues, considerably more benefit was derived from the videotape feedback.

Kernodle and Carlton (1992) further explored the role of attention-focusing cues in optimizing videotape feedback by providing one of two different types of cues to a group of performers attempting to learn the overhand throw. One group received cues intended to focus attention on important aspects of the throwing action ("Focus on the initial position of the body" and "Focus on the hips during the throwing phase"), a second group was presented with error-correcting transitional cues that were intended not only to help the learner identify what component of the skill to change but also to tell the learner how to change the movement in order to accomplish the intended coordination pattern. Performers in this group were likely to receive cues such as "Align your body so the right shoulder faces the target area" and "Rotate the hips from left to right during the throwing phase." The type of cue provided to each learner was based on the type of error made on the previous attempt.

> Novice performers derive greater benefits from videotape feedback when it is supplemented with attention-focusing and error-detecting verbal cues.

As Figure 11.3 shows, the learners who received the error-correcting transitional cues or attention-focusing cues before watching the videotape demonstrated significantly greater improvement in the distance they were able to throw the ball after four weeks of practice when compared to two other groups of learners who received KR or KP alone. More important, the transitional-cues group received the highest movement form rating across all practice sessions when compared to all other feedback groups. The transitional cues were clearly helping these learners modify their movement patterns to achieve the desired action. On the basis of their findings, Kernodle and Carlton concluded that providing KR or KP alone may not be the most potent form of feedback when the skill to be learned is one that involves multiple degrees of freedom.

Allowing a sufficient period of time for learners to view the videotape feedback has also been shown to be important. Learners need time to familiarize themselves with this form of augmented feedback and learn to extract the most useful information. Using videotape feedback over an extended period of time also ensures that the skill to be learned is adequately practiced. On the basis of their review, Rothstein and Arnold recommended that videotape feedback should be presented for at least five weeks in order to be effective. Studies in which videotape feedback was used for a shorter period of time did not result in improved performance.

One final issue related to the use of videotape feedback is that of skill level. On the basis of a number of unpublished doctoral studies, Rothstein and Arnold suggest that novice performers gain less from the use of videotape feedback than players at a more advanced level of performance. Unfortunately, although a number of recent studies have attempted to determine whether this is indeed the case, the results of these studies are inconclusive. Although Rikli and Smith (1980) concluded, on the basis of their findings with novice performers, that videotape feedback may be more effective for intermediate performers attempting to learn the tennis serve, van Wieringen and colleagues (Emmon et al. 1985, van Wieringen, Bootsma, Hoogesteger, & Whiting, 1989) found no benefits of videotape feedback training with a group of intermediate tennis players. The researchers found that neither serving

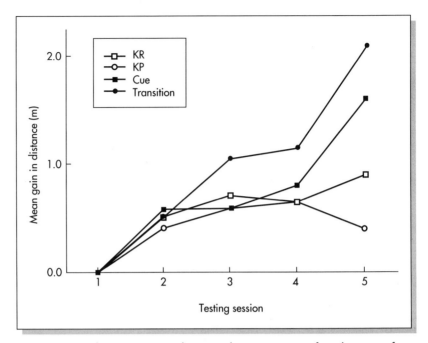

FIGURE 11.3 The mean gain in throwing distance was significantly greater for the group that received error-correcting transitional verbal cues in addition to the videotape feedback.

form nor serving accuracy improved to any greater extent for those players who received the videotape feedback training than for players who received more traditional tennis training. The authors of both studies generally conclude that videotape feedback training may not be as effective as practitioners would like to think. On the basis of these two studies, at least, there is little evidence to suggest that its use is superior to existing teaching methods.

Augmented sensory feedback is designed to amplify and display different types of internal physiological events.

Augmented Sensory Information: Biofeedback

Unlike the more general category of augmented feedback, **augmented sensory feedback** is specifically designed to amplify and display different types of internal physiological events, both normal and abnormal, in an effort to help an individual learn how to control these events. **Biofeedback** is the clinical term often used to describe this form of feedback. In rehabilitation settings, biofeedback is commonly used to inform patients about their own joint displacement, level of muscle activity, force generation, and/or movement of the center of mass. This internally generated information is subsequently presented to the patient in a visual or auditory form and can be used to modify the performance in progress or a subsequent attempt.

Biofeedback techniques are commonly used during the rehabilitation process as a means of facilitating neuromuscular re-education. They are considered a generally effective supplementary tool for re-educating patients with different types of muscle paresis, chronic pain, foot drop following a stroke, cerebral palsy, and Parkinson's disease (Inglis, Campbell, & Donald, 1976; Wolf, 1983). By far the most popular techniques are EMG recordings, goniometry, and various kinetic feedback devices. These different types of devices can provide the patient with feedback that is often more relevant and accurate than that provided by the clinician. The information provided is often more immediate for the performer and can be used to correct errors in performance in a more timely fashion.

> Biofeedback devices provide patients with important feedback that is often more relevant and accurate that that provided by the clinician.

Shumway-Cook and colleagues (Shumway-Cook, Anson, & Haller, 1988) found that the use of visual biofeedback—providing information about the kinetic aspects of postural sway—was particularly effective in the postural retraining of stroke patients. The authors compared two groups of hemiplegic patients who were being taught how to develop a more symmetrical stance. One group received conventional therapy emphasizing tactile and verbal cues, whereas the second group received kinetic biofeedback in the form of foot center of pressure. The results of this study indicated that patients provided with the visual kinetic biofeedback were much more successful in developing a more symmetrical stance. Specifically, the patients in the kinetic biofeedback training group began to increase the loading of their involved limb in order to maintain standing balance more than those patients who received conventional treatment. The authors attributed their findings to the fact that it is extremely difficult for the therapist to infer loading patterns accurately just from observing patient postures or reductions in overall body sway.

Guiding Principles.   As effective as certain types of biofeedback appear to be in the rehabilitation process, it is important that certain principles associated with its use be followed. First, the patient must understand the relationship between the signal presented and the task to be performed. For example, the young child with cerebral palsy who is participating in gait training must know whether the presence of an auditory signal indicates acceptable or unacceptable heel contact performance. Kinetic feedback devices attached to the heel of the child's involved limb may be programmed to emit an auditory signal when the child contacts the floor with the heel during gait (positive feedback) or may emit a continuous signal until the time that the child does contact the floor, at which time the signal stops (negative feedback).

Once the patient understands the relationship between task and signal, practice at controlling the signal should follow while the clinician provides positive verbal reinforcement. Given that this period of the training can often be very tiring and frustrating for the patient, it is also important to limit the use of the biofeedback device to manageable time periods. Finally, once introduced, the device should be used until the task has been learned and the device is no longer needed. At this point in the re-education process, the patient should have begun to equate the biofeedback signal with the appropriate movement sensation.

PRECISION OF AUGMENTED FEEDBACK

Another factor that must be considered when deciding what type of augmented feedback to provide to the learner is the level of precision associated with the feedback. One can logically expect that as the level of precision associated with the augmented feedback increases, so too does the amount of processing required of the learner. It should logically follow, therefore, that as the level of precision associated with the feedback increases, so too should the time provided for the learner to process the information. A number of research investigations devoted to the investigation of the issue of feedback precision (Reeve & Magill, 1981; Rogers, 1974; Smoll, 1972) have also demonstrated that increasing the level of precision associated with the feedback enhances learning only up to a certain point, beyond which performance is negatively affected.

> As the level of KR precision increases, so too should the time provided for the learner to process that more precise information.

The skill level of the learner has also been shown to be an important consideration in how precise the information feedback should be. Magill and Wood (1986) nicely illustrated this relationship by manipulating the precision of the feedback provided to a group of subjects attempting to learn a six-segment movement pattern. The goal of the task was to perform each of the six segments in a particular criterion movement time. One group of subjects received information about the direction of the error (too fast or too slow); a second group also received information about the amount of error produced (number of seconds too fast or too slow).

Figure 11.4 demonstrates two interesting findings that emerged from this investigation. First, both groups performed with similar amounts of error during the early practice trials, irrespective of the type of augmented feedback provided. Second, during the later practice trials, the group receiving the more precise information feedback began to perform significantly better than the group receiving the less precise form of feedback. The performance of the high-precision feedback

FIGURE 11.4 The more precise KR (direction and amount of error) resulted in better performance later in the practice trials, but not during the early trials.

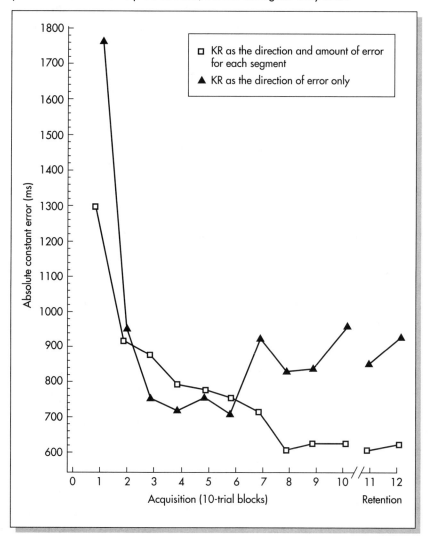

group was also significantly better during a no-KR retention test, which indicated that providing feedback that was more precise positively influenced the learning of the task.

On the basis of their findings, the authors were to conclude that providing more precise levels of feedback early in the learning of a movement skill did not lead to better performance of the task. They suggested that more precise feedback should be withheld until the learner has had enough practice on a task to benefit from detailed information. During the early stages of learning it may be more appropriate to provide general information about the learner's performance until the skill level of the learner and her or his knowledge of the skill's dynamics improves.

> More precise feedback should be withheld until the learner has completed a sufficient amount of practice.

FREQUENCY OF AUGMENTED FEEDBACK

How often should an instructor or clinician provide augmented feedback? If we were to consider only the experimental findings of studies conducted more than thirty years ago, the answer would be "the more the better." This was the conclusion that emerged from a series of studies conducted by Bilodeau and colleagues (Bilodeau & Bilodeau, 1958a, 1958b; Bilodeau, Bilodeau, & Schumsky, 1959) in which the amount of KR provided to a group of learners was manipulated. In one particular study (Bilodeau & Bilodeau, 1958a), subjects attempting to learn a simple lever-pulling task were provided with KR after every third or fourth trial or after every trial. At the conclusion of the practice phase, a comparison of the performances of both KR groups on the task revealed significant differences: The group that received KR after every trial exhibited the least amount of performance error.

The story is somewhat different, however, when the results of later studies are considered (Ho & Shea, 1978; Johnson, Wicks, & Ben-Sira, 1981). Two aspects of the earlier studies were altered during these later studies, and these changes largely account for the reversal of findings observed. First, no-KR retention tests were included in the later studies, which made it possible to differentiate performance from learning effects. Second, the **absolute frequency of KR** (the total number of trials after which KR was provided) was no longer held constant but rather was allowed to vary with the **relative frequency of KR** (the proportion of trials after which KR was provided). This second change eliminated the problems that arose in Bilodeau and Bilodeau's earlier study because the groups received different amounts of practice. Despite the fact that all

> The traditional view, that "the more KR the better," is no longer tenable.

groups received the absolute amount of KR, the group receiving KR after every trial practiced the task only 10 times, whereas the group receiving KR after every fourth trial received 40 practice trials.

Although the results obtained by Ho and Shea were similar when the immediate-performance findings were reviewed, the exact opposite was true when the no-KR retention test results were compared across the different KR frequency groups. The group receiving KR after every trial now performed the task with significantly higher performance error than the other two groups who had received KR less frequently during the acquisition phase. Thus it appears that the benefits associated with providing large amounts of KR are limited to immediate performance. Once the KR is no longer available, the quality of the performance deteriorates quickly. Two theoretical explanations for these disparate findings will be discussed later in this chapter.

> During bandwidth KR practice conditions, a learner who does not receive KR after a practice attempt is being indirectly told that the performance was satisfactory.

Fading-Frequency Schedules of KR

In an attempt to design a KR schedule that might optimize the beneficial effects of low-KR-frequency practice conditions, Winstein and Schmidt (1990) recently conducted a study in which the schedule of KR and no-KR trials was manipulated. Rather than providing KR after a set number of trials during the acquisition phase, they experimented with the idea of providing a higher frequency of KR during the early acquisition trials but then reducing relative KR frequency during later trials. For example, the 50%-relative-frequency-KR group received a relatively high frequency of KR (such as 100%) during the early practice trials, but then the frequency was systematically reduced (to 25%, for example) during the later trials. Although the authors found that the 50%-KR-frequency group performed the complex spatial–temporal movement task only marginally better on an immediate no-KR retention test, the findings were somewhat different when a second no-KR retention test was administered one day later. In the case of this second retention test, the performance of the 50%-KR-frequency group was significantly better than that of the high-relative-KR-frequency group. The results of this study are presented in Figure 11.5.

Bandwidth KR

An alternative instructional strategy for providing KR during the early stages of learning that is also designed to produce practice characterized by reduced KR relative frequency has been developed by Sherwood

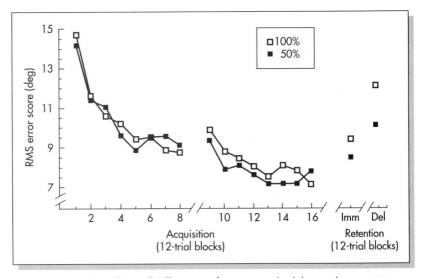

FIGURE 11.5 The effects of different KR-frequency schedules on the acquisition and retention of a tracking task.

(1988). This alternative method of providing feedback is known as **bandwidth KR.** During practice conditions in which bandwidth KR is used, augmented feedback is provided only if errors in performance are outside a given error range. In this practice situation, the learner is informed that the absence of KR after a given trial indicates that his or her performance on the previous trial was acceptable. Not only does the augmented feedback provided during bandwidth practice conditions serve an informational function, but also its absence motivates and/or reinforces the performer. According to Sherwood (1988), learners who do not receive KR after a given practice attempt are being indirectly told that their performance is satisfactory and should be repeated.

The results of a number of research studies (Lee & Carnahan, 1990; Reeve, Dornier, & Weeks, 1990; Sherwood, 1988) devoted to investigating the possible benefits of this practice strategy have demonstrated that compared to high-KR-frequency schedules, bandwidth KR promotes significantly better long-term retention of a skill. Moreover, the superior retention performance demonstrated by subjects who received bandwidth KR has been attributed to more than just a KR-frequency effect. Lee and Carnahan (1990) have also demonstrated that subjects receiving bandwidth KR achieved higher levels of performance consistency during acquisition when compared to subjects who practiced in conditions of reduced KR frequency. Within-subject variability was also significantly lower among subjects in the bandwidth KR group as measured by a

> Bandwidth KR practice conditions promote greater movement consistency.

later retention test. It appears that a second major advantage of bandwidth KR practice conditions over those designed simply to reduce the relative frequency of KR is that the former promote greater consistency of movement.

In a recent review article devoted to a discussion of the application of various motor learning principles to physical therapy, Schmidt (1991) points out yet another beneficial feature of bandwidth KR that should make it easy to implement in practical settings. He suggests that bandwidth KR provides an automatic fading schedule in that early practice attempts are more likely to produce performance errors that exceed the established error range. Larger errors will therefore result in a higher frequency of KR being provided. As practice continues, however, and performances become more consistent, the sizes of the performance errors are reduced to the extent that they now fall within the band of acceptable performance. The frequency with which augmented feedback is provided to the learner therefore decreases, producing a low relative frequency of KR. Thus the primary responsibility of the practitioner using this type of feedback condition is choosing a bandwidth that is large enough to ensure that only the positive guiding effects of KR are evident. Reducing the bandwidth as practice progresses may serve a similar function.

Reversed Bandwidth KR

More recently, a group of researchers have begun to explore a variation of bandwidth KR in which augmented feedback is provided when a learner is performing within a given range of error as opposed to outside of that range (Cauraugh, Chen, & Radlo, 1993). These researchers were particularly interested in comparing the effectiveness of traditional bandwidth KR with that of **reversed bandwidth KR** in the learning of a simple timing task. Unlike the traditional bandwidth method, which produces a low-KR-frequency schedule (such as 35% relative frequency) because augmented feedback is provided only when the performer exceeds a range of error, the reversed bandwidth KR condition would create a considerably higher KR frequency condition (such as 65% relative frequency). Although a review of the changes in absolute performance that occurred during acquisition indicated that the two bandwidth groups adopted different performance strategies for improving their performance accuracy, both groups performed equally well on a no-KR retention test. Cauraugh et al. concluded that whether augmented feedback was provided after an accurate response (reversed bandwidth KR) or after an inaccurate response (traditional bandwidth

KR) was immaterial: Both groups of learners demonstrated similar levels of learning.

Summary KR

A third method of reducing the frequency of augmented feedback was first investigated by Lavery (1962) and involved the withholding of feedback from a learner for a number of practice attempts. When finally presented to the learner, the information described the outcome achieved on each of the trials in which no feedback was provided. In some movement situations, the learner performed as many as twenty trials on a given movement task before any feedback was provided. This augmented feedback schedule came to be known as a **summary KR** schedule. This type of schedule differs from schedules based on the relative frequency of KR, in which a learner practices a skill for a certain number of attempts before receiving feedback related to the last practice trial only. The amount of information provided to the learner after a number of no-feedback practice trials have been completed is what differentiates these two feedback schedules.

> The amount of information provided to a learner after a given trial is what primarily differentiates summary KR from reduced-frequency KR schedules.

Lavery and several other investigators have since found Schmidt, Swinnen, Young, & Shapiro, 1989; Schmidt, Lange, & Young, 1990) that the effectiveness of providing augmented feedback according to a summary schedule is most evident when performances on a no-KR retention test are compared (see Figure 11.6). As Lavery's results demonstrate, the performance of the summary KR group was significantly better on no-KR retention tests conducted on days 7 through 10 when compared to a second group who received feedback after every trial or to a third group who received a combination of both schedules (KR after every trial in addition to summary KR after twenty trials). If one were to consider only performance during the course of six days of practice, however, the same conclusion would not be reached. During the acquisition phase, the performance of the summary KR group was significantly worse than that of either higher-frequency-KR group.

Schmidt and colleagues (Schmidt, Swinnen, Young, & Shapiro, 1989) were to extend the early work of Lavery by searching for the optimal number of trials to summarize. They varied the length of the summary KR period from five to fifteen trials and then compared the relative effectiveness of each summary KR interval to that of an immediate-feedback schedule. The most effective learning was observed in the group that practiced according to the longest summary KR schedule (fifteen trials), and the least effective learning was associated with the

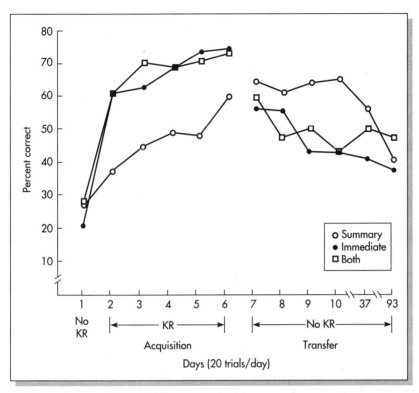

FIGURE 11.6   The effects of different KR schedules on performance during acquisition and retention. The performance of a group receiving KR after every 20 trials (Summary) was compared to that of a group receiving KR after every trial (Immediate) and to that of a third group receiving both KR schedules (Both).

immediate-feedback group. Providing a fifteen-trial summary schedule was not to prove as effective as shorter summary periods (such as five trials), however, when a more complex task was to be learned in a subsequent study (Schmidt, Lange, & Young, 1990). In fact, in these more complex learning situations, an inverted-U relationship was evident between the length of the summary KR period during acquisition and performance during a no-KR retention phase. The optimal summary KR length is therefore influenced by the characteristics of the skill to be learned.

Average Knowledge of Results

Although the collective findings of these laboratory-based studies provide support for the use of summary KR schedules, the usefulness of this type of feedback schedule in more practical settings is questionable. How likely is it, for example, that a practitioner will watch a performer

Applying Motor Learning Principles to Clinical Settings

A technique that clinicians commonly use when teaching partial-weight-bearing skills to patients is to provide concurrent augmented feedback (through auditory feedback devices worn in the shoe, for example, or bathroom scale monitoring of limb loading) during the acquisition phase. Unfortunately, providing concurrent augmented feedback has proved to be an unsatisfactory method of teaching such skills. This is perhaps not a surprising outcome in light of what we now know about the effectiveness of different KR presentation schedules in the learning of various motor skills. Although providing KR to a learner during and/or after every practice trial appears to enhance *performance* of a skill, it does little to facilitate *retention* of that skill. In fact, a number of researchers have concluded that providing KR on every practice trial fosters over dependence on the externally presented feed-back at the expense of the learner's attending to her or his own internal sources of feedback.

Applying motor learning principles, particularly those related to the provision of augmented feedback, Winstein and colleagues (Winstein, Christensen, & Fitch, 1993) conducted a clinical study in which they attempted to teach a group of forty healthy adults how to put no more than 30% of their total body weight on one leg while learning to walk with crutches. During the eighty-trial acquisition phase, the researchers manipulated the amount of KR provided according to four different summary KR schedules (KR after one, five, ten, or twenty trials). KR was presented in the form of a bar graph similar to the one shown here, which indicated the degree to which the subject overshot or undershot the 30% weight-bearing goal. Two days after completion of the acquisition phase, each adult completed a no-KR

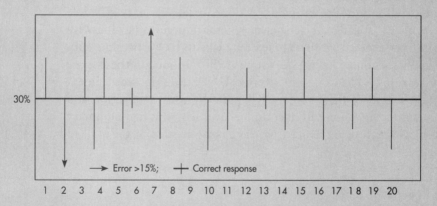

Example of a KR summary graph. KR was presented in the form of a bar graph that indicated the degree to which the subject overshot or undershot the 30% weight-bearing goal. KR was provided according to four different summary KR schedules.

retention test. Recall that this test is commonly used by researchers to measure the degree to which a particular skill has been learned.

In contrast to previous laboratory studies, the results of this more applied study indicated that the weight-bearing performance of *all* the KR groups improved significantly during the acquisition phase, irrespective of the summary KR schedule followed. Both the absolute amount of error (AE) recorded and the variability of that error (VE) decreased significantly during acquisition. The KR-1 group did, however, demonstrate significantly lower amounts of error when compared to the group that received KR after twenty practice trials during acquisition. How did the results for the retention trials compare to those of previous studies investigating the effectiveness of different summary KR schedules? Once again, the retention results were at odds with previous studies in that no significant differences for AE or VE were observed among the four summary KR groups during the retention phase. Although the group receiving KR after every five practice trials now performed with the highest level of performance accuracy, the difference was not significant.

Although the learning of the partial-weight-bearing task used in this study did not appear to be influenced by the frequency with which the feedback was provided, the findings do suggest that the task can be learned as efficiently with less feedback than is commonly provided in clinical settings. Receiving feedback as little as once every twenty practice attempts resulted in the same level of learning as that observed for a group receiving KR after every practice trial. This finding alone certainly proves that more is not always better.

practice a movement skill for a number of trials and then provide information about his or her performance on each of the attempts just completed? It is much more common for a practitioner to watch portions of several trials and then provide one or two pieces of information that describe the essence of the learner's overall performance.

A variation of summary KR is currently being investigated by a group of researchers who share a similar practical concern. Rather than information about each no-KR trial being provided at the conclusion of a summary KR period, in an **average KR** schedule only one piece of information representing an averaged performance score is provided to the learner after several no-KR practice attempts. The effectiveness of average KR schedules has been demonstrated by Young and Schmidt (1992), who compared the retention test performance of an average KR group with that of a group who received KR

> When average KR schedules are used, only one piece of information is provided to learners following multiple no-KR practice attempts.

in the form of a kinematic visual display after every trial. Wood and colleagues (Wood, Gallagher, Martino, & Ross, 1992) also found average KR schedules for a group of experienced golfers attempting to improve the dynamics of their golf swing to be more beneficial when compared to a second group of golfers who received no feedback at all during practice.

More recently, Weeks and Sherwood (1994) directly compared the effectiveness of average KR to summary KR schedules in the acquisition of a static force production task. Kinetic feedback describing the level of force generated was provided either after every trial, following a block of five no-KR practice trials according to a summary KR schedule, or at the completion of the same number of no-KR trials according to an average KR schedule. In general, the findings for both an immediate-retention and a delayed-retention test indicated greater response consistency among the two groups receiving either a summary or an average KR schedule when compared to the group receiving KR after every trial.

In contrast, the level of response bias demonstrated among the groups was significantly different only for the test of short-term retention. In comparing the relative effectiveness of the two lower-frequency-feedback conditions alone, the authors concluded that a summary KR feedback schedule and an average KR feedback schedule were equally effective in promoting greater response consistency and less response bias among the group of subjects tested. Given the unlikelihood that a teacher or clinician can devote enough attention to a single learner during practice to implement a summary KR schedule, it is comforting to know that a practice already in widespread use among practitioners appears to be equally effective.

THEORETICAL EXPLANATIONS OF THE FREQUENCY EFFECT

Guidance Hypothesis

Several theoretical explanations have been advanced to account for the KR frequency and scheduling effects just described. Let's look at two of the more contemporary views developed to explain exactly why the learner benefits from practice conditions wherein less augmented feedback is provided. The first hypothesis developed to account for the superiority of practice conditions that feature a low frequency of KR is the **guidance hypothesis** (Salmoni, Schmidt, & Walter, 1984). According to this hypothesis, the presentation of KR may have both beneficial and detrimental effects on learning. That is, although practice conditions that include high frequency of KR guide the learner toward the correct performance very quickly, such practice conditions may also lead to overdependence on this form of augmented feedback. The provision of too much augmented feedback is thought to prevent the processing of other information related to the inherent dynamics of the task. Remember that the overuse of manual guidance techniques (discussed in Chapter 10) also produces negative consequences. Certainly, the type of cognitive processing used will be different in these two diverse practice conditions. Whereas low-KR-frequency practice conditions seem to foster increased problem solving and independent exploration of a task's dynamics, high-KR-frequency practice conditions apparently do little to promote such activities on the part of the learner.

> Low-KR frequency practice conditions foster more problem solving and independent exploration of the skill's dynamics than do high-KR frequency conditions.

Consistency Hypothesis

The **consistency hypothesis** is a second theoretical explanation advanced to account for the learning benefits associated with fading-frequency and bandwidth KR practice conditions. According to this hypothesis, providing learners with high relative frequency of KR leads them to adjust their performance continually on the basis of each new piece of information provided to them. This constant short-term correction of performance is believed to prevent the learner from developing a stable plan of action and is reflected in a high level of performance variability. You will recall that subjects in the Lee and Carnahan (1990) study who practiced according to a bandwidth KR schedule not only performed the timing task as accurately during a retention test as subjects who received KR after every trial but also demonstrated less within subject variability in their performance. The benefits of bandwidth KR were therefore twofold: increased performance accuracy and greater consistency.

> Providing learners with large amounts of KR causes them to make continuous short-term corrections that hinder the development of a stable action plan.

THE TIMING OF KNOWLEDGE OF RESULTS

Yet another issue that has been investigated by a number of researchers interested in the area of knowledge of results is when to provide KR following a given practice trial. To investigate this issue, researchers have systematically manipulated the time that elapses between the completion of a practice trial and the presentation of performance-related feedback. This interval of time has been referred to as the **KR delay interval**. It has been hypothesized that the longer the delay between the completion of a practice attempt and the presentation of feedback, then as a result of increased forgetting, the more detrimental that delay will be to the learning of a task. Alternatively, it has been suggested that very short KR delay intervals may be equally detrimental to learning by not allowing sufficient time for the learner to engage in important cognitive operations necessary for developing error-detection and -correction abilities (Salmoni, Schmidt, & Walter, 1984). Providing a KR delay interval that optimizes the amount of time available for the learner to engage in important processing activities, while preventing the tendency to forget what has just been practiced, is clearly an important issue for the practitioner.

Fortunately, the results of a number of research studies generally indicate that increasing the KR delay interval does not negatively influence learning (Bilodeau, & Bilodeau, 1958). Conversely, Swinnen and colleagues (Swinnen, Schmidt, Nicholson, & Shapiro, 1990) have recently demonstrated that very short KR delay intervals can have a detrimental effect on learning. When the retention test performance of a group of subjects who received KR immediately following each practice trial was compared to that of a group who received KR following an eight-second unfilled interval, the delayed-KR group performed significantly better, particularly when the retention test was conducted two days after the acquisition phase.

What is of perhaps greater interest to the practitioner is the fact that a third group who was asked to estimate their error verbally during a similar eight-second delay interval performed significantly better than the first two groups during the same retention test (see Figure 11.7). This finding suggests that providing KR immediately following a practice attempt prevents the learner from engaging in important error detection and correction during practice. The negative effects of this practice become apparent, however, only when the learner is asked to perform the skill again in the absence of that feedback. In contrast, delaying the presentation of KR during practice also encourages learners to evaluate the accuracy of their previous practice attempt during the delay, and it results in considerably better performance when augmented feedback is no longer provided. This particular result supports a similar finding reported in a much earlier study by Hogan and Yanowitz (1978). These researchers were particularly interested in

> Providing KR immediately after a practice attempt prevents the learner from engaging in important error detection and correction.

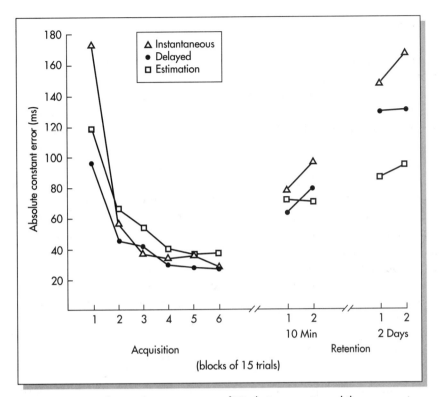

FIGURE 11.7   Delaying the presentation of KR during practice, while encouraging learners to estimate their error during the delay, resulted in the best performance on the no-KR retention trials.

knowing whether subjective estimates of error facilitated the learning of a motor skill. They also demonstrated superior retention performance for a group of subjects who were required to estimate the amount of error following each practice trial.

Such research suggests that it is important for the practitioner to provide the learner with enough time after each practice attempt to process internally generated response-related information. This approach facilitates the learner's development of important skills in error detection and correction. Encouraging learners to identify possible errors in a performance by asking them such questions as "What do you think you may have done incorrectly?" during that interval also appears to be a valuable practice activity. Of course, just how much time should be provided after each practice attempt depends on the complexity of the skill being learned, the skill level of the learner, and other associated factors.

AUGMENTED FEEDBACK AND MOTIVATION

Given that feedback serves many functions, it is important that a practitioner consider when feedback should be used to give the learner error-correction information about the performance and when it should be used to motivate the performer. Although it is now clear that learners require less augmented feedback about their performance than was previously thought, that should not preclude the use of less specific feedback intended to motivate learners or patients to keep up their good efforts. When sincerely conveyed, simple phrases such as "You are really working hard to improve your performance" and "Nice try!" can do much to improve or maintain a learner's interest in the movement skill being taught. The use of bandwidth KR schedules would also seem to provide an opportunity to motivate performers. Remember that instructors who use this schedule provide learners with error-correcting feedback only when their performance does not fall within a predetermined range of acceptable performance. Therefore, on those practice attempts for which an instructor does not provide any feedback, he or she is conveying the idea that the performance was good. This type of KR schedule, then, not only serves as a valuable method of conveying error-related information but also offers a way of motivating the learner.

Unfortunately, the need to provide feedback for the purpose of motivating the performer is often overlooked by the practitioner who is preoccupied with improving the quality of performance. I witnessed a situation a few years ago in which a young man who was a promising rifle shooter reacted negatively to the skill-specific comments repeatedly offered by his coach. As the coach walked away, the performer could be overheard asking a nearby performer why the coach didn't like him. When the coach learned of the comments made, he was very disturbed. He had simply wanted to help the performer, in whom he saw excellent potential, develop his shooting abilities. The coach's intentions were good, but his failure to buffer his skill-related comments with motivating remarks had been interpreted negatively by the performer. Stories such as this remind us that we must never forget the importance of motivation, not only as a precursor to learning but also during the practice that leads to the learning of skills.

SUMMARY

Feedback provided to learners from an external source (such as an instructor or video) is intended to augment, or add to, the information that is naturally available to the learners from their own internal sensory sources. Augmented feedback may be provided in many different forms (verbally, via graphical displays, and so on), and it may be offered during performance, immediately following a movement, or some time after a movement has been completed.

Information provided about the outcome of an action is called knowledge of results (KR), whereas knowledge of performance (KP) is information provided about the quality of the movement pattern produced. Whether it is desirable to provide one or both types of augmented feedback is largely determined by the characteristics of the learner (skill level, past experiences, and the like) and the nature of the task being learned (such as whether the movement involved entails one or several degrees of freedom).

Information feedback describing the kinematic and/or kinetic aspects of a movement can give the performer useful information about what to do on the next practice attempt, whereas more traditional forms of KR (such as movement time and absolute error) provide only information about what *not* to do on a subsequent attempt. This latter type of feedback appears to be less effective as the number of degrees of freedom associated with a particular skill increases.

The use of augmented sensory information, or biofeedback, has proved to be a valuable technique in clinical settings because it conveys information to a patient about otherwise unobservable events (level of muscle activity, force generation, movement of the center of mass). This type of feedback gives patients immediate information about their performance, and that information is often more relevant and accurate than information provided by the clinician.

Recent research into the optimal amount of feedback to give a learner suggests that "more is not better." Although the initial performance of a skill is facilitated when augmented feedback is provided after every practice attempt, its subsequent removal leads to diminished performance and poor retention. According to the guidance hypothesis, although high-KR-frequency practice conditions guide the learner toward the correct performance very quickly, such practice conditions also promote over dependence on this externally presented information. In contrast, low-KR-frequency practice conditions foster increased problem solving and independent exploration of the skill's inherent dynamics and results in better retention of the skill in the long term.

Feedback schedules that provide learners with more feedback during the early stages of learning, and with less as they progress in the learning of the skill, are particularly useful. Fading-frequency and bandwidth schedules of feedback are examples of such schedules. According to the consistency hypothesis, these types of schedules promote the development of a stable plan of action, which, in turn, leads to increased accuracy and consistency of performance. Bandwidth KR schedules also provide learners with two different types of feedback: (1) feedback that motivates and/or reinforces the performer by virtue of its not being presented and (2) feedback that serves an important error-correction function when a particular performance falls outside a predetermined error range.

Summary KR and average KR schedules have also been shown to enhance the learning of movement skills. Unlike other low-KR-frequency schedules, a learner practices a skill for a certain number of attempts before receiving feedback related to the last practice trial (summary KR) or information that provides an averaged performance score of all no-KR practice attempts (average KR). Research has demonstrated that each of these schedules promotes greater performance consistency and less response bias.

Research has also demonstrated that very short KR delay intervals do not provide learners with enough time to engage in important cognitive activities associated with error detection and correction. Conversely, providing larger KR delay intervals, during which the learner is encouraged to identify the errors made on a previous attempt, is particularly beneficial for movement skill learning.

It is important to remember that augmented feedback can also serve to motivate learners when less specific feedback is interspersed with more specific skill-related feedback. Certain reduced-KR-frequency schedules (bandwidth) can also serve a motivating function by virtue of how they are structured.

IMPORTANT TERMINOLOGY

After completing this chapter, readers should be familiar with the following terms and concepts.

absolute frequency of KR	guidance hypothesis
augmented feedback	kinematic feedback
augmented sensory feedback	kinetic feedback
average KR	knowledge of performance (KP)
bandwidth KR	knowledge of results (KR)
biofeedback	KR delay interval
consistency hypothesis	relative frequency of KR
fading-frequency schedules	reversed bandwidth KR
of KR	summary KR

SUGGESTED FURTHER READING

Krebs, D.E., & D. Wolf Behr 1994. Biofeedback. In *Physical Rehabilitation: Assessment and Treatment,* ed. S.B. O'Sullivan & T.J. Schmitz, pp. 707–724. Philadelphia, PA: F.A. Davis

Magill, R.A. 1994. The influence of augmented feedback on skill learning depends on characteristics of the skill and the learner. *Quest,* 46: 314–327.

Winstein, C.J. 1991. Knowledge of results and motor learning—Implications for physical therapy. *Physical Therapy,* 71 (2): 140–149.

TEST YOUR UNDERSTANDING

1. Identify each of the different types of augmented feedback and provide one example of each type.

2. Briefly explain why kinetic and kinematic visual displays are a more valuable form of augmented feedback than traditional forms of augmented feedback. In what types of learning situations are these displays likely to be less effective?

3. Outline three guidelines a practitioner should follow when using videotape as a form of augmented feedback.

4. Briefly describe the advantages associated with the use of kinetic biofeedback devices. Provide one research example that demonstrates the advantage of these devices.

5. Cite four principles that one should follow when using biofeedback devices in clinical settings.

6. What factors should be considered by a practitioner when deciding how precise the augmented feedback that is provided to a learner should be?

7. Briefly explain how the research findings that emerged from studies conducted in the 1950s differed from those presented in later studies investigating the issue of how often to provide KR to learners. What may account for these differences?

8. How does a fading-frequency schedule differ from a bandwidth KR schedule? Outline the major benefits associated with the use of each of these KR schedules in the acquisition of movement skills.

9. Briefly describe how augmented feedback is provided according to a summary KR schedule. How does the use of this feedback schedule affect the quality of performance and learning of movement skills?

10. Compare and contrast two theoretical explanations advanced to account for the KR frequency and scheduling effects.

11. Briefly explain why very short KR delay intervals appear to be detrimental to learning.

12. Briefly describe how augmented feedback can be used to motivate the learner.

13. Identify five general guidelines a practitioner should follow when providing augmented feedback to a patient in a clinical setting or to students in a physical education class.

About the Quote

Adams appears to be extending the statement by Bernstein quoted at the opening of the last chapter. Adams suggests that the information a learner receives after each attempt at a skill underlies his or her ability to solve the motor problem. The contribution of knowledge of results to the acquisition of motor skills has been extensively studied by Adams and a number of other prominent researchers in the area of motor learning. Of course, although there is little doubt that KR has an important influence on learning, how often and in what form it is presented to the learner often determines whether it constitutes a positive or a negative influence. "More is better" does not necessarily apply.

REFERENCES

Abernethy, B., & Russell, D.G. (1984). Advance cue utilisation by skilled cricket batsmen. *The Australian Journal of Science and Medicine in Sport, 16, 2,* 2–10.

Abernethy, B., & Russell, D.G. (1987). The relationship between expertise and visual search strategy in a racquet sport. *Human Movement Science, 6, 283–319.*

Abernethy, B., Burgess-Limerick, R., & Parks, S. (1994). Contrasting approaches to the study of motor expertise. *Quest, 46, 186–198.*

Adams, J.A. (1977). Feedback theory of how joint receptors regulate the timing and positioning of a limb. *Psychological Review, 84, 504–523.*

Adams, J.A. & Goetz, E.T. (1973). Feedback and practice as variables in errror detection and correction. *Journal of Motor Behavior, 5, 217–224.*

Adams, J.A. (1966). Some mechanisms of motor responding: An examination of attention. In E.A. Bilodeau (ed.), *Acquisition of skill.* (pp. 169–200). New York: Academic Press.

Adams, J.A. (1971). A closed-loop theory of motor learning. *Journal of Motor Behavior, 3, 111–149.*

Adams, J.A. (1987). Historical review and appraisal of research on the learning, retention, and transfer of human motor skills. *Psychological Bulletin, 101,* 41–74.

Aggleton, J.P., & Mishkin, M. (1983). Memory impairments following restricted medial thalamic lesions in monkeys. *Experimental Brain Research, 52, 199–209.*

Alderson, G.J.K., Sully, D.J., & Sully, H.G. (1974). An operational analysis of a one-handed catching task using high speed photography. *Journal of Motor Behavior, 6, 217–226.*

Allard, F., & Starkes, J.L. (1980). Perception in sport: Volleyball. *Journal of Sport Psychology, 2, 22–33.*

Allard, F., Graham, S., & Paarsalu, M.E. (1980). Perception in sport: Basketball. *Journal of Sport Psychology, 2, 14–21.*

Anderson, J.R. (1981). A theory of language based on general learning mechanisms. *Proceedings of the Seventh International Joint Conference on Artificial Intelligence.* pp. 97–103.

Anderson, J.R. (1982). Acquisition of cognitive skill. *Psychological Review, 89, 4,* 369–406.

Anderson, J.R. (1987). Skill acquisition: Compilation of weak-method problem solutions. *Psychological Review, 94,* 192–210.

Anderson, J.R., & Reder, L.M. (1979). An elaborative processing explanation of depth of processing. In L.S. Cermak and F.I.M. Craik (eds.), *Levels of processing in human memory* (pp. 385–403). Hillsdale, NJ: Erlbaum.

Annett, J. (1959). Learning a pressure under conditions of immediate and delayed knowledge of results. *Quarterly Journal of Experimental Psychology, 11, 3–15.*

Annett, J. (1979). Memory for skill. In M. Gruneberg and P. Morris (eds.), *Applied problems in memory,* (pp. 215–247). London: Academic Press.

Anson, J.G. (1982). Memory drum theory: Alternative tests and explanations for the complexity effects on simple reaction time. *Journal of Motor Behavior,* 14, 228–246.

Anson, J.G. (1989). Effects of moment of inertia on simple reaction time. *Journal of Motor Behavior,* 21, 60–71.

Atkinson, R.C., & Shiffrin, R.M. (1968). Human memory: A proposed system and its control processes. In K.W. Spence and J.T. Spence (eds.), *The psychology of learning and motivation: Advances in research and theory* (vol. 2, pp. 90–196). New York: Academic Press.

Atkinson, R.C., & Shiffrin, R.M. (1971). The control of short-term memory. *Scientific American,* 225, 82–90.

Baddeley, A.D. (1978). The trouble with levels: A re-examination of Craik and Lockhart's framework for memory research. *Psychological Review,* 85, 139–152.

Baddeley, A.D. (1981). The concept of working memory: A view of its current state and probable future development. *Cognition,* 10, 17–23.

Baddeley, A.D. (1990). *Human memory. Theory and practice.* Boston, MA: Allyn and Bacon.

Baddeley, A.D., & Hitch, G. (1974). Working memory. In G.H. Bower (ed.), *The psychology of learning and motivation: Advances in research and theory* (vol. 8, pp. 47–89). New York: Academic Press.

Baddeley, A.D., & Longman, D.J.A. (1978). The influence of length and frequency of training session on the rate of learning to type. *Ergonomics,* 21, 627–635.

Bahill, A.T., & LaRitz, T. (1984). Why can't batters keep their eyes on the ball? *American Scientist,* 72, 249–252.

Bahrick, H.P., & Phelphs, E. (1987). Retention of Spanish vocabulary over eight years. *Journal of Experimental Psychology: Learning, Memory and Cognition,* 13, 344–349.

Bandura, A. (1977). Self-efficacy: Toward a unifying theory of behavioral change. *Psychological Review,* 84, 191–215.

Bandura, A. (1986). *Social foundations of thought and action: A social cognitive theory.* Englewood Cliffs, NJ: Prentice-Hall.

Bandura, A., Jeffrey, R.W., & Bachica, D.L. (1974). Analysis of memory codes and cumulative rehearsal in observational learning. *Journal of Research in Personality,* 7, 295–305.

Barclay, C.D., Cutting, J.E., & Kozlowski, L.T. (1978). Temporal and spatial factors in gait perception that influence gender recognition. *Perception and Psychophysics,* 23, 145–152.

Bard, C., & Fleury M. (1981). Considering eye movement as a prediction of attainment. In I.M. Cockerill and W.W. MacGillivray (eds.), *Vision and Sport* (pp. 28–41). Cheltenham, UK: Stanley Thornes Publishers.

Baron, R.A. (1970). Attraction toward the model and model's competence as determinants of adult initiative behavior. *Journal of Personality and Social Psychology,* 14, 345–351.

Battig, W.F. (1972). Intratask interference as a source of facilitation in transfer and retention. In R.F. Thompson and J.F. Voss (eds.), *Topics in learning and performance,* (pp. 131–159). New York: Academic Press.

Battig, W.F. (1979). The flexibility of human memory. In L.S. Cermak and F.I.M. Craik (eds.), *Levels of processing in human memory* (pp. 23–44). Hillsdale, NJ: Erlbaum.

Bernstein, N. (1967). *The co-ordination and regulation of movement.* London: Pergamon Press.

Beuter, A., & Garfinkel, A. (1985). Phase plane analysis of limb trajectories in non-handicapped and cerebral palsied subjects. *Adapted Physical Activity Quarterly,* 2, 214–227.

Bilodeau, E.A., & Bilodeau, I.M. (1958a). Variable frequency of knowledge of results and the learning of a simple skill. *Journal of Experimental Psychology,* 55, 379–383.

Bilodeau, E.A., & Bilodeau, I.M. (1958b). Variation of temporal intervals among critical events in five studies of knowledge of results. *Journal of Experimental Psychology,* 55, 603–612.

Bilodeau, E.A., Bilodeau, I.M., & Schumsky, D.A. (1959). Some effects of introducing and withdrawing knowledge of results early and late in practice. *Journal of Experimental Psychology:* 58, 142–144.

Bird, A.M., & Rikli, R. (1983). Observational-learning and practice variability. *Research Quarterly for Exercise and Sport,* 54, 1–4.

Bobath, B. (1965). *Abnormal postural reflex activity caused by brain lesions.* London: Heinemann Medical Books.

Bobath, B. (1978). *Adult hemiplegia: Evaluation and treatment,* (2nd Edition). London: Heineman Medical Books.

Bootsma, R.J., & van Wieringen., P.C.W. (1990). Timing an attacking forehand drive in table tennis. *Journal of Experimental Psychology: Human Perception and Performance,* 16, 21–29.

Borgeaud, P., & Abernethy, B. (1987). Skilled perception in volleyball defense. *Journal of Sport Psychology,* 9, 400–406.

Bransford, J.D., Franks, J.J., Morris, C.D., & Stein, B.S. (1979). Some general constraints on learning and memory research. In L.S. Cermak and F.I.M. Craik (eds.), *Levels of processing in human memory.* (pp. 331–354). Hillsdale, NJ: Erlbaum.

Brooks, V.B. (1984). Cerebellar functions in motor control. *Human Neurobiology,* 2, 251–260.

Brooks, V.B. (1986). *The neural basis of motor control.* New York: Oxford University Press.

Burgess, P.R., & Clark, F.J. (1969). Characteristics of knee joint receptorsin the cat. *Journal of Physiology,* 203, 317–335.

Carroll, W.R., & Bandura, A. (1982). The role of visual monitoring in observational learning of action patterns: Making the unobservable observable. *Journal of Motor Behavior,* 14, 153–167.

Carroll, W.R., & Bandura, A. (1985). The role of visual monitoring and motor rehearsal in observational learning of action patterns. *Journal of Motor Behavior,* 17, 269–281.

Carroll, W.R., & Bandura, A. (1990). Representation guidance of action production in observational learning: A causal analysis. *Journal of Motor Behavior,* 22, 85–97.

Carron, A.V. (1969). Performance and learning in a discrete motor task under massed vs. distributed practice. *Research Quarterly,* 40, 481–489.

Cauraugh, J.H., Chen, D., & Radlo, S. (1993). Effects of traditional and reversed bandwidth knowledge of results on motor learning. *Research Quarterly for Exercise and Sport,* 64, 4, 413–417.

Chase, W.G., & Ericsson, K.A. (1982). Skill and working memory. In G.H. Bower (ed.), *The psychology of learning and motivation* (vol. 16., pp. 1–58). New York: Academic Press.

Chase, W.G., & Simon, H.A. (1973). Perception in chess. *Cognitive Psychology,* 4, 55–81.

Chi, M.T.H. (1976). Short-term memory limitations in children: Capacity of processing deficits? *Memory and Cognition,* 4, 559–572.

Chi, M.T.H. (1977). Age differences in memory span. *Journal of Experimental Child Psychology,* 23, 266–281.

Chi, M.T.H., & Koeske, R.D. (1983). Network representation of a child's dinosaur knowledge. *Developmental Psychology,* 19, 29–39.

Chi, M.T.H., Feltovich, P.J., & Glaser, R. (1981). Categorization and representation of physics problems by experts and novices. *Cognitive Science,* 5, 121–152.

Christina, R.W. (1992). The 1991 C.H. McCloy Research Lecture: Unraveling the mystery of the response complexity effect in skilled movements. *Research Quarterly for Exercise and Sport,* 63, 3, 218–230.

Christina, R.W., & Bjork, R.A. (1991). Optimizing long-term retention and transfer. In D. Druckman and R.A. Bjork (eds.), *In the mind's eye: Enhancing human performance* (pp. 23–56). Washington, DC: National Academy Press.

Christina, R.W., & Corcos, D.M, (1988). *Coaches guide to teaching sport skills.* Champaign, IL: Human Kinetics.

Christina, R.W., & Rose, D.J. (1985). Premotor and motor reaction time as a function of response complexity. *Research Quarterly for Exercise and Sport,* 56, 306–315.

Christina, R.W., & Shea, J.B. (1988). The limitations of generalization based on restricted information. *Research Quarterly for Exercise and Sport,* 59, 291–297.

Christina, R.W., & Shea, J.B. (1993). More on assessing the retention of motor learning based on restricted information. *Research Quarterly for Exercise and Sport,* 64, 2, 217–222.

Christina, R.W., Fischman, M.G., Vercruyssen, M.J.P., & Anson, J.G. (1982). Simple reaction time as a function of response complexity: Memory drum theory revisited. *Journal of Motor Behavior,* 14, 301–321.

Clark, F.J., & Burgess, P.R. (1975). Slowly adapting receptors in the cat knee joint: Can they signal joint angle? *Journal of Neurophysiology,* 38, 1448–1463.

Clark, F.J., Matthews, P.B.C., & Muir, (1979). Anesthesizing skin. The role of cutaneous receptors.

Clark, J.E., & Ewing, M. (1985). A meta-analysis of gender differences and similarities in the gross motor skill performances of prepubescent children. *Paper presented at the annual meeting of the North American Society for the Psychology of Sport and Physical Activity.* Gulf Port, MS.

Clark, J.E., Whitall, J., & Phillips, S.J. (1988). Human interlimb coordination:

The first 6 months of independent walking. *Developmental Psychobiology,* 21, 445–456.

Colley, A.M. (1989). Learning motor skills: Integrating cognition and action. In A.M. Colley and J.R. Beech (eds.), *Acquisition and performance of cognitive skills* (pp. 167–189). New York: Wiley.

Colley, A.M., & Beech, J.R. (1988). Grounds for reconciliation: Some preliminary thoughts on cognition and action. In A.M. Colley and J.R. Beech (eds.), *Cognition and action in skilled behaviour* (pp. 1–11). Amsterdam: North-Holland.

Connor, N.P., & Abbs, J.H. (1991). Sensorimotor contributions of the basal ganglia: Recent advances. In J.M. Rothstein (ed.), *Movement Science* (pp. 112–120). Alexandria, VA: American Physical Therapy Association.

Cook, D.G., & Kesner, R.P. (1984). Memory for equocentric spatial localization in an animal model of advanced Huntington's disease. *Neuroscience Abstracts,* 10, 133.

Cooke, J.D. (1979). Dependence of human arm movements on limb mechanical properties. *Brain Research,* 165, 366–369.

Craik, F.I.M., & Lockhart, R. (1972). Levels of processing: A framework for memory research. *Journal of Verbal Learning and Verbal Behavior,* 11, 671–676.

Craik, F.I.M., & Tulving, E. (1975). Depth of processing and the retention of words in episodic memory. *Journal of Experimental Psychology: General,* 104, 268–294.

Cuddy, L.J., & Jacoby, L.L. (1982). When forgetting helps memory: An analysis of repetition effects. *Journal of Verbal Learning and Verbal Behavior,* 21, 451–467.

Cutting, J.E. (1978). Generation of synthetic male and female walkers through manipulation of a biomechanical invariant. *Perception,* 7, 393–405.

Cutting, J.E., & Kozlowski, L.T. (1977). Recognising friends by their walk: Gait perception without familiarity cues. *Bulletin of the Psychonomic Society,* 9, 353–356.

Cutting J.E., & Proffitt, D.R. (1982). Gait perception as an example of how we may perceive events. In R. Walk and H.L. Pick, Jr. (eds.), *Intersensory perception and sensory integration* (pp. 32–47). New York: Plenum Press.

DeGroot, A.D. (1966). Perception and memory vs. thought. In B. Kleinmuntz (ed.), *Problem solving research methods and theory* (pp. 19–50). New York: Wiley.

Del Rey, P. (1989). Training and contextual interference effects on memory and transfer. *Research Quarterly for Exercise and Sport,* 60, 342–347.

Del Rey, P., Whitehurst, M., & Wood, J. (1983). Effects of experience and contextual interference on learning and transfer. *Perceptual and Motor Skills,* 56, 581–582.

Del Rey, P., Wughalter, E., & Whitehurst, M. (1982). The effects of contextual interference on females with varied experience in open skills. *Research Quarterly for Exercise and Sport,* 53, 108–115.

Del Rey, P., Whitehurst, M., Wughalter, E., & Barnwell, J. (1983). Contextual interference and experience in acquisition and transfer. *Perceptual and Motor Skills, 57,* 241–242.

Della Sala, S.D., Lorenzo, G.D., Giordano, A., & Spinnler, H. (1986). Is there a specific visuo-spatial impairment in parkinsonians? *Journal of Neurology, Neurosurgery, and Psychiatry, 49,* 1258–1265.

Delong, M.R., & Georgopoulos, A.P. (1981). Motor functions of the basal ganglia. In J.M. Brookhart (ed.), *Handbook of physiology: The nervous system* (pp. 1017–1061). Bethesda, MD: American Physiological Society.

Denny-Brown, D. (1949). Interpretation of the electromyogram. *Archives of Neurology and Psychiatry, 61,* 99–128.

Dewhurst, D.J. (1967). Neuromuscular control system. *IEEE Transactions on Biomedical Engineering, 14,* 167–171.

Doody, S.G., Bird, A.M., & Ross, D. (1985). The effect of auditory and visual models on acquisition of a timing task. *Human Movement Science, 4,* 271–281.

Dudai, Y. (1989). *The neurobiology of memory. Concepts, findings, trends.* Oxford, England: Oxford University Press.

Edwards, J.M., Elliott, D., & Lee, T.D. (1986). Contextual interference effects during skill acquisition and transfer in Down's syndrome adolescents. *Adapted Physical Activity Quarterly, 3,* 250–258.

Emmon, H.H., Wesseling, L.G., Bootsma, R.J., Whiting, H.T.A., & van Wieringen, P.C.W. (1985). The effect of video-modelling and video-feedback on the learning of the tennis serve by novices. *Journal of Sport Sciences, 3,* 127–138.

Enoka, R.M. (1994). *Neuromechanical basis of kinesiology* (2nd ed.). Champaign, IL: Human Kinetics.

Enoka, R.M., Miller, D.I., & Burgess, E.M. (1982). Below-knee amputee running gait. *American Journal of Physical Medicine, 61,* 66–84.

Ericsson, K.A., & Polson, P.G. (1984). A cognitive analysis of exceptional memory for restaurant orders. In M. Chi, R. Glaser, and M. Farr (eds.), *The nature of expertise.* Hillsdale, NJ: Erlbaum.

Eyzaguirre, C., & Fidone, S.J. (1975). *Physiology of the nervous system* (2nd ed.). Chicago, IL: Year Book Medical Publishers.

Farr, M.J. (1987). *The long-term retention of knowledge and skills. A cognitive and instructional perspective.* New York: Springer-Verlag.

Feltz, D.L. (1982). The effect of age and number of demonstrations on modeling form and performance. *Research Quarterly for Exercise and Sport, 53,* 291–296.

Feltz, D.L., & Landers, D.M. (1983). The effects of mental practice on motor skill learning and performance: A meta-analysis. *Journal of Sport Psychology, 5,* 25–57.

Fischman, M.G., & Schneider, T. (1985). Skill level, vision, and proprioception in simple one-hand catching. *Journal of Motor Behavior, 17,* 219–229.

Fitts, P.M. (1964). Perceptual-motor skills learning. In A.W. Melton (ed.), *Categories of human learning* (pp. 243–285). New York: Academic Press.

Fodor, J.A., & Pylyshyn, Z.W. (1981). How direct is visual perception? Some reflections on Gibson's "Ecological Approach." *Cognition, 9,* 139–196.

Forssberg, H. (1985). Ontogeny of human locomotor control. I. Infant stepping, supported locomotion, and transition to independent locomotion. *Experimental Brain Research, 57,* 480–493.

Forssberg, H., Grillner, S., & Rossignol, S. (1977). Phasic gain control of reflexes from the dorsum of the paw during spinal locomotion. *Brain Research, 132,* 121–139.

Fournier, E., & Pierrot-Deseilligny, E. (1989). Changes in transmission in some reflex pathways during movement in humans. NIPS 4, 29–32.

Fowler, C., & Turvey, M.T. (1978). Skill acquisition: An event approach with special reference to searching for the optimum of a function of several variables. In G. Stelmach (ed.), *Information processing in motor control and learning* (pp. 1–40). New York: Academic Press.

French, K.E., & Thomas, J.R. (1987). The relation of knowledge development to children's basketball performance. *Journal of Sport Psychology, 9,* 15–32.

Fritsch, G., & Hitzig, E. (1870). Uber die elektrische errebarkeit des grosshirns. *Archives of Anatomical Physiologie, 37,* 300–332. (trans. G. von Bonin). In Some Papers on the Cerebral Cortex. Springfield, IL: Thomas, 1960 (pp. 73–96).

Gabriele, T.E., Hall, C.R., & Buckholz, E.E. (1987). Practice schedule effects on the acquisition and retention of a motor skill. *Human Movement Science, 6,* 1–6.

Gentile, A.M. (1972). A working model of skill acquisition with application to teaching. *Quest,* Monograph XVII, 3–23.

Gentile, A.M. (1987). Skill acquisition: Action, movement, and neuromotor processes. In J.H. Carr, R.B. Shephard, J. Gordon, A.M. Gentile, and J.M. Held (eds.), *Movement science. Foundations for physical therapy in rehabilitation* (pp. 93–154).

Gentner, D. (1982). Are scientific analogies metaphors? In D.S. Miall (Ed.), *Metaphor: Problems and perspectives* (pp. 106–118). Brighton, Sussex, England: Harvester Press, Ltd.

Gerst, M.S. (1971). Symbolic coding processes in observational learning. *Journal of Personality and Social Psychology, 19,* 9–17.

Gibson, J.J. (1966). *The senses considered as perceptual systems.* Boston: Houghton Mifflin.

Gibson, J.J. (1979). *The ecological approach to visual perception.* Boston: Houghton Mifflin.

Gilbert, P.F.C., & Thach, W.T. (1977). Purkinje cell activity during motor learning. *Brain Research, 70,* 1–18.

Glendon, A.I., Mckenna, S.P., Blaylock, S.S., & Hunt, K. (1987). Evaluating mass training in cardiopulmonary resuscitation. *British Medical Journal, 294,* 1182–1183.

Glickstein, M., & Yeo, C. (1989). The cerebellum and motor learning. *Journal of Cognitive Neuroscience, 2,* 2, 69–79.

Goode, S.L. (1986). The contextual interference effect in learning an open motor skill. Unpublished doctoral dissertation, Louisiana State University, Baton Rouge, LA.

Goode, S.L., & Magill, R.A. (1986). The contextual interference effect in learning three badminton serves. *Research Quarterly for Exercise and Sport, 57,* 308–314.

Goode, S.L., & Wei, P. (1988). "Differential effects of variations of random and blocked practice on novice learning an open motor skill" (Abstract). In D.L. Gill and J.E. Clarke (eds.), *Abstracts of research papers, 1988* (p. 80). American Alliance for Health, Physical Education, Recreation and Dance Annual Convention, Kansas City, MO. Reston, VA: AAHPERD.

Goodwin, G.M., McCloskey, D.I., & Matthews, P.B.C. (1972). The contribution of muscle afferents to kinesthesia shown by vibration-induced illusions of movement and by the effects of paralysing joint afferents. *Brain, 95,* 705–748.

Gordon, J. (1987). Assumptions underlying physical therapy intervention: Theoretical and historical perspectives. In J.H. Carr, R.B. Shephard, J. Gordon, A.M. Gentile, and J.M. Held, (eds.), *Movement Science. Foundations for Physical Therapy in Rehabilitation* (pp. 1–30). Rockville, MD: Aspen Publications.

Gordon, W.C. (1989). *Learning and memory.* Pacific Grove, CA: Brooks/Cole.

Gould, D.R. (1980). *The influence of motor task types on model effectiveness.* Unpublished doctoral dissertation, University of Illinois.

Gould, D.R., & Weiss, M.R. (1981). The effects of model similarity and model talk on self-efficacy and muscular endurance. *Journal of Sport Psychology, 3,* 17–29.

Goulet, C., Bard, C., & Fleury, M. (1989). Expertise differences in preparing to return a tennis serve: A visual informa-tion processing approach. *Journal of Sport and Exercise Psychology, 11,* 382–398.

Graham G., Holt/Hale, S., & Parker, M. (1993). *Children moving. A reflective approach to teaching physical education.* Mountain View, CA: Mayfield.

Greene, P.H. (1972). Problems of organization of motor systems. In R. Rosen, & F.M. Snell (eds.), *Progress in theoretical biology* (vol. 2). New York: Academic Press.

Grillner, S. (1975). The role of muscle stiffness in meeting the postural and locomotor requirements for force development by the ankle extensors. *Acta Physiologica Scandinavia, 86,* 92–108.

Grillner, S. (1981). Control of locomotion in bipeds, tetrapods, and fish. In V.B. Brooks (ed.), *Handbook of Physiology.* Vol. 3: *Motor control* (pp. 1179–1236). Bethesda, MD: American Physiological Society.

Grossberg, S., & Kuperstein, M. (1986). *Neural dynamics of adaptive sensory-motor control.* Amsterdam: North-Holland.

Gydikov, A., & Kosarov, D. (1973). Physiological characteristics of the tonic and phasic motor units in human muscles. In A.A. Gydikov, N.T. Tankov, and D.S. Kosarov (eds.), *Motor control* (pp. 75–94). New York: Plenum Press.

Gydikov, A., & Kosarov, D. (1974). Some features of different motor units in human biceps brachii. *Pflugers Archiv, 347,* 75–88.

Hallett, M., Shahani, B.T., & Young, R.R. (1975). EMG analysis of patients with cerebellar deficits. *Journal of Neurology, Neurosurgery, and Psychiatry, 38,* 1163–1169.

Halverson, L., Roberton, M.A., & Langendorfer, S. (1982). Development of the overarm throw: Movement and ball velocity changes by seventh grade. *Research Quarterly for Exercise and Sport, 53,* 198–205.

Hay, J.G. (1988). Approach strategies in the long jump. *International Journal of Sport Biomechanics,* 4, 114–129.

Hebb, D.O. (1949). *The organization of behavior.* New York: Wiley.

Helsen, W., & Pauwels , J.M. (1990). Analysis of visual search activity in solving tactical game problems. In D. Brogan (ed.), *Visual Search* (pp. 177–184). London: Taylor & Francis.

Henneman, E. (1957). Relation between size of neurons and their susceptibility to discharge. *Science, 126,* 1345–1347.

Henneman, E. (1979). Functional organization of motoneuron pools: The size principle. In H. Asanuma and V.J. Wilson (eds.), *Integration in the nervous system* (pp. 13–25). Tokyo: Igaku-Shoin.

Henry, F.M. (1974). Variable and constant performance errors with a group of individuals. *Journal of Motor Behavior, 6,* 149–154.

Henry, F.M., & Rogers, D.E. (1960). Increased response latency for complicated movements and a "memory drum" theory of neuromotor reaction. *Research Quarterly, 31,* 448–458.

Ho, L., & Shea, J. B. (1978). Levels of processing and the coding of position cues in motor short-term memory. *Journal of Motor Behavior, 10,* 113–121.

Hogan, J., & Yanowitz, B. (1978). The role of verbal estimates of movement error in ballistic skill acquisition. *Journal of Motor Behavior, 10,* 133–138.

Holding, D.H. (1976). *The principles of training.* Oxford: Pergamon Press.

Hollerbach, J.M. (1987). *A study of human motor control through analysis and synthesis of handwriting.* Unpublished dissertation, Massachusetts Institute of Technology, Cambridge, MA.

Housner, L., & Hoffman, S.J. (1981). Imagery ability in recall of distance and location information. *Journal of Motor Behavior, 13,* 207–223.

Hubbard, A.W., & Seng, C.N. (1954). Visual movements of batters. *Research Quarterly, 25,* 42–57.

Hurlock, R.E., & Montague, W.E. (1982). *Skill retention and its implications for navy tasks: An analytical review.* NPRDC SR 82–21, San Diego, CA: Navy Personnel Research and Development Center.

Inglis, J., Campbell, D., & Donald, M.W. (1976). Electromyographic feedback and neuromuscular rehabilitation. *Canadian Journal of Behavioral Science,* 8, 299–323.

Jelsma, O., & Pieters, J.M. (1989). Practice schedule and cognitive style interaction in learning a maze task. *Applied Cognitive Psychology,* 3, 73–83.

Jelsma, O., & Van Merrienboer, J.J.G. (1989). Contextual interference interactions with reflection-impulsivity. *Perceptual and Motor Skills, 68,* 1055–1064.

Johansson, G. (1971). Visual motion perception: A model for visual motion and space perception from changing proximal stimulation. *Report from the Department of Psychology, University of Uppsala, No. 98.*

Johansson, G. (1976). Spatio-temporal differentiation and integration in visual motion perception. *Psychological Research*, 38, 379–393.

Johansson, G., von Hofsten, G., & Jansson, G. (1980). Event perception. *Annual Review of Psychology*, 31, 27–63.

Johnson, R.W., Wicks, G., & Ben-Sira, D. (1981). Practice in the absence of knowledge of results: Skill acquistion and retention. In G.C. Roberts and D.M. Landers (eds.), *Psychology of Motor Behavior and Sport*. Champaign, IL: Human Kinetics Publ.

Jones, M.B. (1985). *Nonimposed overpractice and skill retention*. (Contract No. MDA 903-83-K-0246.) Alexandria, VA: Army Research Institute for the Behavioral and Social Sciences.

Jordan, T.C. (1972). Characteristics of visual and proprioceptive response times in the learning of a motor skill. *Journal of Experimental Psychology*, 24, 536–543.

Keele, S.W. (1968). Movement control in skilled motor performance. *Psychological Bulletin*, 70, 387–403.

Kelso, J.A.S. (1977). Motor control mechanisms underlying human movement production. *Journal of Experimental Psychology: Human Perception and Performance*, 3, 529–543.

Kelso, J.A.S., & Tuller, B. (1984). A dynamical basis for action systems. In M.S. Gazzaniga (ed.), *Handbook of cognitive neuroscience* (pp. 321–356). New York: Plenum Press.

Kent, D.L., & Larson, E.B. (1988). Magnetic resonance imaging of the brain and the spine: Is clinical efficacy established after the first decade? *Annals of Internal Medicine*, 108, 402–424.

Kernodle, M. W., & Carlton, L. G. (1992). Information feedback and the learning of multiple-degree-of-freedom activities. *Journal of Motor Behavior*, 24, 2, 187–196.

Kieras, D.E. (1981). *Knowledge representation in cognitive psychology*. (Contract No. N00014-78-C-0509.) Personnel and Training Research Programs, Office of Naval Research. (Tech Report No. 7).

Klapp, S.T. (1975). Feedback versus motor programming in the control of aimed movements. *Journal of Experimental Psychology: Human Perception and Performance*, 104, 147–153.

Knutsson, E. (1983). Analysis of gait and isokinetic movements for evaluation of anti-spastic drugs or physical therapies. In J.E. Desmedt (ed.), *Motor control mechanisms in health and disease* (pp. 1013–1034). New York: Raven Press.

Knutsson, E., & Richards, C. (1979). Different types of distributed motor control in gait of hemiparetic patients. *Brain*, 102, 405–430.

Konoske, P.J., & Ellis, J.A. (1985). *Cognitive factors in learning and retention of procedural tasks*. Paper presented at the meeting of the American Educational Research Association, Chicago, IL.

Kowalski, E.M., & Sherrill, C. (1992). Motor sequencing of boys with learning disabilities: Modeling and verbal rehearsal strategies. *Adapted Physical Activity Quarterly*, 9, 261–272.

Kugler, P.N. & Turvey, M.T. (1987). *Information, natural law and the self-assembly of rhythmic movement*. Hillsdale, NJ: Erlbaum.

Kugler, P.N., Kelso, J.A.S., & Turvey, M.T. (1980). On the concept of coordinative structures as dissipative structures: I. Theoretical lines of convergence. In G.E.

Stelmach & J. Requin (eds.), *Tutorials in motor behavior* (pp. 3–47). Amsterdam: North-Holland.

Kugler, P.N., Kelso, J.A.S., & Turvey, M.T. (1982). On the control and coordination in naturally developing systems. In J.A.S. Kelso and J.E. Clark (eds.), *The development of movement control and coordination* (pp. 5–78). New York: Wiley.

Landers, D.M., & Landers, D.M. (1973). Teacher versus peer models: Effect of model's presence and performance level on motor behavior. *Journal of Motor Behavior, 5,* 129–139.

Lashley, K.S. (1917). The accuracy of movement in the absence of excitation from the moving organ. *The American Journal of Physiology, 43,* 169–194.

Lashley, K.S. (1929). *Brain mechanisms and intelligence.* Chicago: University of Chicago Press.

Lashley, K.S. (1950). In search of the engram. *Symp. Soc. Experimental Biology.* 4, 454–82.

Laszlo, J.I., & Bairstow, E.J. (1983). Kinesthesia: Its measurement, training and relationship to motor control. *Quarterly Journal of Experimental Psychology, 35A,* 411–422.

Lavery, J.J. (1962). Retention of simple motor skills as a function of type of knowledge of results. *Canadian Journal of Psychology, 16,* 300–311.

Lee, D.N. (1976). A theory of visual control of braking based on information about time-to-collision. *Perception, 5,* 437–459.

Lee, D.N. (1978). The functions of vision. In H. Pick and E. Salzmann (eds.), *Modes of perceiving and processing information,* (pp. 159–170). Hillsdale, NJ: Erlbaum.

Lee, D.N. (1980). Visuo-motor coordination in space-time. In G.E. Stelmach and J. Requin (eds.), *Tutorials in motor behavior* (pp. 281–295). Amsterdam: North-Holland.

Lee, D.N., & Aronson, E. (1974). Visual proprioceptive control of standing in human infants. *Perception and Psychophysics, 15,* 527–532.

Lee, D.N., & Lishman, J.R. (1975). Visual proprioceptive control of stance. *Journal of Human Movement Studies, 1,* 87–95.

Lee, D.N., & Young, D.S. (1985). Visual timing of interceptive action. In D. Ingle, M. Jeannerod, and D.N. Lee (eds.), *Brain mechanisms and spatial vision* (pp. 1–30). Dordrecht, Netherlands: Martinus Nijhoff.

Lee, D.N., Lishman, J.R., & Thomson, J.A. (1982). Regulation of gait in long-jumping. *Journal of Experimental Psychology: Human Perception and Performance, 8,* 448–459.

Lee, D.N., Lough, F., & Lough, S. (1984). Activating the perceptuo-motor system in hemiparesis. *Journal of Physiology,* 349, 28P.

Lee, T.D. (1988). Testing for motor learning: A focus on transfer-appropriate processing. In O.G. Meijer and K. Roth (eds.), *Complex motor behavior: "The" motor-action controversy* (pp. 201–215). Amsterdam: Elsevier Science.

Lee, T.D., & Carnahan, H. (1990). Bandwidth knowledge of results and motor learning: More than just a relative frequency effect. *Quarterly Journal of Experimental Psychology, 42A,* 777–789.

Lee, T.D., & Genovese, E.D. (1988). Distribution of practice in motor skill acquisition: Learning and performance effects reconsidered. *Research Quarterly for Exercise and Sport, 59,* 59–67.

Lee, T.D., & Magill, R.A. (1983). The locus of contextual interference in motor skill acquisition. *Journal of Experimental Psychology: Learning, Memory, and Cognition, 9,* 730–746.

Lee, T.D., & Magill, R.A. (1985). Can forgetting facilitate skill acquisition? In D. Goodman, R.B. Wilberg, and I.M. Franks (eds.), *Differing perspectives in motor learning, memory and control* (pp. 3–22). Amsterdam: North-Holland.

Lee, T.D., & White, M.A. (1990). Influence of an unskilled model's practice schedule on observational motor learning. *Human Movement Science, 9,* 349–367.

Lee, T.D., Magill, R.A., & Weeks, D. J. (1985). Influence of practice schedule on testing schema theory predictions in adults. *Journal of Motor Behavior, 17,* 283–299.

Lirgg, C.D., & Feltz, D.L. (1991). Teacher versus peer models revisited: Effects on motor performance and self-efficacy. *Research Quarterly for Exercise and Sport, 62,* 2, 217–224.

Magill, R.A. (1989). *Motor learning: Concepts and applications* (3rd ed.). Dubuque, IA: Wm. C. Brown.

Magill, R.A. (1993). *Motor learning. Concepts and applications* (4th ed.). Dubuque, IA: Wm. C. Brown.

Magill, R.A., & Hall, K. G. (1990). A review of the contextual interference effect in motor skill acquisition. *Human Movement Science, 9,* 241–289.

Magill, R.A., & Wood, C.A. (1986). Knowledge of results precision as a learning variable in motor skill acquisition. *Research Quarterly for Exercise and Sport, 57,* 170–173.

Martens, R., Burwitz, L., & Zuckerman, J. (1976). Modeling effects on motor performance. *Research Quarterly, 47,* 2, 277–291.

Martenuik, R.G., Leavitt, J.L., MacKenzie, C.L., & Athenes, S. (1993). Functional relationship between grasp and transport components in a prehension task. *Human Movement Science,* Vol. 9, pp. 149–176.

Martone, M., Butters, N., Payne, M., Becker, J.T., & Sax, D.S. (1984). Dissociations between skill learning and verbal recognition in amnesia and dementia. *Archives of Neurology, 41,* 965–970.

Matthews, P.B.C. (1981). Proprioceptors and the regulation of movement. In A.L. Towe and E.S. Luschei (eds.), *Motor coordination.* Vol. 5 in *Handbook of behavioral neurobiology* (pp. 93–127). New York: Plenum Press.

McAuley, E. (1985). Modeling and self-efficacy: A test of Bandura's model. *Journal of Sport Psychology, 7,* 283–295.

McCloskey, D.I. (1973). Differences between the senses of movement and position shown by the effects of loading and vibration of muscles in man. *Brain Research, 61,* 119–131.

McCloskey, D.I., Cross, M.J., Honner, R., & Potter, E.K. (1983). Sensory effects of pulling of vibrating exposed tendons in man. *Brain, 106,* 21–37.

McCrea, D.A. (1992). Can sense be made of spinal interneuron circuits? *Behavioral and Brain Sciences, 15,* 4, 633–643.

McCullagh, P. (1986). A model's status as a determinant of attention in observational learning and performance. *Journal of Sport Psychology, 8,* 319–331.

McCullagh, P. (1987). Model similarity effects on motor performance. *Journal of Sport Psychology, 9,* 249–260.

McCullagh, P., & Caird, J.K. (1990). Correct and learning models and the use of model knowledge of results in the acquisition and retention of a motor skill. *Journal of Human Movement Studies, 18,* 107–116.

McCullagh, P., Stiehl, J., & Weiss, M.R. (1990). Developmental considerations in modeling: The role of visual and verbal models and verbal rehearsal in skill acquisition. *Research Quarterly for Exercise and Sport, 61,* 344–350.

McCullagh, P., Weiss, M.R., & Ross, D. (1989). Modeling considerations in motor skill acquisition and performance: An integrated approach. In K.B. Pandolf (ed.), *Exercise and sport science reviews* (vol. 17, pp. 475–513). Baltimore: Williams & Wilkins.

McDonald, P.V., van Emmerik, R.E.A., & Newell, K.M. (1989). The effects of practice on limb kinematics in a throwing task. *Journal of Motor Behavior, 21,* 3, 245–264.

McIntyre, D.R., & Pfautsch, E.W. (1982). A kinematic analysis of the baseball batting swing involved in opposite-field and same-field hitting. *Research Quarterly for Exercise and Sport, 53,* 206–213.

McKenna, S.P., & Glendon, A.I. (1985). Occupational first aid training. Decay in cardiopulmonary resuscitation (CPR) skills. *Journal of Occupational Psychology, 58,* 109–117.

McPherson, S. (1993). The influence of player experience on problem solving during batting preparation in baseball. *Journal of Sport and Exercise Psychology, 15,* 304–325.

McPherson, S.L., & Thomas, J.R. (1989). Relation of knowledge and performance in boy's tennis: Age and expertise. *Journal of Experimental Child Psychology, 48,* 190–211.

Meany, K. S. (1994). Developmental modeling effects on the acquisition, retention, and transfer of a novel motor task. *Research Quarterly for Exercise and Sport, 65,* 1, 31–39.

Meeuwsen, H., & Magill, R.A. (1987). The role of vision in gait control during gymnastics vaulting. In T.B. Hoshizaki, J. Slamela, and B. Petiot (eds.), *Diagnostics, treatment, and analysis of gymnastic talent* (pp. 137–155). Montreal: Sport Psyche Editions.

Meichenbaum, D., & Goodman, J. (1971). Training impulsive children to talk to themselves: A means of developing self-control. *Journal of Abnormal Psychology, 77,* 115–126.

Meijer, O.G., & Roth, K. (eds.) (1988). *Complex motor behavior: "The" motor-action controversy.* Amsterdam: Elsevier Science Publishers B.V. (North-Holland).

Merton, P.A. (1953). Speculations on the servo control of movement. In G.E.W. Wolstenholme (ed.), *The spinal cord.* London: Churchill.

Merton, P.A. (1972). How we control the contraction of our muscles. *Scientific American, 226,* 30–37.

Michaels, C.F., & Carello, C. (1981). *Direct perception.* Englewood Cliffs, NJ: Prentice-Hall.

Milgram, P. (1987). A spectacle-mounted liquid-crystal tachistoscope. *Behavior, Research Methods, Instruments and Computers, 19,* 449–456.

Miller, G.A. (1956). The magical number seven, plus or minus two: Some limits on our capacity for processing information. *Psychological Review, 63,* 81–97.

Mills, V.M. (1988). Traumatic head injury. In S.B. O'Sullivan and T.J. Schmitz (eds.), *Physical rehabilitation: Assessment and treatment* (2nd ed., pp. 495–514). Philadelphia, PA: F.A. Davis.

Mishkin, M. (1978). Memory in monkeys severely impaired by combined but not by separate removal of amygdala and hippocampus. *Nature, 273,* 297–298.

Mishkin, M. (1982). A memory system in the monkey. *Philosophical Transactions of the Royal Society of London. 298,* 85–95.

Moberg, E. (1983). The role of cutaneous afferents in position sense, kinesthesia, and motor function of the hand. *Brain,* 106, 1–19.

Morris, C.D., Bransford, J.D., & Franks, J.J. (1977). Levels of processing versus transfer appropriate processing. *Journal of Verbal Learning and Verbal Behavior,* 16, 519–533.

Morris, C.D., Stein, B.S., & Bransford, J.D. (1979). Prerequisites for the utilization of knowledge in recall of prose passages. *Journal of Experimental Psychology: Human Learning and Memory, 5,* 253–261.

Nashner L.M. (1976). Adapting reflexes controlling human posture. *Experimental Brain Research, 26,* 59–72.

Nashner, L.M., & Grimm, R.J. (1978). Analysis of multiloop dyscontrols in standing cerebellar patients. In J.E. Desmedt (ed.), *Cerebral motor control in man,* (pp. 300–319). Basel: Karger.

Naylor, J., & Briggs, G. (1963). Effects of task complexity and task organization on the relative efficiency of part and whole training methods.

Journal of Experimental Psychology, 65, 217–244.

Newell, K.M. (1974). Knowledge of results and motor learning. *Journal of Motor Behavior,* 6, 235–244.

Newell, K.M. (1985). Coordination, control and skill. In D. Goodman, R.B. Wilberg, and I.M. Franks (eds.), *Differing perspectives in motor learning, memory, and control* (pp. 295–317). Amsterdam: North-Holland.

Newell, K.M. (1991). Motor skill acquisition. *Annual Review of Psychology, 42,* 213–237.

Newell, K.M. & Carlton, M.J. (1987). Augmented information and the acquisition of isometric tasks. *Journal of Motor Behavior,* 19, 4–12.

Newell, K.M., & McDonald, P.V. (1992). Searching for solutions to the coordination function: Learning as exploratory behavior. In G.E. Stelmach and J. Requin (eds.), *Tutorials in Motor Behavior II* (pp. 517–532). Amsterdam: North-Holland.

Newell, K.M., & McGinnis, P.M. (1985). Kinematic information feedback for skilled performance. *Human Learning,* 4, 39–56.

Newell, K.M., & van Emmerik, R.E.A. (1989). The acquisition of coordination: Preliminary analysis of learning to write. *Human Movement Science,* 8, 17–32.

Newell, K.M., & Walter, C.B. (1981). Kinematic and kinetic parameters as information feedback in motor skill acquisition. *Journal of Human Movement Studies,* 7, 235–254.

Newell, K.M., Morris, L.R., & Scully, D.M. (1985). Augmented information and the acquisition of skills in physical activity.

In R.L. Terjung (ed.), *Exercise and Sport Sciences Reviews* (pp. 235–261). New York: Macmillan.

Newell, K.M., Carlton, M.J., Fisher, A.T., & Rutter, B.G. (1989). Whole-part training strategies for learning the response dynamics of microprocessor driven simulators. *Acta Psychologica,* 71, 197–216.

Newell, K.M., Kugler, P.N., van Emmerik, R.E.A., & McDonald, P.V. (1989). Search strategies and the acquisition of coordination. In S.A. Wallace (ed.), *Perspectives on the coordination of movement* (pp. 85–122). Amsterdam: North-Holland.

Newell, K.M., Quinn, J.T., Sparrow, W.A., & Walter, C.B. (1983). Kinematic information feedback for learning a rapid arm movement. *Human Movement Science,* 2, 255–269.

O'Keefe, J., & Nadel, L. (1978). *The hippocampus as a cognitive map.* Oxford, England: Oxford University Press.

O'Sullivan, S.B. (1988). Strategies to improve motor control. In S.B. O'Sullivan and T.J. Schmitz (eds.), *Physical rehabilitation: Assessment and treatment* (pp. 253–280, 2nd ed.). Philadelphia, PA: F.A. Davis.

O'Sullivan, S.B. (1994). Strategies to improve motor control and motor learning. In S.B. O'Sullivan and T.J. Schmitz (eds.), *Physical Rehabilitation: Assessment and Treatment* (3rd ed.). Philadelphia, PA: F.A. Davis (pp. 225–249).

O'Sullivan, S.B., & Schmitz, T.J., eds. (1994). *Physical rehabilitation: Assessment and treatment.* Philadelphia, PA: F.A. Davis.

Ornstein, P.A., Naus, M.J., & Liberty, C. (1975). Rehearsal and organization processes in children's memory. *Child Development,* 26, 818–830.

Osgood, C.E. (1949). The similarity paradox in human learning: A resolution. *Psychological Review,* 56, 132–143.

Owens, J., Bower, G.H., & Black, J.B. (1979). The "soap opera" effect in story recall. *Memory and Cognition,* 7, 185–191.

Oxendine, J.B. (1984). *Psychology of motor learning* (2nd ed.). Englewood Cliffs, NJ: Prentice-Hall.

Parks, S., Rose, D.J., & Dunn, J. (1989). A comparison of fractionated reaction time between cerebral-palsied and non-handicapped youth. *Adapted Physical Activity Quarterly,* 6, 4, 379–388.

Patla, A.E., Prentice, S.D., Robinson, C., & Neufeld, J. (1991). Visual control of locomotion: Strategies for changing direction and for going over obstacles. *Journal of Experimental Psychology: Human Perception and Performance,* 17, 3, 603–634.

Petri, H.L., & Mishkin, M. (1994). Behaviorism, cognitivism and the neuropsychology of memory. *American Scientist,* 82, 30–37.

Pew, R.W. (1974). Levels of analysis in motor control. *Brain Research,* 71, 393–400.

Pew, R.W. (1984). A distributed processing view of human motor control. In W. Prinz and A.F. Sanders (eds.), *Cognition and motor processes* (pp. 19–27). Berlin: Springer.

Piggott, R.E., & Shapiro, D.C. (1984). Motor schema: The structure of the variability session. *Research Quarterly for Exercise and Sport,* 55, 41–54.

Pikler, E. (1968). Some contributions to the study of the gross motor development of children. *The Journal of Genetic Psychology,* 113, 27–39.

Pollock, B.J., & Lee, T.D. (1992). Effects of the model's skill level on observational motor learning. *Research Quarterly for Exercise and Sport,* 63, 1, 25–29.

Poto, C.C., French, K.E., & Magill, R.A. (1987). Serial position and assymetric transfer effects in a contextual interference study. *Paper presented at the annual meeting of the North American Society for the Psychology of Sport and Physical Activity,* Vancouver, B.C., Canada.

Prophet, W.W. (1976). Long-term retention of flying skills: A review of the literature. (HumRRO Final Report 76–35.) Alexandria, VA: Human Resources Research Organization (ADA036077).

Raibert, M.H. (1977). Motor control and learning by the state-space model. Technical Report, Artificial Intelligence Laboratory, Massachusetts Institute of Technology (AI-TR-439), Cambridge, MA.

Reed, E.S. (1982). An outline of a theory of action systems. *Journal of Motor Behavior,* 14, 98–134.

Reeve, T.G., & Magill, R.A. (1981). Role of components of knowledge of results information in error correction. *Research Quarterly for Exercise and Sport,* 52, 80–85.

Reeve, T.G., Dornier, L.A., & Weeks, D.J. (1990). Precision of knowledge of results: Consideration of the accuracy requirements imposed by the task. *Research Quarterly for Exercise and Sport,* 61, 284–290.

Rikli, R., & Smith, G. (1980). Videotape feedback effects on tennis serving form. *Perceptual and Motor Skills,* 50, 895–901.

Roach, N.K., & Burwitz, L. (1986). Observational learning in motor skill acquisition: The effect of verbal directing cues. In J. Watkins and L. Burwitz (eds.), *Sports science: Proceedings of the VIII Commonwealth and International Conference on Sport, Physical Education, Dance, Recreation and Health* (pp. 349–354). London: E. & F.N. Spoon.

Rogers, C.A. (1974). Feedback precision and post-feedback interval duration. *Journal of Experimental Psychology,* 102, 604–608.

Rose, D.J., & Tyry, T. (1994). The relative effectiveness of three model types on the early acquisition of rapid-fire pistol shooting. *Journal of Human Movement Studies,* 26, 87–99.

Rose, D.J., & Clark, S. (1995). Efficacy and transferability of a customized balance training program for "at-risk" older adults. Proceedings of the 5th Asia/Oceania Regional Congress of Gerontology, Hong Kong.

Rosenbaum, D.A., Inhoff, A.W., & Gordon, A.M. (1984). Choosing between movement sequences: A hierarchical editor model. *Journal of Experimental Psychology: General,* 113, 372–393.

Ross, I.D. (1974). Interference in discrete motor tasks: A test of the theory. Unpublished dissertation, University of Michigan.

Rothstein, A.L., & Arnold, R.K. (1976). Bridging the gap: Application of research on videotape feedback and bowling. *Motor skills: Theory into Practice,* 1, 36–61.

Rumelhart, D.E., & McClelland, J.L. (1986). *Parallel distributed processing. Explorations in the microstructure of cognition* (vol. 1). Cambridge, MA: M.I.T. Press.

Salmoni, A.W., Schmidt, R.A., & Walter, C. B. (1984). Knowledge of results and motor learning: A review and reappraisal. *Psychological Bulletin,* 95, 355–386.

Sawle, G.V., & Myers, R. (1993). The role of positron emission tomography in the assessment of neurotransplantation. *Trends in Neuroscience,* 16, 5, 172–176.

Schendel, J.D., Shields, J., & Katz, M. (1978). *Retention of motor skills: Review.* (Technical Paper 313.) Alexandria, VA: U.S. Army Research Institute for the Behavioral and Social Sciences.

Schmidt, R.A. (1975). A schema theory of discrete motor skill learning. *Psychological Review,* 82, 225–260.

Schmidt, R.A. (1976). Control processes in motor skills. *Exercise and Sport Sciences Reviews,* 4, 229–261.

Schmidt, R.A. (1982). More on motor programs. In J.A.S. Kelso (ed.), *Human motor behavior. An introduction* (pp. 189–207). Hillsdale, NJ: Erlbaum.

Schmidt, R.A. (1982). The schema concept. In J.A.S. Kelso (ed.), *Human motor behavior: An introduction* (pp. 219–235). Hillsdale, NJ: Erlbaum.

Schmidt, R.A. (1988). *Motor control and learning: A behavioral emphasis* (2nd ed.). Champaign, IL: Human Kinetics.

Schmidt, R.A. (1988). Motor and action perspectives on motor behavior. In O.G. Meijer and K. Roth (eds.), *Complex motor behavior: "The" motor-action controversy* (pp. 3–44). Amsterdam: North-Holland.

Schmidt, R.A. (1991). *Motor learning and performance. From principles to practice.* Champaign, IL: Human Kinetics.

Schmidt, R.A. (1991). Frequent augmented feedback can degrade learning: Evidence and interpretations. In G.E. Stelmach and J.Requin (eds.), *Tutorials in motor neuroscience* (pp. 59–75). Norwell, Mass: Kluwer Academic Publishers.

Schmidt, R.A. (1992). Motor learning principles for physical therapy. In Lister M. (ed.), *Contemporary Management of Motor Problems. (Proceedings of the II STEP Conference,* pp. 65–76). Alexandria, VA: Foundation for Physical Therapy, Inc.

Schmidt, R.A., & White, J.L. (1972). Evidence for an error-detection mechanism in motor skills: A test of Adams' closed-loop theory. *Journal of Motor Behavior,* 4, 143–153.

Schmidt, R.A., & Young, D.E. (1987). Transfer of motor control in motor skill learning. In S.M. Cormier and J.D. Hagman (eds.), *Transfer of learning* (pp. 47–79). Orlando, FL: Academic Press.

Schmidt, R.A., Lange, C.A., & Young, D.E. (1990). Optimizing summary knowledge of results for increased skill learning. *Human Movement Science,* 9, 325–348.

Schmidt, R.A., Young, D.E., Swinnen, S., & Shapiro, D.C. (1989). Summary knowledge of results for skill acquisition: Support for the guidance hypothesis. *Journal of Experimental Psychology: Learning, Memory, and Cognition,* 15, 352–359.

Schunk, D.H., & Hanson, A.R. (1985). Peer models: Influence on children's self-efficacy and achievement. *Journal of Educational Psychology, 77*, 313–322.

Schunk, D.H., Hanson, A.R., & Cox, C.D. (1987). Peer-model attributes and children's achievement behaviors. *Journal of Educational Psychology, 79*, 54–61.

Scully, D.M. (1986). Visual perception of technical execution and aesthetic quality in biological motion. *Human Movement Science, 5*, 185–206.

Scully, D.M., & Newell, K.M. (1985). Observational learning and the acquisition of motor skills: Toward a visual perception perspective. *Journal of Human Movement Studies, 11*, 169–186.

Seefeldt, V., & Haubenstricker, J. (1982). Patterns, phases, or stages: An analytical model for the study of developmental movement. In J.A.S. Kelso and J.E. Clark (eds.), *The development of movement control and coordination* (pp. 309–318). New York: Wiley.

Shallice, T. (1964). The detection of change and the perceptual-moment hypothesis. *British Journal of Statistical Psychology Record, 17*, 113–135.

Shapiro, D.C. (1978). *The learning of generalized motor programs.* Unpublished doctoral dissertation, University of Southern California, Los Angeles.

Shapiro, D.C., & Schmidt, R.A. (1982). The schema theory: Recent evidence and developmental implications. In J.A.S. Kelso and J.A. Clark (eds.), *The development of movement control and coordination,* (pp. 113–150). New York: Wiley.

Shapiro, D.C., Zernicke, R.F., Gregor, R.J., & Diestel, J.D. (1981). Evidence for generalized motor programs using gait-pattern analysis. *Journal of Motor Behavior, 13*, 33–47.

Sharp, R.H., & Whiting, H.T.A. (1974). Information processing and eye movement behavior in a ball-catching skill. *Journal of Human Movement Studies, 1*, 124–131.

Shea, J.B., & Morgan, R.L. (1979). Contextual interference effects on the acquisition, retention, and transfer of a motor skill. *Journal of Experimental Psychology: Human Learning and Memory, 5*, 179–187.

Shea, J.B., & Zimny, S.L. (1983). Context effects in memory and learning in movement information. In R.A. Magill (ed.), *Memory and control of action* (pp. 345–366). Amsterdam: North-Holland.

Shea, J.B., & Zimny, S.T. (1988). Knowledge incorporation in motor representation. In O.G. Meijer and K. Roth (eds.), *Complex motor behaviour: "The" motor-action controversy* (pp. 289–314). North-Holland: Elsevier.

Sheffield, F.D. (1961). Theoretical considerations in the learning of complex sequential tasks from demonstration and practice. In A.A. Lumsdaine (ed.), *Student Response in Programmed Instruction* (pp. 13–32). Washington, DC: National Academy of Science–National Research Council.

Sheridan, M.R. (1984). Planning and controlling simple movements. In M.M. Smyth and A.L. Wing (eds.), *The psychology of movement* (pp. 47–82). London, UK: Academic Press.

Sherrington, C.S. (1906). *The integrative action of the nervous system.* New Haven: Yale University Press (reprinted 1947).

Sherwood, D.E. (1988). Effect of bandwidth knowledge of results on movement consistency. *Perceptual and Motor Skills, 66*, 535–542.

Shumway-Cook, A., Anson, D., & Haller, S. (1988). Postural sway biofeedback: Its effect on reestablishing stance stability in hemiplegic patients. *Archives of Physical Medicine and Rehabilitation, 69*, 395–400.

Sidaway, B., McNitt-Gray, J., & Davis, G. (1989). Visual timing of muscle preactivation in preparation for landing. *Ecological Psychology, 1*, 253–264.

Singer, R.N. (1980). *Motor learning and human performance* (3rd ed.). New York: Macmillan.

Skinner, B.F. (1938). *The behavior of organisms.* New York: Appleton-Century.

Smith, E., & Goodman, L. (1984). Understanding instructions: The role of explanatory material. *Cognition and Instruction, 1*, 359–396.

Smith, J.L. (1969). *Fusimotor neuron block and voluntary arm movement in man.* Unpublished dissertation, University of Wisconsin, Madison, WI.

Smoll, F.L. (1972). Effects of precision of information feedback upon acquisition of a motor skill. *Research Quarterly, 43*, 489–493.

Smyth, M.M., & Marriott, A.M. (1982). Vision and proprioception in simple catching. *Journal of Motor Behavior, 14*, 143–152.

Snoddy, G.S. (1926). Learning and stability. *Journal of Applied Psychology, 10*, 1–36.

Sparrow, W.A. (1983). The efficiency of skilled performance. *Journal of Motor Behavior, 15*, 237–261.

Sparrow, W.A., & Irizarry-Lopez, V.M. (1987). Mechanical efficiency and metabolic cost as measures of learning a novel gross motor task. *Journal of Motor Behavior, 19*, 240–264.

Starkes, J.L., & Deakin, J.M. (1984). Perception in sport: A cognitive approach to skilled performance. In W.F. Straub and J.M. Williams (eds.), *Cognitive Sport Psychology* (pp. 115–128). Lansing, NY: Sport Science Associates.

Starkes, J.L., Edwards, P., Dissanayake, P., & Dunn, T. (1995). A new technology and field test of advance cue usage in volleyball. *Research Quarterly for Exercise and Sport, 66*, 2, 162–167.

Stelmach, G.E., Garcia-Colera, A., & Martin, Z.E. (1989). Force transition control within a movement sequence in Parkinson's disease. *Journal of Neurology, Neurosurgery and Psychiatry, 50*, 296–303.

Stelmach, G.E., Worringham, C.J., & Strand, E.A. (1986). Movement preparation in Parkinson's disease: The use of advance information. *Brain, 109*, 1179–1194.

Stelmach, G.E., Worringham, C.J., & Strand, E.A. (1987). The programming and execution of movement sequences in Parkinson's disease. *International Journal of Neuroscience, 36*, 55–65.

Sternberg, S., Monsell, S., Knoll, R.L., & Wright, C.E. (1978). The latency and duration of rapid movement sequences: Comparisons of speech and typewriting. In G.E. Stelmach (ed.), *Information processing in motor control and learning* (pp. 117–152). New York: Academic Press.

Strick, P.L. (1983). The influence of motor preparation on the response of cerebellar neurons to limb displacements. *Journal of Neuroscience, 3*, 2007–2020.

Swinnen, S.P., Schmidt, R.A., Nicholson, D.E., & Shapiro, D.C. (1990). Information feedback for skill acquisition: Instantaneous knowledge of results degrades learning. *Journal of Experimental Psychology: Learning, Memory, and Cognition, 16,* 706–716.

Swinnen, S.P., Walter, C.B., Lee, T.D., & Serrien, D.J. (1993). Acquiring bimanual skills: Contrasting forms of information feedback for interlimb decoupling. *Journal of Experimental Psychology: Learning, Memory, and Cognition, 19,* 6, 1328–1344.

Tarver, S., Hallahan, D., Kauffman, J., & Ball, D. (1976). Verbal rehearsal and selective attention in children with learning disabilities: A developmental lag. *Journal of Experimental Child Psychology, 22,* 375–385.

Taub, E., & Berman, A.J. (1968). Movement and learning in the absence of sensory feedback. In S.J. Freedman (ed.), *The neuropsychology of spatially oriented behavior* (pp. 173–192). Homewood, IL: Dorsey Press.

Taub, E., & Berman, A.J. (1968). Movements in nonhuman primates deprived of somatosensory feedback. *Exercise and Sport Sciences Reviews, 4,* 335–374.

Thach, W.T. (1978). Correlation of neural discharge with pattern and force of muscular activity, joint position, and directon of the intended movement in motor cortex and cerebellum. *Journal of Neurophysiology, 41,* 654–676.

Thelen, E. (1986). Development of coordinated movement: Implications for early human development. In H.T.A. Whiting and M.G. Wade (eds.), *Motor develop-* *ment in children: Aspects of coordination and control* (pp. 107–124). Dordrecht, Netherlands: Martinus Nijhoff.

Thelen, E., & Smith, L.B. (1994). A dynamic systems approach to the development of cognition and action. Cambridge, MA: M.I.T. Press.

Thomas, J.R. (1980). Acquisition of motor skills: Information processing differences between children and adults. *Research Quarterly, 51,* 158–173.

Thomas, J.R., & Gallagher, G.D. (1986). Memory development and motor skill acquisition. In Seefeldt, V. (ed.), *Contributions of physical activity to human well-being* (pp. 125–139). Reston, VA: AAHPERD Publications.

Thomas, J.R., French, K.E., & Humphries, C.A. (1985). Knowledge development and sport skill performance: Directions for motor behavior research. *Journal of Sport Psychology, 8,* 259–272.

Thomas, J.R. (1984). Children's motor skill development. In J.R. Thomas (ed.), *Motor skill development during childhood and adolescence* (pp. 91–104). New York: McGraw-Hill.

Thompson, R.F. (1980). The search for the engram, II. In D.McFadden (ed.), *Neural mechanisms in behavior: A Texas symposium* (pp. 172–222). New York: Springer-Verlag.

Thorndike, E.L. (1914). *Educational psychology: Briefer course.* New York: Columbia University Press.

Thorndike, E.L. (1927). The law of effect. *American Journal of Psychology, 39,* 212–222.

Thorndike, E.L., & Woodworth, R.S. (1901a). The influence of improvement in one mental function upon the efficiency of other functions. *Psychological Review,* 8, 247–261.

Titzer, R., Smith, L., & Thelen, E. (1995). The effects of infants' experience on the visual cliff and a reaching task. *Journal of Sport and Exercise Psychology,* 17, supplement, 103.

Tourangeau, R., & Sternberg, R. (1982). Understanding and appreciating metaphors. *Cognition,* 11, 203–244.

Tulving, E. (1983). *Elements of episodic memory.* Oxford, England: Clarendon Press/Oxford University Press.

Tulving, E. (1985). How many memory systems are there? *American Psychologist,* 40, 385–398.

Tulving, E., & Thomson, D.M. (1973). Encoding specificity and retrieval processes in episodic memory. *Psychological Review,* 80, 352–373.

Turvey, M.T. (1974). Perspectives in vision: Conception or perception. In D.D. Duane and M.B. Rawson (eds.), *Reading, perception and language,* (pp. 131-194). Baltimore, MD: York Press.

Turvey, M.T. (1977). Preliminaries to a theory of action with reference to vision. In R. Shaw and J. Bransford (eds.), *Perceiving, acting, and knowing* (pp. 211–265). Hillsdale, NJ: Erlbaum.

Turvey, M.T. (1990). Coordination. *American Psychologist,* 45, 938–953.

Turvey, M.T., & Carello, C. (1981). Cognition: The view from ecological realism. *Cognition,* 10, 313–321.

Turvey, M.T., & Carello, C. (1988). Exploring a law-based ecological approach to skilled action. In A.M. Colley and J.R. Beech (eds.), *Cognition and action in skilled behavior* (pp. 247–253). Amsterdam: North-Holland.

Turvey, M.T., Fitch, H.L., & Tuller, B. (1982). The Bernstein perspective: I. The problems of degrees-of-freedom and context-conditioned variability. In J.A.S. Kelso (ed.), *Human motor behavior: An introduction* (pp. 239–252). Hillsdale, NJ: Erlbaum.

van Emmerik, R.E.A., den Brinker, B.P.L.M., Vereijken, B., & Whiting, H.T.A. (1989). Preferred tempo in the learning of a gross cyclical action. *The Quarterly Journal of Experimental Psychology,* 41, 251–262.

Van Rossum, J.H.A. (1990). Schmidt's schema theory: The empirical base of the variability of practice hypothesis. *Human Movement Science,* 9, 387–435.

van Wieringen, P.C.W. (1988). Discussion: Self-organization or representation? Let's have both! In A.M. Colley and J.R. Beech (eds.), *Cognition and action in skilled behaviour* (pp. 247–253). Amsterdam: North-Holland.

van Wieringen, P.C.W., Emmen, H.H., Bootsma, R.J., Hoogesteger, M., & Whiting, H.T.A. (1989). The effect of video-feedback on the learning of the tennis serve by intermediate players. *Journal of Sport Sciences,* 7, 153–162.

Vereijken, B. (1991). The dynamics of skill acquisition. Unpublished dissertation, Free University, Netherlands.

Vereijken, B., & Whiting, H.T.A. (1988). A comparison of echokinetic and synkinetic paradigms in the learning of a complex cyclical action. *Pre-proceedings of the Second Workshop on Imagery and Cognition.*

Vereijken, B., van Emmerik, R.E.A., Whiting, H.T.A., & Newell, K.M. (1992). Free(z)ing degrees of freedom in skill acquisition. *Journal of Motor Behavior*, 24, 1, 133–142.

Vickers, J.N. (1988). Knowledge structure of expert-novice gymnasts. *Human Movement Science*, 7, 47–72.

Warren, W.H., Jr., Young, D.S., & Lee, D.N. (1986). Visual control of step length during running over irregular terrain. *Journal of Experimental Psychology: Human Perception and Performance*, 12, 259–266.

Weeks, D.L., & Sherwood, D.E. (1994). A comparison of knowledge of results scheduling methods for promoting motor skill acquisition and retention. *Research Quarterly for Exercise and Sport*, 65, 2, 136–142.

Weiskrantz, L., Warrington, E.K., Sanders, M.D., & Marshall, J. (1974). Visual capacity in the hemianopic field following a restricted cortical ablation. *Brain*, 97, 709–728.

Weiss, M.R. (1983). Modeling and motor performance: A developmental perspective. *Research Quarterly for Exercise and Sport*, 54, 190–197.

Weiss, M.R., & Klint, K.A. (1987). "Show and tell" in the gymnasium: An investigation of developmental differences in modeling and verbal rehearsal of motor skills. *Research Quarterly for Exercise and Sport*, 58, 234–241.

Weiss, M.R., Ebbeck, V., & Rose, D.J. (1992). "Show and tell" in the gymnasium revisited: Developmental differences in modeling and verbal rehearsal effects on motor skill learning. *Research Quarterly for Exercise and Sport*, 63, 292–301.

Whiting, H.T.A. (1970). An operational analysis of a continuous ball-throwing and catching task. *Ergonomics*, 13, 445–454.

Whiting, H.T.A., Bijlard, M.J., & den Brinker, B.P.L.M. (1987). The effect of the availability of a dynamic model on the acquisition of a complex cyclical action. *The Quarterly Journal of Experimental Psychology*, 39, 43–59.

Whiting, H.T.A., Gill, E.B., & Stephenson, J.M. (1970). Critical time intervals for taking in flight information in a ball-catching task. *Ergonomics*, 13, 265–272.

Wightman, D.C., & Lintern, G. (1985). Part-task training strategies for tracking and manual control. *Human Factors*, 27, 267–283.

Williams, A.M., Davids, K., Burwitz, L., & Williams, J.G. (1992). Perception and action in sport. A review. *Journal of Human Movement Studies*, 22, 147–204.

Winstein, C.J., & Garfinkel, A. (1985). Qualitative dynamics of disordered human locomotion: A preliminary investigation. *Journal of Motor Behavior*, 21, 4, 373–391.

Winstein, C.J, & Schmidt, R.A. (1990). Reduced frequency of knowledge of results enhances motor skill learning. *Journal of Experimental Psychology: Learning, Memory, and Cognition*. 16, 677–691.

Winstein, C.J., Christensen, S., & Fitch, N. (1993). Effects of summary knowledge of results on the acquisition and retention of partial weight bearing during gait. *Physical Therapy Practice*, 2, 4, 40–51.

Winther, K.T., & Thomas, J.R. (1981). Developmental differences in children's labeling of movement. *Journal of Motor Behavior*, 13, 77–90.

Wolf, S.L. (1983). Electromyographic feedback for spinal cord injured patients: A realistic perspective. In J.V. Basmaijian (ed.), *Biofeedback: Principles and practice for clinicians,* (pp. 130–134). Baltimore, MD: Williams & Wilkins.

Wolpaw, J.R., & Carp, J.S. (1990). Memory traces in spinal cord. *Trends in Neuroscience,* 13, 4, 137–142.

Wood, C.A., Gallagher, J.D., Martino, P.V., & Ross, M. (1992). Alternate forms of knowledge of results: Interaction of augmented feedback modality on learning. *Journal of Human Movement Studies,* 22, 213–230.

Wrisberg, C.A., & Mead, B.J. (1983). Developing coincident-timing skill in children: A comparison of training methods. *Research Quarterly for Exercise and Sport,* 54, 67–74.

Young, D.E., & Schmidt, R.A. (1990). Units of motor behavior: Modifications with practice and feedback. In M. Jeannerod (ed.), *Attention and Performance XIII* (pp. 763–795). Hillsdale, NJ: Erlbaum.

Young, D.E., & Schmidt, R.A. (1992). Augmented kinematic feedback and motor learning. *Journal of Motor Behavior,* 24, 261–273.

CREDITS

p. 226 Weiss, M.R., Ebbeck, V., & Rose, D.J. (1992). "Show and tell" in the gymnasium revisited: Developmental differences in modeling and verbal rehearsal effects on motor skill learning. *Research Quarterly for Exercise and Sport, 65,* 2, 127–135. Reprinted with permission.

p. 229 *Journal of Motor Behavior,* 24, 1, 133–142, (1992). Reprinted with permission of the Helen Dwight Reid Educational Foundation. Published by Heldref Publications, 1319 Eighteenth St., N.W., Washington, D.C. 20036–1802. Copyright © 1992.

p. 250 Stelmach, G.E. (1969). Efficiency of motor learning as a function of intertrial rest. *Research Quarterly,* 40, 2, 198–202. Reprinted with permission.

p. 268 Swinnen, S.P., Walter, C.B., Lee, T.D., & Serrien, D.J. (1993). Aquiring bimanual skills: Contrasting forms of information feedback for inter-limb decoupling. *Journal of Experimental Psychology: Learning, Memory, and Cognition,* 19, 6, 1328–1344. Copyright © by the American Psychological Association. Reprinted with permission.

p. 270 Kernodle, M.W., & Carlton, L.G. (1992). Information feedback and the learning of multiple-degree-of-freedom activities. *Journal of Motor Behavior,* 24, 2, 187-196. Reprinted with permission of the Helen Dwight Reid Educational Foundation. Published by Heldref Publications, 1319 Eighteenth St., N.W., Washington, D.C. 20036–1802. Copyright © 1992.

p. 273 Magill, R.A., & Wood, C.A. (1986). Knowledge of results precision as a learning variable in motor skills acquisition. *Research Quarterly for Exercise and Sport,* 57, 2, 170–173. Reprinted with permission

p. 276 Winstein, C.J., & Schmidt, R.A. (1990). Reduced frequency of knowledge of results enhances motor skill learniung. *Journal of Experimental Psychology: Learning, Memory, amd Cognition,* 16, 677–691. Reprinted with permission.

p. 279 Lavery, J.J. (1962). Retention of simple motor skills as a function of type of knowledge of results. *Canadian Journal of Psychology,* 16, 4, 300–311. Copyright © 1964. Canadian Psychological Association. Reprinted with permission.

p. 285 Swinnen, S., Schmidt, R.A., Nicholson, D.E., & Shapiro, D.C. (1990). *Journal of Experimental Psychology: Learning, Memory, and Cognition,* 16, 706–716. Reprinted with permission.

AUTHOR INDEX

A

Abbs, J.H., 46
Abernethy, B., 26, 50, 139, 176, 177, 178, 181, 187
Adams, J.A., 105, 145, 146, 167, 179, 249, 264, 290
Aggleton, J.P., 195
Alderson, G.J.K., 131
Allard, F., 176, 181
Anderson, J.R., 197, 198, 202
Annett, J., 201, 253
Anson, D., 271
Anson, J.G., 30, 31, 32
Arnold, R.K., 267, 268, 269
Aronson, E., 128
Athenes, S., 38
Atkinson, R.C., 191, 192, 194, 197

B

Bachica, D.L., 222
Baddeley, A.D., 193, 196, 207, 212
Bahill, A.T., 132
Bahrick, H.P., 207
Bairstow, E.J., 109
Ball, D., 224
Bandura, A. 222, 225, 227, 228
Barclay, C.D., 228
Bard, C., 176, 178
Barnwell, J., 243
Baron, R.A., 221
Battig, W.F., 207, 241, 247
Becker, J.T., 196
Beech, J.R., 19

Ben Sira, D., 274
Berman, A.J., 8, 146
Bernstein, N., 13, 22, 23, 148, 152, 166, 237, 243, 262, 290
Beuter, A., 45
Bijlard, M.J., 230
Bilodeau, E.A., 171, 274, 284
Bilodeau, I.M., 171, 274, 284
Bird, A.M., 148, 163, 164, 223
Bjork, R.A., 199, 201, 203, 212
Black, J.B., 206
Blaylock, 200
Bobath, B., 8, 253
Bootsma, R.J., 132, 133, 134, 269
Borgeaud, P., 176, 181
Bower, G.H., 206
Bransford, J.D., 142, 161, 165, 168, 193, 206
Briggs, G., 255
Brooks, V.B., 4, 46, 53, 58, 82, 83, 106, 110, 144, 218
Buckholz, E.E., 148
Burgess, E.M., 41
Burgess, P.R., 105
Burgess-Limerick, R., 139, 181
Burke, D., 115
Burwitz, L., 125, 139, 180, 219, 221

C

Caird, J.K., 220, 221
Campbell, D., 271
Carello, C., 13, 124, 148
Carlton, L.G., 268, 269
Carlton, M.J., 258
Carnahan, H., 276, 283

317

SUBJECT INDEX